POWERNOMICS

Economics and Strategy
After the Cold War

Edited by
Clyde V. Prestowitz, Jr.
Ronald A. Morse
Alan Tonelson

D1314348

Economic Strategy Institute
Washington, D.C.

Copyright © 1991 by Economic Strategy Institute

Published by Madison Books
4720 Boston Way
Lanham, Maryland 20706

Distributed by National Book Network
JK

Library of Congress Cataloging-in-Publication Data

Powernomics : economics and strategy
after the Cold War
Includes bibliographical references .
1. United States—Economic policy—1981-
I. Prestowitz, Clyde V., 1941-
II. Morse, Ronald A.
III. Tonelson, Alan, 1953-
IV. Economic Strategy Institute.
HC106.8.P68   1990
338.97390-13040

ISBN 0–8191–8038–6
ISBN 0–8191–8039–4 paper

Contents

Preface

Ideas matter, and Americans owe a debt of gratitude to Ronald Reagan for reminding them of this truth. As the 1990s begin and a new century approaches, however, the ideas shaping our national economic future seem to be profoundly wrong. In fact, because of today's conventional economic wisdom—what we call the Orthodoxy—our nation's leading politicians and economic experts regularly hail challenges to America's well-being that other countries would consider alarming—the rise of powerful global competitors, the loss of major industries, mounting dependence on foreign resources, a significant loss of control over the national economy.

It was to bring new ideas to the national economic policy debate and develop new approaches for assuring America's future that the Economic Strategy Institute was founded. As its staff and supporters began to set priorities and objectives, it quickly became clear that an impressive body of new (and not so new) ideas about economics and strategy were already challenging the status quo. Yet these writings were so widely scattered that few Americans had the opportunity to learn about them. The Institute decided that publishing some of the best examples of this new economic thinking in one volume would provide an important national service.

Powernomics was produced with the help of many individuals aside from the editors. Steven A. Schoenfeld skillfully put together a series of internal staff seminars instrumental in framing the issues for *Powernomics* to address. Robyn Vogel took charge of the difficult task of securing dozens of copyright permissions in scant weeks and, along with Alexandra Fischer, efficiently collected the hundreds of books, articles, and reports from which the readings were culled. Gioia Marini deftly handled numerous last-minute administrative and editorial tasks. Tim Morris, Andrea Qu, and Maureen Jais-Mick coordinated a complex production task without missing a beat.

Outside friends who lent a hand editorially and administratively include Helen Loerke, Elizabeth Dixon, Terry Erb, and Marie Anderson. Outside specialists providing valuable advice in focusing the volume were David Calleo, Robert Cohen, David Denoon, Eliot Konopko, and Robert Kuttner. Special thanks in this vein are also due to several members of ESI's Advisory Board: Saburo Okita, George C. Lodge, William C. Norris, Joel Popkin, Owen Bieber, Jacques Gansler, Moriya Uchida, and J. Richard Iverson. Finally, the editors would like to thank Jill Keeley and the rest of the staff at the University Press of America for patiently guiding the Institute through its maiden voyage in publishing.

Introduction

On August 2 1990, Iraqi dictator Saddam Hussein sent his battle-hardened, poison-gas-armed, million-man army into the neighboring, oil-rich sheikdom of Kuwait. The invasion set in motion forces that will redraw the map of the Middle East and change the shape of the post-Cold War world. Saddam also brought to life in the most dramatic fashion possible the principal message of this book.

If the human drama teaches countries anything, it is that national security, substantial national freedom of action, and the ability to fulfill societal promises are anchored in economic vitality, and that such vitality does not occur by accident and cannot be left to chance.

Of course, the West's response to the Persian Gulf crisis has several objectives. But it is primarily to keep the price of oil relatively low that much of an excessively petroleum-dependent world finds itself at the brink of war in the Arabian desert. Had the United States pursued policies aimed at greater energy independence and more diverse sources of supply over the past 15-plus years, it would not be necessary to send massive military forces halfway around the world and to make young Americans hostages to the byzantine politics of the Arab world today.

But the United States did not do that. Rather, believing that such economic matters should always be left to "market forces," and warmly embracing the concept of "interdependence," U.S. leaders left development and control of the commodity most important to its economic well-being—oil—to chance. That is, until the crunch. Then, after twenty years of laissez-faire, Washington decided that chance is something too fragile on which to base the future of the American way of life. But having dawdled for so long in developing a realistic strategy, American leaders found that the only one left was to put American lives on the line. Surely there is a better way.

This volume is about finding such a way. The title, *Powernomics*, is meant to highlight the tight link between economics and other aspects of national welfare. It was conceived in order to define an American response to the end of the Cold War and to the dawn of a new era in which national security will increasingly be defined in economic terms, and in which the United States will face unprecedented challenges without the benefit of past superiority in industry, technology, and finance.

Recent events in the Middle East are only the most dramatic example of a broader phenomenon. For the past 45 years, the overwhelming advantages in productivity with which America emerged from the Second World War have allowed the nation to ignore the links between national welfare and leadership in technology and productivity. Indeed, often in this period we subordinated economic interests and consciously traded technological leadership for greater dependency in order to secure geopolitical objectives. Obviously, we can no longer afford to do this. In fact, we need to recognize that we do not face a choice between building military strength and creating freedom of action on the one hand, and cultivating economic strength on the other. Both sets of goals depend on each other.

This means that in the new world rapidly unfolding before us, it will be essential for America to have an economic strategy that is an integral part of its overall strategy. God may indeed watch over little boys and the United States of America. But Heaven also helps those who help themselves.

Powernomics has three main purposes. First, it presents in a helpful way basic works that explain to readers how national and global developments are affecting America's well-being—and their own. Second, its sections are arranged to guide readers through a thought process that reveals the magnitude of the challenges confronting us, and explains why the conventional wisdom has been so slow to recognize them—and, in fact, continues to deny that they exist. Third, the volume spotlights the questions that need to be asked in order to meet these challenges.

Taken in toto, the readings provide benchmarks for developing a strategy aimed at restoring America's economic leadership while creating the kind of freedom of action that great powers need in a still perilous world. The basics of this strategy are easily understandable as well—and flow from common sense as much as from sophisticated theory. They involve increasing investments in future strength—not only in factories and tools but in people and infrastructures. They involve ensuring that America continues to have a well-balanced economic structure, producing the entire range of products that any advanced economy needs to thrive today—not just glamorous supercomputers and spacecraft but jackhammers and jigsaws and automobiles. They involve making sure that our businesses have the game-plans and assets they need to compete in world markets. And they involve a trade policy that deals with the world as it is, not as academic economists and bureaucrats would like it to be. The ultimate goal is to assure America's long-term leadership in productivity. Only in this way can we be certain of having the resources to keep our living standards rising as rapidly or more so than those of other countries, solve our social problems, defend our values, and realize our national dreams.

Adding up these proposals provides an idea of the kind of economic strategy that America needs today. Moreover, speaking in terms of this kind of comprehensive strategy allows us to rise above the sterile debate in which American economic policy is currently trapped. Discussion about economics today seems to take place only at the extremes. Too often, the choices are restricted to complete laissez-faire or 1930s-style protectionism; complete deregulation or Soviet-style planning. Yet life tends to be lived somewhere between these proposals. The proposals in *Powernomics* present a way of devising a practical strategy for the real world in which we live.

An ill-fitting orthodoxy

This approach is, of course, a direct challenge to the mainstream Orthodoxy that has placed a dead hand on the current American economic debate. For the Orthodoxy denies not only the need for a strategy, but also the possibility of developing a strategy as well as its potential effectiveness of one if it could be introduced. Fostered by the hot-house environment of the post-World War II Pax Americana, the conventional wisdom has come to rest on three particular concepts that are increasingly insupportable.

First is the idea that economics and economic policy are things that exist and should exist outside and apart from values, mores, psychology, political and social institutions, and, most important, international power relationships. Thus, for example, the possibility that foreign investment in the U.S. economy could reduce America's geopolitical freedom of action or result in the foreign manipulation of domestic politics is not considered relevant in judging its effects. Conversely, the trading away of leading-edge technology to economic competitors in an effort to achieve interoperable military systems is considered irrelevant both to economic policy and national security. This utopianism is nicely captured by a prominent Republican party economist, who describes the view of his Nixon administration colleagues thus:

> The world economic order was to be universalist and private. We were floaters and free traders. In a strict sense, there would be no economic relations between countries. There would be economic relations between individuals who happened to live in different countries but who operated in a world market that didn't distinguish between friend and foe.[1]

In other words, the world of the Orthodoxy is divided into states, but outside the Soviet bloc (clearly an economic basket case), these states have no economic significance. There is competition, but the competition is not between states because they are all assumed to be guided by the same principles of the separation of power and economics.

The second pillar of the Orthodoxy buttresses the first. It involves the argument that what a nation produces doesn't matter. As long as full employment is achieved, how it is achieved—whether by chopping down trees and selling logs or by producing airplanes and supercomputers—allegedly is of no consequence. This view has best been articulated by the Director of the U.S. Office of Management and Budget, Richard Darman, and by the Chairman of the President's Council of Economic Advisors, Michael Boskin. In 1985, at the height of a round of massive dumping of semiconductors in the U.S. market, Darman remarked to a group of Cabinet officials, "Why do we want a semiconductor industry? If our guys can't hack it, let them go." At a later date, Boskin made the comment, "Computer chips, potato chips, what's the difference? They're all chips. One hundred dollars of potato chips and one hundred dollars of computer chips are both one hundred dollars."

This view has several implications. But in terms of the national scene and national strategy, it means that even if other nations, by some odd chance, do not share this view, there is no reason for concern. If in pursuit of an industrial policy, the Europeans subsidize the Airbus and the Japanese come to dominate the world semiconductor market by underpricing their exports, not to worry. Loss of these industries doesn't mean America is losing. The United States will simply shift to some other economic activity, like shipping scrap aluminum or waste paper (New York harbor's biggest export item).

Thus, the world of the Orthodoxy is not a strategic world. This belief is responsible for its third pillar—the belief that a country's relative economic performance is unimportant as long as its absolute performance is increasing. In other words, Americans should not worry if, say, Germany is growing at an annual rate of 5 percent while the U.S. economy is expanding at 3 percent each year.

Consequently, only private-sector actors should have strategies. Only they can be trusted to ignore such sentimental and ultimately destructive concerns as national welfare, political values, social and cultural preferences—and power. Because losing or trailing means so little to a nation, strategy has no necessary or legitimate place in national economic policymaking. For strategy is nothing more than a blueprint for catching up.

The Orthodoxy's first precept is far too simplistic to be of any use to policymakers. Economics and international power relationships are part and parcel of each other. Military power, political power, and economic power are all mutually reenforcing. And when any one of these varieties of power is in short supply, the others will be diminished. If enough economic independence is lost, a real erosion of political independence will not be far behind. Nor is it enough to deal with national security as a great exception to the dream world envisioned by the Orthodoxy. Instead, a strategic perspective, acknowledging the reality of a high-stakes, unavoidable competition between countries, must be integrated into all aspects of American public policy.

The Orthodoxy's second precept neglects the truth that certain kinds of industries generate many more economic (and thus national security) benefits than others. Through linkages with numerous other industries, and through the spillover effects of research and development, these industries can help countries sustain and enhance their economic potential and their economic position for decades.

The problem with the third pillar of the Orthodoxy is that in a world of power, relative performance can determine absolute performance. And relative position is especially important given the rapid technological change characterizing the late-20th century, and given the huge costs of competing effectively in global markets in the knowledge-intensive technologies of the future. Countries on the rise will find it relatively easy to remain on the rise. Countries on the wane will face enormous difficulties reversing decline. Former Japanese Finance Minister Korekiyo Takahashi got it right back in 1936: "It is much harder to nullify the results of an economic conquest than those of a military conquest."

In other words, a huge irony is at work. Over any period longer than the short run, the Orthodoxy cannot meet even its own tests of generating wealth and achieving efficiency. Its built-in short-term focus can tell us only how to get rich quickest, not how to lay the foundations for enduring economic success. It tells us how to make accountants happy, but not how to assure our future. Therefore, although the Orthodoxy can teach our national leaders a great deal—specifically about the short-term material consequences of their actions, it cannot be trusted to set our priorities for us. Political leaders—especially in democracies—need broader and richer advice.

The orthodoxy in tatters

Because its components describe reality so poorly, at the outset of the 1990s the case for the Orthodoxy no longer seems airtight. Perhaps most disturbing, because it lacks a strategic dimension, this ideology cannot even recognize a series of grave new threats to America's economic future, much less respond effectively.

For example, the Orthodoxy's most effective spokesmen—found on both ends of the political spectrum—ridicule alarm over America's shrinking economic edge by observing that the new winners are America's friends—notably the newly unified Germany and Japan; that their success is a triumph for postwar American strategy; and that growth throughout the free world continues. Besides, they say, look at the Soviets.

Similar arguments belittle the issue of the resulting decline of American political power and freedom of action. The beneficiaries of this trend, after all, are the same friendly countries. And relying on friends for export markets, and for loans to underwrite our budget deficit as well as millions of jobs, is something that our leaders say we should be happy about. This is the essence of interdependence.

America's vanishing productivity and technology leads, meanwhile, are viewed by the Orthodoxy in two ways. The first is as just desserts for America's lazy workers and shortsighted business leaders. The second is as part of a welcome transition to a "mature," service-centered economy. Economic theory tells us that national economies are supposed to evolve from farming, to producing primitive, ungainly goods like steel and ships, to turning out sleeker, high-tech products like computers, to the supposed pinnacle of economic activity—banking, hotel administration, and the like.

But most of the best-paying jobs in any economy—which produce what economists call high-technology, value-added products—are in the manufacturing sector. If manufacturing becomes extinct, these jobs become extinct as well. Further, even though the theory of the evolving economy predicts that America should be excelling in services, the numbers tell a different story. Most economists view productivity performance in most of the service sector as a disaster. The main problem seems to be an inability to use new information technologies efficiently. And the problem is concentrated in the service sector's equivalent of the shop floor, where most of employees work. By all accounts, the folks in the front office—including, by the way, many economists—are doing fine. In either case, official remedies are considered unnecessary. And in either case, the Orthodoxy's advice is the same: As long as America can sell the world enough insurance and soybeans to finance computer imports purchases, we'll have all the technology we need.

Finally, the Orthodoxy sees America's new dependence on foreign capital either as a sign of the world's confidence in the United States, or as a purely symbolic punishment for our sins on the budget and savings fronts. And to the extent that any of these developments are viewed as problems by the Orthodoxy, the same old prescriptions are dredged up: Improve American management, balance the budget, keep lowering the exchange rate of the dollar.

It was to add a strategic dimension to American economic policymaking and thinking—and an economic dimension to American strategic thinking—that the Economic Strategy Institute was founded. It staff, supporters, and allies believe that the Orthodoxy is no longer enough to halt a slide into second-class economic status that will eventually sap the health and happiness of American society. As the readers make their way through its pages, we hope that they will begin to understand why the Orthodoxy's alternatives of either laissez-faire or piecemeal tinkering with exchange rates, taxes, interest rates, or money supply will no longer do, and why the United States needs nothing less than a comprehensive economic strategy.

Powernomics

As anyone who watches the evening news can see, the U.S. economy is in deep trouble. Recognizing this is the first step toward developing an economic strategy. The changes buffeting our economy need to be treated as a set of problems urgently requiring solutions, not as signs from Above that we should sit back and enjoy. As indicated by the readings comprising *Part One*, the last decade has witnessed especially drastic deterioration—despite the long but modest expansion and low inflation lauded by the Orthodoxy. The underlying economy is much weaker than is commonly supposed. Many of the gains of the 1980s stemmed from factors (such as cheap oil) whose effects are starting to wear off. And the disappearance of U.S. technological and productivity edges and economic independence are nearing crisis proportions.

Winning and losing in the global economic competition are vitally important to a nation's security and welfare. In other words, economic failure can have epochal consequences. And the nations with the best chance of winning will be those keeping the most control over their own fate. These beliefs form the second step in developing a strategy.

Part Two explains why the optimistic mainstream description of America's recent economic lag no longer washes—if it ever did. Two related reasons stand out. First, we still live in a strategic world. For all the talk that global interdependence has made the nation-state obsolete, nations still find that they have their own particular sets of interests and that these will not always coincide. With some degree of conflict inevitable, nations will remain locked in a struggle for the closely related goals of security and prosperity.

Second, without nurturing durable economic strength—as opposed to breakneck consumption—no society can succeed over the long run. No country can achieve whatever goals it sets for itself. And no political faction or social group can hope to see its agenda carried out. Although the relationship between long-term economic power and national success seems too obvious to harp on, it nonetheless is no longer reflected in America's current set of national priorities. Yet having the resources—the economic strength—needed to fulfill national ambitions is especially important for a country like America. For America is not simply a country but an idea. And the health of American society is inseparable from the ability to fulfill our historical promise of offering haven and hope and the opportunity for a better life to Americans and to all wishing to be Americans.

Successful economies today all seem to have a certain look to them. They all seem to make—or want to make—the same kinds of products. They all seem to be going after the same markets. Nor is a doctorate in economics needed to figure out why: Certain kinds of products create more benefits throughout the whole economy than others. Countries strong in, say, computer chips will be strong in practically any industry relying heavily on these chips—in other words, practically any industry. Countries strong in timber will be lucky to corner the world market in bowling pins.

These insights can be summed up in the expression "composition counts." As shown in *Part Three*, this idea—that the composition of a country's economy goes a long way towards determining its performance—lies at the heart of any successful economic strategy. It recognizes that certain sectors are more important to economic well-being than others. Knowing what these industries are and how they contribute to economic dynamism is also the key to preventing an economic strategy from degenerating into an exercise in political porkbarrelling. Thinking about composition can produce the master plan capable of vaccinating national leaders against the special pleading of narrow interests.

As discussed, it is widely believed that there is something fundamentally un-American about the notion of economic strategy; it clashes with the belief in Americans as a Chosen People. Others argue that American politics and society are simply too fragmented to come up with a coherent economic policy. *Part Four* debunks both beliefs, and demonstrates that Americans have thought and acted strategically in the past.

From the country's founding, American leaders recognized the links between economic prowess and national security, as well as the importance of certain industries to both objectives. Nor has strategic thinking been restricted to the Republic's early years, when it faced three European empires on its borders and its infant industries could not compete with foreign rivals. Even during the heyday of our post-World War II Orthodoxy, the U.S. government actively promoted many of the industries and technological advances that cemented U.S. predominance since the end of World War II. Just think of the space program. Clearly, thinking strategically is deeply ingrained in American traditions and practices.

Past American policymakers, in other words, understood that in an unforgiving world environment, economic success cannot be left to chance. As *Part Five* illustrates, America's major economic competitors understand this, too. Not only Japan but Germany, the rest of the European Community, South Korea, and others think strategically. In addition, the readings show that America's competitors realize that the composition of their economies counts. They know that the kinds of goods they produce matters a great deal to their economic futures.

Unfortunately, most American leaders today have forgotten these critical maxims of economic strategy. This is clear from regulatory policies that needlessly handcuff business activity; from tax policies that reward consumption (e.g., deductions on home mortgage deductions and credit card interest payments) and penalize production and investment; from executive suite attitudes that give short-shrift to product quality and long-term planning; from schools that turn out illiterate graduates; and from numerous other obstacles to improved U.S. economic performance. As described in *Part Six*, these obstacles reveal that America as a society is not well organized to achieve faster productivity growth. Far-reaching change will be needed in practically every aspect of the American Way of Life. The readings in Part Six also indicate that attacking these obstacles piecemeal will not suffice. Injecting new, longer-term perspectives into America's boardrooms, for example, will accomplish little if U.S. industry is strapped with excessive or misconceived regulation.

As *Part Seven* explains, U.S. foreign policy also reveals a failure to take economic success seriously enough. Our elite foreign policy establishment has long put fighting communism over cultivating economic power. In part, our leaders simply assumed that America would always be Number One economically. Therefore, we could afford to buy allied loyalty with economic favors. In part, they naively believed that advanced industrialized democracies would simply never have major quarrels over economic issues. In some instances, these priorities were right. But in too many cases they were disastrously wrong. As a result, for example, the United States spent nearly 15 years crippling its economy in order to defeat peasant communists in Southeast Asia—all the while neglecting many pressing domestic needs bearing directly on the welfare of the American people—fixing and maintaining roads and bridges, improving schools, modernizing factories, etc.

Societies must value economic excellence. They must act as if their futures depended on it—for they do. But as our Founding Fathers knew and our current competitors recognize today, such excellence cannot be left to chance. Without vision, leadership, and coordination—without a strategy—excellence will never be achieved. And these are qualities that the private sector alone, for all its strengths, cannot provide. *Part Eight* presents examples of the kinds of proposals that would comprise an economic strategy. However wide-ranging, these readings all recognize that spurring productivity growth and technological progress are vital to assuring America's economic security, and that imaginative new forms of government-business cooperation are an indispensable part of this strategy. This section also examines the politics of competitiveness. It assays the electoral obstacles faced and opportunities enjoyed by American political leaders as they chart a new economic course for the country. And it describes how voters can be mobilized behind a compelling but daunting set of new economic priorities.

As American politics heads into another Presidential election cycle, the belief in a trade-off between military strength and economic well-being dominates the debate over our nation's future. But unless Americans understand the relationships between both kinds of strength, they will have neither. *Powernomics* is a first step towards refocusing the debate on long-neglected fundamentals. Readers will find that none of the contributors to this volume has all the answers. We hope they come away persuaded that they are starting to ask the right questions.

Notes

1. Quoted in Alan Tonelson, "A Manifesto for Democrats," *The National Interest* 16 (Summer 1989), p. 38.

I

Dimensions of Economic Decline

During the late 1970s, many Americans took to calling the Soviet Union a giant with feet of clay. Moscow boasted all of the obvious attributes of superpower status—especially military. But even then considerable rot was apparent in Soviet society and the Soviet economy. The parallel is hardly exact, but entering the 1990s, despite outward signs of prosperity, great cracks are apparent in the economic foundations of American power.

The problems go much deeper than can be identified by monthly or yearly changes in America's rates of growth, inflation, and employment, or in its trade balance. Instead, mounting evidence shows that the sources of America's economic strength are at risk.

This distinction is vitally important to policymakers. If our Orthodoxy is correct, the best response is no response. After all, if the failures of individual consumers, private enterprises, and officials are the cause of economic problems, and if losing the global economic competition need not have lasting consequences, nature should be allowed to take its course. In other words, whatever comes down will come up; we can afford to wait; and we needn't worry even if they stay down.

Yet the readings in Part One show that the problems faced today both by the U.S. economy as a whole and by individual sectors and industries themselves prevent recovery. They threaten, in fact, to plunge the country into second-class status for decades to come, and even threaten America's security and independence.

Clyde V. Prestowitz, Jr's. overview describes the especially rapid erosion in America's international economic, technological, and financial position over the last decade. Just as important, he provides a reminder that, thanks to the Orthodoxy's confidence that new, high tech sources of American comparative advantage are always just around the corner, the United States is running out of industries to lose.

The Orthodoxy's confidence in non-interference today also flows from its reading of the 1980s as an unalloyed triumph for laissez-faire economics. Lawrence Chimerine exposes the "supply-side miracle" as a fairy tale. In fact, he reveals that the decade's modest expansion masked an alarming deterioration in the U.S. economy's underlying strengths.

As Part One demonstrates, the economy's weakness shows up in specific industries as well. MIT's Commission on Industrial Productivity reports that the American machine tool industry may be in terminal decline, with leadership passing to well-financed rivals in Japan and the European Community. According to the Commerce Department, the U.S. electronics sector—the country's traditional technology leader and today its largest employer—could soon be eclipsed by foreign challenges in fields ranging from computers to electronic instruments.

Finally, Douglas P. Woodward illuminates a striking symptom of America's economic lag—the spectacular growth in foreign investment in the United States since the mid-1980s. As Woodward notes, the foreign investment boom reflects America's "inability to create a strong foundation for home-grown, globally competitive industry." And it may be helping to dig the United States into a deeper and deeper economic hole.

In a Single Decade

Clyde V. Prestowitz, Jr.

As recently as 1981 the United States was a leader in per capita output. It was the leader in virtually all areas of high technology. It had the highest productivity levels in most industries. It was the largest supplier of capital to the world. It had the strongest military forces.

In this new decade, the United States still has strong military forces. On every other point of comparison it has fallen behind, and shows few signs of reversing its decline. It has dropped to number five in GNP per capita. It is falling behind in productivity growth. It has lost the lead in many key technologies: semiconductors, silicon, semiconductor equipment, consumer electronics, and advanced materials. It is losing the lead in most others. There is not a single high technology area in which the relative American position was strengthened in the 1980s. Even in aerospace, the area of greatest American dominance, its position is being eroded.

In 1981 the United States was the world's largest creditor nation. At the end of the decade it was the world's largest debtor, and faces the prospect of paying three to five percent of national output to foreign leaders by the mid-1990s.

In the world arena the erosion of the relative U.S. economic position as completed the invalidation of the premises of the *Pax Americana*, the era in which the United States was able to subordinate its international economic interests to its geopolitical interests. This process has undermined the productivity base upon which the security and living standards of future Americans must rest, hampered its freedom to act independently on the world scene, hamstrung its efforts to keep pace with the industrial and financial power centers now rapidly emerging in Europe and Asia, and constrained its

---

Clyde V. Prestowitz *is founder and President of the Economic Strategy Institute. The author of* Trading Places: How We Are Giving Our Future to Japan and How To Reclaim It *(1988), he previously served as Counselor for Japan Affairs to the Secretary of Commerce, 1983-1986.*

ability to help the new democracies of Eastern Europe as well as the debt-laden countries of Latin America and Africa.

At the dawn of the post-World War II era, when the shattered countries of Europe and Asia set about the unprecedented task of rebuilding themselves, their approach differed from that of the United States. Working on different sides of the globe, the nations of Asia, and to a lesser extent Western Europe, persistently put production needs first and consumer needs second. Reasoning that if their peoples were to prosper, their industries and financial structures must prosper first, they developed policies designed to foster national successes in world markets. Achieving these economic goals to the great delight of the United States, these nations were seen as American success stories—visible proof, we thought, of the principles we so ardently espoused.

On the surface, the nations of the new Europe and the new Asia looked much like the United States. They were democratic free-market societies. In fact, they differed sharply from the American book of industrial success in World War II. Their governments created and fostered close government-labor-management-financial links-ties designed to assure that their respective countries would join the first rank of nations in the shortest possible time span. And this they achieved.

Other countries began to follow the economic trails blazed by the new leaders of Europe and Asia. Creating production-oriented policies of their own, the Pacific Basin nations of Korea, Taiwan, and Singapore added mightily to the international flow of trade in goods and services. The cumulative effect of these powerful, production-oriented strategies began to change the setting of the world economic stage. These international changes were accompanied by major economic shifts inside the United States—shifts that included the alteration of the nation's industrial base, and changes in the composition of its workforce.

Textiles In the late 1950s the United States' textile industry began to experience competitive difficulties. Imports surged, trade friction rose, and the industry secured protection. Outside the industry there was little concern, however. Many believed America's future had no room for such old, mature, labor intensive industries. It seemed harmless—and in fact proper—to let textiles migrate to other countries while Americans turned to more productive tasks.

Consumer Electronics In the early 1960s the consumer electronics industry ran into serious trouble. American radio production collapsed first—quickly followed by stereos, then black and white television, and VCR's. That is to say, the American consumer electronics industry was first driven out of the less sophisticated areas of the market, and then from the top end of the market. This pattern was repeated in other industries, but Americans continued to think that each situation was separate and distinct, and that products requiring labor-intensive assembly were better suited to production in less-developed countries. America, it was thought, would simply move on to more advanced industries and technologies.

Steel and Automobiles In the early 1970s, the steel industry became the focus of national attention, followed by the auto industry in the late 1970s. Losses in these industries caused more concern than those in textiles or consumer electronics. They lay at the heart of industrial America. Nevertheless, steel and automobiles were widely considered to be old, "rust-belt" industries plagued by troglodyte unions and neanderthal management. Many—with some justification—believed these industries had created their own troubles and were only reaping what they had sowed. Discounting the problems in Detroit and Pittsburgh, many Americans looked to the West, believing they had found the country's golden future in California's high technology Silicon Valley.

Semiconductors As the steel and automobile industries declined, Silicon Valley was in its heyday. The U.S. semiconductor industry was booming. In the span of a few short years, it had spawned dozens of companies in the San Francisco Bay area—a whole new culture based on informality, technology, and the American entrepreneurial spirit—far from the bureaucracies of Washington and New York.

By the mid-1980s the semiconductor industry appeared to be going the way of textiles, consumer electronics, steel and autos. Having earlier spurned Washington as hopelessly bureaucratic, Silicon Valley executives reluctantly turned to government for help. In doing so, they were the first to make the case that their industry was not competitive because the American system itself was not competitive. The response was cool. Policy makers, pundits, and academics alike continued to blame management for industry's troubles. There was little concern because the United States was thought to be moving into a post-industrial period. The invisible global hand would ensure that America could pay for imported manufactured goods with the earnings of its strong service industries.

Services By the late 1980s, it became apparent that the United States was not competitive in services, either. Japanese and European banks and financial companies began to make major inroads into U.S. financial service markets. Japanese banks gained over sixty percent of the market for municipal letters of credit while steadily increasing their share of U.S. corporate lending. In the construction industry more and more projects in the United States began to be awarded to foreign contractors, and the United States began to run a trade deficit in construction services of over $3 billion annually. By late 1989 the United States even had a trade deficit in housing.

Looking for root causes

As our great industries faltered and began to decline, many explanations were offered, but no root causes were found—only individual, discrete, unrelated problems peculiar to each industry: poor management in one, expensive labor in another, and sometimes just bad luck. There was no attempt to place the problem in a larger context. During these decades of change, policy makers and others wanted to believe that all was essentially well in America. But plainly this was not the case. It may be possible to blame the problems of individual companies, industries, or clusters of industries on management problems, labor problems or shifting world markets. But when many companies and industries find themselves unable to compete, it is time to look for more fundamental causes. The truth is that the current American system itself is not competitive because it is based upon four outmoded concepts. These concepts are that:

> Increasing consumption, without regard for production, is the main object of economic policy.

> Government should act only as a regulator and economic referee rather than a business promoter.

> Corporations are collections of assets deployed almost exclusively for the further enrichment of shareholders.

> International trade in the extension overseas of the rules of the American market.

These concepts served the United States well when it stood head and shoulders above the rest of the world, but the country now has many strong competitors, and such ideas are no longer valid.

We must come to grips with a rapidly growing number of socioeconomic problems: failing city infrastructures, a failing educational system, a large and growing underclass, a stream of immigrants that appears to be increasingly difficult to assimilate, and a lack of unanimity as to what the nation is and what it should become in the 21st Century.

In New York City there are dangerous streets, a wheezing public transportation, and the near-failure of essential services: water supply and sewage systems at the breaking point, decaying interstates, and airports barely able to handle the traffic increase. New York City's unfunded maintenance bills have soared into the *billions* of dollars, and similar bills continue to mount in such cities as Pittsburgh, Detroit, and Akron. Hundreds of American cities are literally falling apart, and it will take *trillions* of dollars to fix them.

American literacy rates have actually declined in the last 20 years. The United States is the only major nation to experience this phenomenon—not Japan, not Korea, not West Germany, not even the far less developed nations of Latin America. In Washington, D.C., capital of the richest, most powerful country the world has ever seen, half the children will not graduate from high school and of those who do, a large percentage are barely able to read or write. The figures are roughly the same in all of our major metropolitan school systems. On a national basis, about 25% of our students drop out of high school, consigned to a social and economic scrap heap before they even begin their adult lives. The United States is the only major nation of the world that tolerates such human waste.

American policy has encouraged emigration from all nations of the world; the new arrivals brought their skills and productive capacities to a country that welcomed them and was ready to put them to work. They, in turn, helped the country grow and prosper. With a declining economy there may be little room for immigrants, and a resentment may mount among the many native-born Americans who fear that new arrivals may replace them in the ever tighter American labor market. If so, this would represent a basic reversal of traditional American values.

These are pressing concerns in purely social terms, but each has an equally pressing economic dimension. When urban infrastructures fail, business conditions deteriorate. Materials are slow to move in and products slow to move out. Employees do not want to work in such places and manufacturers also look for greener pastures. Will they look in a suburb, another state—or another country?

Manufacturing jobs require ever greater technical knowledge, and American employers find fewer and fewer qualified candidates graduating from U.S. schools. Many have had to develop expensive remedial education programs—for old as well as new employees. Typically, these programs teach such basic concepts as decimal calculation—a concept normally taught in elementary school. Can such companies be expected to remain in the United States when well-educated labor forces await them elsewhere in the world?

Immigrants are to America what flour is to bread, its most vital ingredient. They have plowed the fields, built the factories, made and consumed the products, enriched the culture, and given it strength. An America that believes it can no longer absorb newcomers, an America that can no longer provide the jobs that will help immigrants become useful, productive citizens integrated into the mainstream of our society, is an America that may have lost faith in itself.

These are but a few of the dozens of socio-economic issues that face a declining America at the end of the 20th century—the American Century—and no amount of mere policy tinkering can solve them. The country needs to make economic leadership a matter of high national priority and pursue that goal with a strong and determined will based on a comprehensive economic strategy—a multi-dimensional strategy aimed at restoring economic excellence.

What "Supply-Side Miracle"?

Lawrence Chimerine

Although the economic expansion of the 1980s may be over, it will still stand as one of the longest peacetime expansions in U.S. history. This steady seven and one-half year performance has of course engendered the claim that Ronald Reagan's supply-side and deregulation policies have transformed the U.S. economy. If they are continued, we are told, prosperity will continue through the 1990s. Supply-siders acknowledge that the economy is very soft at the moment, but they dismiss the problem as a short term aberration caused largely by extremely tight Federal Reserve policies and/or by the jump in oil prices following the Iraqi invasion of Kuwait.

Yet the expansion of the 1980s was anything but a supply-side miracle. Superficial prosperity has masked a steady worsening of the underlying economic fundamentals. These problems were only temporarily hidden by a recovery that was largely cyclical in nature and aided by a several factors that are turning out to be transitory. Indeed, despite the recent expansion, the U.S. economy's fundamentals are perhaps at their lowest point since the end of World War II. It is essential to understand the real economic story of the 1980s and where we stand economically at present in order to make reasonable projections about the future, identify whatever problems lie ahead, and develop effective solutions.

Supply-side economics promised that cuts in marginal tax rates would increase economic incentives so dramatically that economic growth would spurt and savings and investment would rise. Moreover, deregulation and spending cuts would remove the last shackles restraining corporate performance. And many supply-siders insisted that economic activity would

Lawrence Chimerine, *a Fellow of the Economic Strategy Institute, is president of Radnor Consulting Services and Senior Advisor, Data Resources, Inc. Previously he was chairman and CEO of The WEFA Group, chairman, CEO and chief economist of Chase Econometrics, and manager of U.S. Economic Research and Forecasting for IBM Corporation.*

even expand enough to create additional tax revenues despite lower rates, and more than offset any revenue loss. Thus, they predicted that the large tax cuts of the early 1980s, especially if coupled with modest spending cuts, would actually improve the budgetary outlook instead of causing the large deficits so widely forecast. Did the long expansion result directly from the incentive-creating policies that have been labeled supply-side economics? A careful review of the evidence exposes these claims as fairy tales.

Incentives for what?

In the first place, the labor force did grow fairly rapidly during much of the 1980s—even faster than population growth. Yet the increase in the so-called participation rates (the percentage of the population actually working or looking for work) was no greater in the 1980s than in previous decades. Participation rates for adult men remained flat, as is normally the case, but the rates for women continued to rise sharply, extending a long-term trend deeply rooted in social factors and economic pressures. In fact, female participation probably continued to rise in the 1980s in part because job cuts, a loss of high-paying jobs, wage freezes and give-backs, and other factors created a real earnings squeeze for many during the decade. Thus, many women (and probably some teenagers) joined the labor force not because of any supply-side incentive (that is, because a lower tax rate increased the after-tax return from working). Rather, stagnant real incomes forced many families to seek a second income source to maintain the living standards to which they had grown accustomed.

What these trends in fact imply is a downward sloping supply curve for labor—in other words, lower tax rates may reduce labor supply by enabling many families to earn the same after-tax income with less work. More important, there is no evidence from earlier years that reduced tax rates boost labor supply. Thus, the so-called incentive effects for labor were not a significant factor in the expansion of the 1980s.

Perhaps the biggest incentive effect anticipated by supply-siders was the propensity of a sharp reduction in marginal tax rates to boost household savings. Yet exactly the opposite occurred. U.S. personal savings rates during the 1980s remained far below not only those in virtually every other major industrialized country, but far below the U.S. average for the 1945-1980 period. This development is even more remarkable considering several other developments. For instance, the extraordinarily high real interest rates of the 1980s should have stimulated more frugality by increasing the after-tax return on such savings. The introduction of IRAs, Keoghs, 401Ks, and other new savings vehicles; the phasing out of the deductibility of consumer interest; and other similar tax changes should have had the same effect. Yet the personal saving rate plummeted. This not only indicates that saving is not positively affected by the after-tax returns on such saving, but that the reverse may be the case—just as it was for workforce participation. Perhaps what the supply-siders missed is that many people base their savings behavior on achieving a targeted level of savings at some future time. If so, a higher after-tax return would actually reduce the amount of new savings necessary to reach the target. Again, the evidence is mixed. It simply cannot support the claim that the savings supply is in fact negatively sloped. But neither the data nor the experience of the 1980s supports the supply-side view that the savings supply is strongly positively sloped and that supply-side incentives actually work. The soundest conclusion seems to be that the tax system has little or no effect on savings patterns and that savings for most families are more of a residual—rather than a direct—decision variable. Thus, the weakness in real incomes coupled with the desire of many families to maintain and improve their living standards actually caused a decline in personal savings in the 1980s despite the new incentive structure.

If investment is largely determined by the amount of savings, then the savings drop-off must have curbed the growth of business investment during the 1980s. Therefore, supply-side incentives not only failed to deliver on its promise of a big increase in personal savings, but by creating enormous budget deficits, supply-side policies actually caused the sharp decline in national savings that made a big increase in investment impossible. Indeed, as will be discussed below, the 1980s was not a period of strong investment, despite the long expansion. In fact, the decline in national savings and the relatively high real interest rates caused by supply-side economics produced exactly the opposite effect—they deterred net investment.

Supply-siders also predicted that their incentives would revive productivity growth. Yet, as is now well documented, productivity growth has continued to lag, despite a whole raft of forces that should have made a difference.

Supply-side theory promised that lower marginal tax rates, by stimulating saving, investment, productivity, and the like, would improve America's competitive position in world markets and ultimately enhance national economic security. Unfortunately, the 1980s witnessed the largest trade deficits in U.S. history and losses of market share in virtually every manufacturing industry. The supply-siders remained undaunted. True, they acknowledged, they did not anticipate these deficits. But they actually portrayed the trade gap as a sign of supply-side success. It supposedly reflects the strength of the U.S. economy, plus the higher returns on investment in America made possible by lower tax rates and other supply-side innovations. This is a complete misreading of U.S. trade and competitiveness in the 1980s.

The erosion in U.S. trade signals serious deterioration in U.S. competitiveness, not American success. It results first and foremost from the steady shrinkage of America's lead in world productivity growth and is producing a disturbing and, in turn, economically damaging shift in innovation and product development abroad. And, far from showing an improvement in U.S. competitiveness, the recent narrowing of the trade deficit indicates exactly the opposite. For this gap remains enormously high (currently a $90 billion annual rate) despite very strong growth overseas, despite a flattening out of the U.S. economy over the last 18 months, despite a sharp decline in the U.S. dollar since 1985, and despite a host of trade actions and supposed market-opening initiatives vis-à-vis other countries.

U.S. productivity and technology advantages were so large during the early postwar years that the United States could maintain dominance in world markets and generate large ongoing trade surpluses despite funding much of the free world's defense, despite keeping its markets very open, and despite toleration of cultural and trade barriers that limited access to some other markets. Yet, even though U.S. manufacturing has remained relatively stable as a share of GNP, these basic advantages have been narrowed dramatically, primarily by rapid productivity growth among traditional foreign competitors, and by the emergence of many highly-productive new competitors in the last 15 years.

These developments reflect:

> the speedier transfer of U.S.-developed technology to the rest of the world;

> a more rapid rate of innovation in many other countries than in earlier years;

> a strong foreign emphasis on product quality and design;

> high saving and investment rates abroad;

> the rebuilding of World War II-ravaged infrastructures with the most modern equipment (and the use of such equipment in the newly industrializing countries);

> the increased mechanization of foreign agriculture;

> the lower base from which many foreign countries started; and

> an emphasis on rapid growth, both domestically and in exports, in order to generate the higher profits necessary to fund additional investment, and research and development.

During the same time, productivity growth in the United States was slowing relative to the earlier postwar years. In fact, average productivity levels in many tradable-goods industries are actually now higher in Japan and some other countries than they are in the United States (although not on an overall economy basis, because U.S. productivity levels remain higher in various other industries).

As a result, relatively high U.S. wage and capital costs can no longer be justified by productivity differences, and represent an enormous competitive disadvantage. The combination of these developments has ended U.S. dominance in world markets for most manufactured and agricultural goods, and spurred massive trade deficits and rapidly growing foreign debt. These trends have been aggravated by the enormous U.S. budget deficits, the overvalued dollar and slow growth overseas in the early 1980s, and the Third World debt crisis. The decline in fundamental competitiveness (i.e., in relative productivity) and its likely effect on future economic growth have been hidden or unrecognized for several reasons.

First, the ratio of manufacturing/GNP (in real terms) has remained relatively stable, suggesting that the United States is not de-industrializing. Yet the apparent stability of manufacturing output as a share of real GNP during the 1980s may be based on faulty data. And even if this ratio did remain stable, this development would constitute another sign of the erosion of U.S. competitiveness. For it would have to be viewed in the context of the rapid rebound in the demand for manufactured goods (relative to total demand) in the United States, reflecting the large turnaround in consumer durables and the procurement-dominated military buildup.

In fact, the surge in demand for goods in the early 1980s was so strong that it prevented the manufacturing/GNP ratio from declining despite the loss of U.S. market shares (and the related influx of imports and slowdown in exports). Without the change in relative competitiveness, the manufacturing output/GNP ratio would have risen sharply during the 1980s. This also explains why manufacturing output grew more rapidly in America than in the rest of the world during the initial stages of the recovery—the U.S. market, in which American producers have a relatively large (but declining) share, simply grew much more rapidly than markets overseas. Finally, maintaining a near-stable manufacturing/GNP ratio (the trend at cyclical peaks has actually been slightly negative) over the last 15 years was made possible only in part by the steadily declining dollar of the 1970s, which offset some of the widening unit-labor -cost differentials at that time.

Second, the U.S. economy grew more rapidly than most other industrialized countries during much of the 1980s. This is often cited as the primary cause of large U.S. trade deficits. Yet although faster economic growth in the United States obviously increased the trade imbalance in some years, it does not account for the sharp rise in import penetration rates (as opposed to simple import levels), and the decline in U.S. exports in real terms after 1980 (even though modest economic growth did occur abroad). These shifts combined to cause the sharp decline in the U.S. share of worldwide production in most industries referred to earlier, and of overall world trade, during much of the decade. Further, the U.S. trade imbalance continued to rise even as U.S. demand and overall economic growth slowed in 1985 and 1986. The size of the gap in the last year has been especially noteworthy, given strong growth overseas and slow growth at home.

Third, the onset of massive trade deficits has coincided with large budget deficits, indicating to many that the budget imbalance, by pushing up interest rates and the dollar exchange rate, caused most of our trade problem. Yet as best evidenced by the rapid rate of increase in the U.S. trade deficit with Japan, and the steady decline in the U.S. dollar relative to the yen and other industrialized-country currencies, our trade problems were developing well before the 1980s. The full extent of underlying deteriorating competitiveness at that time was temporarily masked by the surge in exports to Latin America (financed by unsustainable U.S. bank lending, much of this in turn tied to exports), by rising exports to OPEC countries (in response to oil-revenue-financed development and construction programs), and by the relatively weak dollar. Large U.S. budget deficits clearly made the trade deficits worse in the early 1980s, both by pushing up the U.S. dollar and by directly stimulating demand. Yet foreign competitive pressures would have mounted even in the absence of unbalanced U.S. fiscal policies. Thus, the prediction that U.S. competitiveness would improve as a result of supply-side economics was flat wrong.

Perhaps the strongest indictment of supply-side economics centers on the strength of the 1980s' recovery. Despite the nearly 8-year expansion, average economic growth during the decade as a whole actually lagged behind growth in each of the preceding three decades—including the stagflation years of the 1970s. Two factors are primarily responsible. First, as will be discussed further below, to a great extent the long expansion simply represented a catch-up period following two deep recessions. Consequently, the expansion benefited from an extremely low starting point. And second, average economic growth since 1982 has actually lagged considerably behind the average growth rate registered in previous recoveries. These modest growth rates completely contradicted the supply-siders' bold prediction.

In sum, there was no supply-side miracle in the 1980s. Other explanations are required for the long but relatively modest expansion. Moreover, contrary to the supply-siders' expectations, the budget picture has been a disaster. Reagonomics brought massive deficits, not healthy surpluses. Nor can the deficits be blamed on excessive spending by Congress. Non-defense discretionary expenditures were reduced by approximately 2 percent of GNP, and are now about $100 billion less than they would have been had they retained their 1980 share of GNP. Further, total spending did not significantly exceed the administration's budget requests during the 1980s. What changed was simply the mix between defense and non-defense programs—the former swelling, the latter shrinking.

The other real cause of large budget deficits was on the tax side. Despite large social security tax increases, tax revenues have trailed the growth of GNP, reflecting the revenue loss produced by the deep cuts of the early 1980s. Tax receipts, moreover, also lagged because the economy did not grow as rapidly as the supply-siders had projected.

Finally, it has become clear that the budget problem has been feeding on itself. The big supply-side-created deficits have remained large, and are now becoming even larger because of their effect on the national debt. America's debts are rising so rapidly that interest payments on the debt are now one of the fastest growing components of government spending. The supply-side legacy of extraordinarily high interest rates and monumental budget deficits will damage the U.S. economy for years to come.

What did happen during the 1980s?

The soundest explanation for the long expansion during the 1980s is rather simple. It was a cyclical expansion. It lasted longer than others because of its low starting point and its relatively slow growth rate. In addition, the expansion was helped along by several transitory factors on which the economy can no longer depend.

As is well known, the 1980s began with two recessions in only three years. The first began in 1980 and extended through the fall of that year. After a brief recovery lasting into the spring of 1981, a second, relatively deep recession began. The essential point about these recessions is that they were separated by only six months rather than by the historical norm of three to four years. The short recovery after the first recession, coupled with the magnitude and length of the second, in turn explains the extremely low starting point for the economic expansion. By virtually any measure of macroeconomic performance (e.g., the unemployment rate, capacity utilization in most industries, the gap between actual GNP and potential GNP) the economy at the outset of the recovery was operating at or close to its nadir for the entire post-World War II period. Thus, there was enormous room to grow without straining resources.

Further, enormous pent-up demand was created during the recessions. Millions of Americans, for example, were unable to replace an automobile or other goods. They lacked the financial wherewithal, or were concerned about their future, and thus did not want to incur major new financial liabilities. Similarly, many corporations were unable to replace older equipment because they were either losing money or suffering from weak profitability at best. And, of course, extremely high real interest rates and tight credit made it difficult to finance these expenditures by borrowing, even if the will to do so had existed.

The length of the expansion, however, cannot be explained entirely by normal cyclical factors. It was also aided along by temporary factors that helped translate unused resources and pent-up demands into rising economic activity. Several factors stand out. First is the massive fiscal stimulus resulting from the large military buildup plus big tax cuts. Yet such stimulus had nothing to do with supply-side incentives. Essentially, it represents old-fashioned demand stimulus. And this description is especially apt for the military buildup.

As economic jargon puts it, military expenditures create a very large multiplier effect because they involve direct purchases of goods and services by the federal government rather than transfer payments or changes in tax liabilities. Many industries throughout the country enjoyed Reagan-era booms due to the direct (and indirect) impact of this enormous rise in military procurement. The relative contribution made by rising military expenditures to the recovery (as opposed to tax changes) has long been understated. But it is now becoming clear as the military buildup shifts into reverse. Several regions are already in recession, almost completely as a result of the defense cuts now being implemented.

Second, the two oil shocks of the 1970s hurt economic growth in a number of ways: by diverting purchasing power away from other goods and services; by creating sporadic energy shortages; by directly pushing up interest rates; and ultimately by leading to one of the tightest periods of monetary policy in U.S. history. During most of the 1980s many of these trends were reversed. In particular, oil prices dropped from a peak of about $40 per barrel in 1980 to near single digits by 1986. Unquestionably, dramatically declining oil prices gave a tremendous boost to overall U.S. economic performance.

Third, partly because of lower oil prices, and partly because of the slack in the economy created during the two earlier recessions, overall inflation also fell sharply during the 1980s, from a peak of about 14 percent (as measured by the Consumer Price Index) to as low as 1.1 percent in 1986. This also was very favorable for economic activity.

Fourth, lower inflation and an easier monetary stance led to significantly lower nominal interest rates in the 1980s and helped spur a major rebound in housing, other construction, and other interest-sensitive goods. But real interest rates remained relatively high. Massive supply-side-generated budget deficits and America's related increasing dependence on foreign capital deserve most of the blame. On balance, however, interest rate trends during the 1980s helped economic growth. But rates fell despite supply-side economics, not because of it.

Fifth, of all the unanticipated developments of the 1980s, one of the most significant was the increased willingness of all U.S. economic sectors to incur significant increases in debt. In particular, the enormous increase in private debt—by households, corporations, farmers, etc.—stimulated the expansion process by boosting demand and spending.

Admittedly, much of the debt buildup was used to replace equity and for financial transactions unrelated to increases in demands for goods and services. But the willingness to finance spending by borrowing at a higher rate than existed before (especially by consumers, because real incomes were not rising rapidly enough to finance all desired spending), and the willingness of foreigners to provide that money, played a critical role in perpetuating the expansion of the 1980s.

Where we stand

As indicated by most of the major economic statistics, as well as anecdotal evidence, the economy has slowed markedly since mid-1989. The economy may have already moved from slow growth into recession. Many will blame the unfolding slump on Federal Reserve and/or the recent oil price surge resulting from Iraq's invasion of Kuwait. Yet this near-recession, which began more than a year ago, is largely an outgrowth of many of the developments responsible for the expansion of the 1980s, and should have been anticipated. And slow growth seems likely to continue for many years into the future whether genuine recession develops or not, for many reasons.

The end of this unspectacular expansion spells serious economic trouble for America. For the failures of supply-side economics entailed far more than a failure to strengthen the economy's fundamentals. The supply-side experiment gravely weakened them. And as these weakened fundamentals loom ever larger in our economic future, many of the transitory factors that stimulated growth during the 1980s are now becoming impediments to growth.

First are the cyclical factors. It has become obvious over the past year or two that the large pent-up demands created during the early 1980s have been largely satisfied. Trends in consumer durables in particular support this conclusion. Statistical analysis shows clearly that some of the recent declines in auto sales, household appliances, furniture and other consumer durables stem from a decline in replacement demand. Put very simply, these industries thrived in the mid-1980s because many consumers replaced older products with new ones. Now this major boon to the recovery has generally come to an end.

In addition, at least until recently, a large amount of the idle resources created during the 1980s had essentially been absorbed by early or mid-1989. Capacity utilization in manufacturing rose from less than 70 percent to almost 85 percent on average as of that time. In fact, in a relatively large number of industries, capacity conditions at that time can only be described as relatively tight with very limited, if any, spare capacity. Further, the national unemployment rate dropped from nearly 11 percent in 1982 to slightly above 5 percent during the late 1980s. Not only had massive joblessness faded, but in a sizeable number of geographic areas, the main problem had become one of labor scarcity, particularly of relatively skilled workers and other very specialized employees. Thus, in cyclical terms, the economy is operating nearly at its limits. Most of the fuel for new growth is already being used.

Second, the recent slowdown has been compounded by a fading out of the numerous stimulants discussed earlier that helped translate the large potential for growth that resulted from cyclical forces into real performance. For example, the enormous fiscal stimulus provided by the civilian and military halves of Reaganomics in the early 1980s has long since passed. The large deficits are still rising. But they are now choking off growth by helping to prop up real interest rates at a time when these rates are beginning to bite ever deeper. Large budget deficits hamper growth in several ways: by squeezing out more productive investment; by increasing our dependence on foreign capital; and by creating ongoing uncertainty in capital markets. Further, the nominal deficit continues to rise—because of rising interest payments, because of the increased cost of the savings-and-loan bailout, and because slow growth depresses tax revenues.

Cuts in defense spending and restraint in other expenditure programs are exerting an actual fiscal drag. Meanwhile, the shifting of many Federal programs to state and local governments is forcing sizeable increases in state and local taxes, which further depress economic activity. And of course any deficit reduction package that may be implemented—including additional spending cuts and/or tax increases—would only slow growth even more.

The large private debt overhang accumulated during the 1980s has also become an obstacle to economic growth. Put very directly, we borrowed from the future during the 1980s, not only at the Federal government level but in the private sector as well. The cost of servicing the debt already accumulated by households and corporations has reduced the leeway to borrow to finance new spending commitments. It is thus also now restraining economic activity—especially sales of autos and other credit-sensitive products.

Third, the weakness in the financial system caused by excessive risk-taking in the 1980s and other structural factors is dampening economic activity as well. Rising credit-quality problems coupled with the need to increase capital levels are forcing nearly all financial institutions to become extremely cautious. In order to improve their balance sheets and cut down on their nonperforming assets, they will now make credit tighter than usual even for their most reliable customers. The construction of office buildings, hotels, and condominiums fueled growth in the 1980s, but it has also left the economy extremely overbuilt today. As a result, new activity for most types of construction has fallen very sharply and these low levels have become an additional drag on growth.

Oil is another factor slowing the economy now after helping to speed it up in the 1980s. Even before the Iraqi invasion of Kuwait, oil prices were on the way back up. And although the impact on inflation and economic activity to date has been far smaller than it was when oil prices skyrocketed during the 1970s, a major stimulant to early 1980s growth no longer exists. Now, of course, the latest price surge is becoming a brake on the economy.

Partly reflecting energy prices, the overall inflation rate has also stopped declining and has in fact experienced a mild upswing since the low point of 1986. It is difficult to prove that inflation has significantly hurt the economy over the last year or two. But it is clear that the economy is no longer benefitting from declining inflation as it had earlier.

Virtually the same observations can be made about interest rates. After declining sharply in nominal terms over a six year period, interest rates have begun to climb in recent years, particularly in the long end of the market. Again, rates have not risen enough to halt the expansion. Yet whatever stimulus the economy previously received from declining rates is no longer available. Further, as mentioned earlier, real interest rates remain extremely high, and their bite is becoming ever deeper because the highest rate of return investments have already been made, and because those investments that are less important or that will produce lower returns tend to be more heavily affected by interest rates.

The long-term outlook

Now that the cyclical forces are spent and many of the temporary stimulants have now been reversed, how fast the U.S. economy grows in the future will depend largely on long-term factors—the overlooked or previously obscured fundamentals. As mentioned earlier, these underlying determinants of growth have remained relatively poor during the 1980s despite superficial signs of economic health, and in fact in many cases have deteriorated.

Of critical importance is the sharp slowing of productivity growth during the past two years. This slowdown followed a brief period of improvement that was largely cyclical in nature and mostly caused by one-time adjustments. Now that most previously idle workers are back in the labor force, the only way to spark faster growth in the future is by getting more productivity out of this existing labor force.

On top of this, the factors that determine productivity are weakening, too, strongly indicating that no upswing is likely any time soon. The growth in private, nondefense research and development continues to slow dramatically, in part because of high debt levels in the corporate sector. In addition, by virtually all measures, the quality of American education, particularly in math and science, has not improved from the relatively dismal levels to which it sank in the 1970s. And in inner-city schools in particular, the situation seems to be getting worse.

Finally, not only is the level of investment in the United States still unacceptably low and in net terms still below the levels in the 1950s and 1960s, but the mix of investment has been anything but optimal. Too much U.S. investment has gone into building shopping centers and office buildings, and toward purchases of personal computers and information gathering equipment. Not nearly enough has gone into the types of equipment that would improve efficiency and productivity.

The weakness in productivity is, moreover, occurring at the same time that demographic factors are reducing labor-force growth. Sluggish labor-force growth will only compound the weakness in productivity and further depress overall economic growth. Even more disturbing, the limited labor-force growth in the 1990s will come primarily from segments of the population with relatively little education and few skills.

And, as discussed earlier, U.S. competitiveness in world markets remains extremely poor at a time when global economic integration penalizes laggard countries ever more sharply. Unless U.S. domestic demand plummets further, no significant additional improvement can be expected in the trade account without higher productivity levels and better product quality. And the competitiveness problems facing the U.S. economy will surely be magnified by the enormous research-and-development and investment booms now underway in Japan and the rest of the Far East, which are likely to bring sharp increases in productivity and many new products in the 1990s. In addition, economic integration in Europe ultimately is likely to raise productivity levels—by weeding out cumbersome regulations and creating economies of scale in many industries. The increasing use of relatively low cost labor from southern and Eastern Europe may further enhance Europe's competitive position. Thus, today's apparently complacent American attitudes regarding trade are misplaced—the more so because the massive military buildup and construction boom that offset our deteriorating trade position in the 1980s will not exist in the 1990s. Any weakness in trade cannot fail to affect overall economic activity much more profoundly than it did during the 1980s. Lastly, as mentioned above, the U.S. savings rate remains relatively low, with very little evidence of any rebound—let alone any movement toward catching up with the other industrialized countries.

The overall picture is as clear as it is worrisome. Moreover, in virtually every case, we have begun to lag considerably behind most other leading countries. And several of the factors that are now holding the economy down, even below the limited potential for growth that remains, are likely to persist for a relatively long period.

In particular, it is likely to take a relatively long period of time to: stabilize the financial system; absorb the excess building of the 1980s; bring private debt burdens down to levels where they no longer retard economic growth; reduce the Federal deficit to acceptable levels; lower real interest rates; reduce our dependence on imported oil; and improve our competitiveness in world markets.

In effect, the deterioration in the factors that determine long-term economic growth (savings, investment, quality of education, etc.) has reduced the growth in potential output to a rate far below the historical norm for the United States. Reversing the excesses of the 1980s, moreover, will probably hold the economy even below this modest potential for many more years. The net effect: the U.S. economy seems to be headed for an extremely long period of subpar performance unless many of the underlying trends are changed.

We are now just entering a painful adjustment process. It could continue for many years. In turn, a weakened U.S. economy will lag far behind the rest of the world in the 1990s, with obvious implications for America's political clout.

Numerous warning signs already in place suggest that this long period of both absolute and relative economic decline may have already started, despite the expansion of the 1980s. For example, not only did real incomes stagnate in the last decade, but many American workers are worse off now than they were ten years ago—either their wages have not kept pace with inflation, or they were laid off from a high wage job and forced to take one at lower wages. Rising oil prices and higher tax burdens will only aggravate the squeeze on real incomes in the 1990s. Moreover, some basic needs such as housing, education, and health care, have become increasingly unaffordable for a rising share of the population. Even before the recent slowdown, delinquencies, bankruptcies, and foreclosures reached levels that were in many cases higher than those at the troughs of previous recessions. It is not difficult to imagine how these problems could multiply in a prolonged period of slow or no growth. Similarly, the savings-and-loan crisis, coupled with rising bank failures, developed even while the expansion was still proceeding, again suggesting fundamental weaknesses in the system that were at least partially hidden.

In addition, the distribution of income became much more unequal during the 1980s. And the budget deficit can only be described as being completely out of control, with federal spending aimed toward building for the future essentially being crowded out by debt servicing. Reliance on foreign capital continues unabated at a time when the need for such capital has increased elsewhere in the world, and therefore the price has risen. Finally, virtually every study shows that the sharp deterioration of America's infrastructure [*See Part VI*] has become one of the biggest obstacles to better U.S. productivity.

The final blow is that economic policy has become virtually inoperable or ineffective in America. Massive budget deficits have eliminated fiscal policy as a stabilization tool. And the enormous dependence on foreign capital has reduced the Federal Reserve's control over long-term interest rates, thus curbing the Fed's flexibility in the use of monetary policy.

The United States is not headed for complete economic disaster. But the policies of the 1980s, coupled with the neglect, indifference and greed that permeated American politics, society, and business, have worsened our economy's long-term outlook even though in the short-term they fostered a long economic recovery. Unless some of the underlying trends are reversed promptly, the 1990s shape up as a most difficult decade for America.

The Rusting Machine Tool Sector

The machine-tool industry stands at the heart of the nation's manufacturing infrastructure, and it is far more important than its relatively small size might suggest. All industries depend on machine tools to cut and shape parts. The entire industrial economy suffers if a nation's machine tools are too slow, cannot hold tight tolerances, break down often, or cost too much. If American manufacturers must turn to foreign sources for machine tools (or for other basic processing systems, such as those for fabricating semiconductors or making steel), they can hardly hope to be leaders in their industries, because overseas competitors will often get the latest advances sooner. . . .

Growing American dependence on foreign machine-tool vendors is already putting some U.S. manufacturers behind their foreign competitors. . . . Thus, if U.S. manufacturing industries want to lead rather than be perpetually trying to catch up, a strong American machine-tool industry will be essential.

Much of the American machine-tool industry has been in decline for a decade or two. The Commission found a pattern of interrelated causes for the decline, most of which are characteristic of the entire industrial economy. In other words, not just the builders of machine tools are responsible; the buyers and users are too. Briefly, the causes are these:

- A sharply declining interest in the manufacturing process as a strategic advantage within industry and as an intellectual keystone within universities;

- Weak user demand for innovation and declining user sophistication in new process technologies and equipment;

- Short-term investment strategies fostered by Wall Street;

Excerpted with permission from Made In America: Regaining the Productive Edge *by Michael L. Dertouzos, Richard K. Lester, Robert M. Solow and the MIT Commission on Industrial Productivity (Cambridge, Mass.: MIT Press, 1989).*

- The absence of commercially oriented government policies.

Although a few American machine-tool makers remain leaders or contenders, broad leadership has been taken over by Japan and Europe; within the European community, West Germany is the leader. The West Germans and the Japanese have taken quite different approaches to advancing their machine-tool industries. German firms stress high precision and special capabilities, whereas the Japanese concentrate on offering fast delivery of reliable, standard machines at low prices. Contrasting the recent history of the industry in the United States with these more successful nations, however, reveals some common elements for success, including an export orientation, continuous innovation with rapid adoption of advanced technology, mechanisms to propagate information across the industry, high levels of cooperation, and sophisticated user communities.

Structure of the U.S. industry

The U.S. machine-tool industry has historically been fragmented, with small firms, mostly family-owned, clustered in regions where user industries are concentrated. Each firm tended to specialize in a narrow product line for a particular market. . . .

Since the mid-1960s the industry has been consolidating as smaller companies have been bought by larger firms, particularly conglomerates. By 1982, 85 percent of machine-tool production companies had become concentrated in just 12 firms, and the number of active companies had shrunk steadily until only about 500 remained. Even with the consolidation, however, nearly two-thirds of domestic machine-tool builders still have fewer than 20 employees. The acquiring firms, for the most part, have continued to operate their acquisitions as separate units rather than rationalizing product lines, integrating manufacturing facilities, and combining marketing efforts.

Performance of the industry

After a worldwide economic boom that crested between 1979 and 1981, orders and shipments for machine tools nose-dived. Orders have been rising again since the mid-1980s, but the industry has rebounded less strongly in the United States than in the other major producing nations. . . . U.S. shipments peaked at $5.1 billion in 1981, and after the slump of the early 1980s they rose to only $2.8 billion in 1986. From being the world's largest producer with over a fourth of world production in the 1960s, the U.S. industry's share had shrunk to less than 10 percent by 1986. Japan, meanwhile, with only 7.5

percent of world production in 1968, exceeded 24 percent in 1986.

A major problem facing American machine-tool builders is that demand by U.S. manufacturers appears to have permanently shrunk. Many metalworking companies in a broad ranger of industries have shut down domestic factories. Other materials, such as plastics and fiber composites, are increasingly replacing metal. Some process improvements (such as powder-metal near-net-shape casting) have reduced the need for machining. . . .

At the same time the share of imported machine tools in the U.S. market rose from 4 percent in the mid-1960s to nearly 50 percent in 1986. . . . Penetration has been greatest in metal-cutting machines, which are about three-fourths of the market, especially in CNC lathes and machining centers in the low- and mid-price ranges. That was the first sector of the American market targeted by the Japanese. In contrast, for grinding and polishing machines, imports are strongest at the high-price end of the market, because the United States depends on precision equipment from Europe in this category.

Globalization of the business has also worked against the American industry, which has not been export-oriented. During the past two decades the share of worldwide machine-tool production that is exported rose from less than 30 percent to almost half. All European countries trade extensively, especially with one another, based on special strengths in particular types of machines. The European companies have been strong in precision, custom-engineered machines that often have unique capabilities. Japan, which is now the world's largest producer of machine tools, is challenging West Germany's position as the top exporter. The Japanese, initially lacking skills in precision machining, aimed first to build standard, low-cost, reliable products that could be used by almost any metal working manufacturer or machine shop. In recent years such newly industrialized countries as South Korea, Taiwan, and Brazil have begun to displace Japan in low-cost lathes and drills; most recently these new entrants in the market have begun to switch more of their production to numerically controlled (NC) machines. The Japanese, meanwhile, have been moving toward higher precision with more advanced computer controls, and they are building highly integrated machining systems.

Recognizing the importance of overseas plants for marketing and supporting specialized equipment and systems, the Japanese and some European companies are building plants in the United States. Moreover, American machine-tool companies have entered into licensing and distribution agreements with Japanese firms to sell foreign-built machines in the American market, especially at the low end of the American manufacturers' lines. This strategy produces higher profits for the U.S. companies in the short run, but the long-term effect will be loss of the skills needed to design and build competitive low-cost machines. . . .

The outlook for the U.S. industry

Without a coordinated, national effort the prospects for machine-tool builders in this country are not good. The United States has not established a global market niche as the Europeans, the Japanese, and more recently, even some of the newly industrialized countries have done. The funds needed to make the American machine-tool makers competitive again cannot be generated internally by this fragmented, cyclical industry. U.S. machine-tool companies are not export-oriented, and so they do not have the pressures to be innovative felt by their foreign competitors, and government controls discourage exporting. The status accorded to manufacturing by most managers and professionals remains low, and little has been done to make it an important part of engineering education.

Two recent efforts to help the industry catch up, both fostered by the Department of Defense, fall far short of what is needed. The Air Force, through its Manufacturing Technology (ManTech) program, has encouraged research on manufacturing processes rather than products; the companion Technological Modernization (TechMod) program supplies seed money to get contractors to install advanced equipment. . . .

The second effort is the National Center for Manufacturing Sciences (NCMS), located in Ann Arbor, Michigan. More than 110 companies across a broad spectrum of machine-tool builders and users had joined by mid-1988. . . . NCMS aims to set a national agenda for manufacturing research and then promote the dissemination and commercialization of results. Research will be conducted by groups of members, sometimes in collaboration with universities or other research institutions. After a promising start, NCMS is working to build up funding to levels where it can become effective in upgrading American manufacturing.

Although these small programs are encouraging, they are not nearly enough. Without a strong, commercially focused national policy, it is difficult to see how this critical industry can be turned around. And that does not bode well for American industry as a whole, since excellent machine tools are a key to the nation's manufacturing strength.

The Browning-out of U.S. Electronics

The U.S. electronics sector has been historically and remains today the overall leader in the world by many measures. In terms of output, employment, innovation, and technology base, the United States is number one. However, in terms of the growth of these measures and others, such as exports, Japan and Korea are quickly reducing the U.S. advantage. In fact, if current relative growth rates continue, the Japanese will be the world's number one electronics producer and trader by the early 1990s.

U.S. suppliers of a broad range of electronic products have seen their worldwide market shares rapidly decline over the last several years—from silicon wafers and DRAMs (memory chips) to computer displays and telecommunications network switches. The situation is even bleak for some of the newest technologies: X-ray lithography, optical storage devices, and flat panel displays.

Thus, U.S. leadership in electronics is under serious challenge and may very well be eclipsed unless continued tenacity by the U.S. private sector is accompanied by a higher degree of consensus within the industry and improved coordination with academia, federal, state and local governments.

The importance of electronics to the nation

Electronics is the major growth area in the U.S. economy—in terms of employment, output, exports, and innovation. In 1988, the sector employed nearly 2 million workers and shipped $200 billion in products, of which $39 billion was exported. Electronic inventions received 40 percent of all patents, and the sector conducted 20 percent of all U.S. industry's research. These facts suggest that any further erosion in this sector's competitive status could have serious implications for the health of the U.S. economy and the standard of living of Americans generally.

Electronics is also vital to the nation's defense and security since our

Excerpted from The Competitive Status of the U.S. Electronics Sector: From Materials to Systems *(Washington, D.C.: U.S. Department of Commerce, 1990).*

military advantage is based on technological superiority, not the quantity of the weapons in our arsenals.

Causes of the competitive challenge

The causes can be found both domestically and internationally. Domestically, the electronics sector is disadvantaged relative to other nations in such areas as the higher cost and lower availability of finance capital, weaknesses in vocational training and science and engineering education, and stricter antitrust laws. Although these issues affect many other U.S. industries, electronics is particularly vulnerable, since the sector is one of the most capital intensive, is extremely dependent on scientists and engineers throughout its operations, and may be forced to move toward joint manufacturing efforts in some products to counter foreign dominance.

Internationally, the sector faces targeting by many foreign governments which have identified electronics as crucial to their economic destinies. They have instituted policies to foster their domestic industries, including restricting domestic markets, funding joint R&D projects, and forcing the transfer of technology from foreign suppliers to domestic firms. Electronics firms have been hurt by unfair trade practices such as dumping and intellectual property rights violations.

In contrast to these foreign governments, the U.S. Government has not had a coordinated set of policies directed at this sector. In general, the United States has followed an ad hoc approach, the effect of which has been to place the U.S. electronics sector at a competitive disadvantage . . . .

The electronics sector itself is the origin of some of the reasons for its declining competitiveness. As is true of U.S. corporations in general, management of electronics companies has been forced by their equity structure to take a less strategic view of the market than have their foreign competitors, who often emphasize market share over return on investment. The smaller capitalized, entrepreneurial character of companies comprising over 90 percent of the firms in this sector makes them more vulnerable to price discounting tactics frequently employed by foreign competitors. Some U.S. electronics firms are not as efficient as their Japanese competitors in transferring research and development results to the market. Moreover, the Japanese lead in manufacturing techniques, giving them an edge in producing low-cost, high-quality products. The Japanese have made substantial market gains through their focus on making incremental improvements on existing products . . . .

In terms of growth rates since 1984 . . . . [t]he United States fell to last place, with an average of only 1 percent per year, compared with 8 and 6 percent for Japan and the EC [European Community], respectively. In short, if Japan and the United States maintained their respective growth rates, Japanese electronics production would surpass that of the United States in 1994. The newly industrialized countries (NICs)—South Korea, Taiwan, Singapore, Brazil, and India—all had double digit average growth rates, although from much smaller bases.

Several factors contributed to the relative decline . . . . In addition to some softness in the U.S. market, the growing strength of the dollar until 1985. . .weakened overseas demand for U.S. products. Finally foreign competition increased, in terms of price, reliability, and level of technology.

. . . . Japan not only was the leading electronics exporter in volume ($42 billion) in 1987, but also outstripped the United States in export growth by a ratio of 3 to 1. Although representing about 23 percent of the world's electronics trade in 1987 (the most recent year available across these countries), the United States had a $4.8 billion trade deficit and ranked last among the selected countries in terms of the rate of improvement in its balance of trade. . . .

While U.S. electronics exports grew substantially from 1980-87, with some impetus from a weakening dollar, their growth was outstripped by that of U.S. electronics imports . . . . The principal source of these imports was the Far East. Some of this deficit was attributable to the movement offshore of U.S. production, some to outsourcing by U.S.-based firms (including affiliates of foreign companies) from both U.S. overseas subsidiaries and foreign suppliers.

. . . . The United States also had the largest electronics market in 1988, with a 40 percent share of world consumption. Japan and the EC followed with 20 and 26 percent, respectively. As in the case of production, other markets have been growing faster, placing the U.S. market in last place in terms of growth. . . .

These figures show that Japan and Europe taken together surpass the U.S. market in value, underscoring the fact that U.S. electronics companies must not only compete successfully in their own market, but in these overseas markets as well if they are to survive. The sector cannot depend only on its domestic market for future growth. Flowing from this is the implication that these foreign markets must be free of trade and investment barriers for U.S.

electronics firms to compete fairly.

. . . . The United States has the largest electronics work force, but electronics employment in other countries, such as Japan and Korea, has grown more rapidly. While employment in the U.S. electronics sector has shown steady gains, growth since 1982 has slowed. Within this overall growth, the number of production workers remained virtually unchanged, reflecting the movement to offshore production and the increasing use of automation.

. . . . A country's physical and human infrastructures are vital to the support of a high technology sector, such as electronics. As a proxy for the physical infrastructure, telephones and computers per capita will be compared. The rationale is that these products are fundamental elements of an environment that provides not only communications, but also the computational resources to design, develop, and manufacture sophisticated product technologies. The United States leads in physical infrastructure, while Singapore, with its high concentration of foreign operations, is the leading developing country.

In terms of the human infrastructure, the situation is different. While the United States has the largest number of scientists and engineers of any country (787,400), according to U.N. data, Japan has the highest concentration of scientists and engineers (4,712 per million of population). Korea has the largest number of scientists and engineers among the NICs. . . .

The number of U.S. electronics patents granted from 1963 to 1987 was used as the proxy for these countries' technological know-how. Patents awarded by the United States usually reflect the most advanced technologies developed worldwide and the technological prowess of competitors in the U.S. market. As expected, the United States has the predominant share, although this has declined from 80 percent of the total prior to 1974 to 55 percent in 1987. There has been a significant surge recently in the number of foreign-owned patents granted, with most of these going to Japan. Taiwan has the largest number of patents (1 percent of the total) among the developing countries; however, data show that relative latecomers, like South Korea, have increased their activity substantially in recent years. The Japanese have more than doubled the number of U.S. electronics patents they were awarded when compared with the mid-1970s, and their patents have been cited more frequently than those of their U.S. counterparts. Japanese companies also held the top three positions for U.S. electronics patents received in 1987 . . . .

Specific electronics technologies

This downward trend in the U.S. share of patents is reflected in the declining capabilities of U.S. firms relative to the Japanese in the research and development phases of bringing key electronics technologies to market. In process materials, U.S. firms lag behind the Japanese in nearly all areas. Their Japanese competitors are now the dominant suppliers of high-quality semiconductor materials and the only source of ceramic packaging materials and quartz glass for mask blanks. U.S. companies also trail in many processing equipment technologies, particularly those required to produce sub-micron semiconductor devices.

At the component level, U.S. firms lead only in microprocessors and custom/semicustom logic and are behind in several key memory technologies and optoelectronics. The United States has seen its lead eroded in many systems-level products. In the computer area, U.S. firms are roughly at parity with the Japanese in hardware design although they still have a slight, but dwindling, advantage in the development of parallel, multiprocessor systems.

In telecommunications, a panel of government and industry experts reported in 1986 that the United States had generally lost ground to the Japanese in advanced research and product development in telecommunications wire and radio systems. But the United States remained strong in basic research on networks and networking subsystems.

World market shares

. . . . Table 10 [page 36] shows that dramatic erosion occurred from 1984 to 1988 in the share of worldwide shipments of U.S. companies across a broad range of major products corresponding to many of these technologies. Another perspective can be seen by narrowing the view to computers. . . . [O]ver the 1977 to 1986 period, U.S. computer companies, while showing revenue growth, lost market share to local and third-country suppliers in [the five leading foreign markets for computers: France, Italy, the United Kingdom, West Germany, and Japan]. The loss was particularly startling in Japan, where the U.S. market share dropped from about 50 to 22 percent over this period. . . .

Future competitive trends

Unfair trade practices at the company level will likely spread to new segments of the sector. For example, dumping of computer software and integrated systems is likely to occur as foreign suppliers progress technically and begin to move into these markets. Overseas, violations of intellectual property rights (IPR) will continue where foreign governments do not institute effective intellectual property laws or do not adequately enforce existing laws. In the U.S. market, IPR violations could increase, if both the U.S. Government and industry do not remain diligent . . . . Smaller U.S. electronics firms will be most vulnerable . . . .

The main competition in the world's electronics markets should come from the Far East and Europe. Japanese suppliers are becoming more multinational in character, establishing manufacturing facilities to serve local customers in the United States and key European nations. They are also expanding their R&D operations overseas to take advantage of foreign research talent. The Europeans are hoping to emerge as a stronger force in the world market for electronics products through their national and regional R&D projects and the 1992 initiatives. The developing countries generally have targeted the production of low-end equipment (personal computers, peripherals, and customer premises equipment). However, as their technological know-how improves, they should move upstream into more capital-intensive areas (semiconductors) and knowledge-intensive areas (software and services) . . . .

Computers

Japan is already the United States' main competitor in almost all product segments. The United States is still ahead in some—microcomputers, workstations, and high performance computer systems; Japan leads in others— optical storage, video displays, and laser printers. South Korea and Taiwan are becoming very competitive in microcomputers and peripherals. The EC may play a significant role in several areas, such as parallel processors, but much of this will depend upon the outcome of their R&D efforts, such as ESPRIT.

Software

Japan may also emerge as the leading competitor in software, based on the amount of resources it is putting into the TRON and SIGMA projects and into software engineering research. Japan is seeking to exploit the synergism between microprocessors and software through these R&D efforts and through becoming a leading force in the important area of technical and market standards. To obtain the necessary programming talent, Japanese companies are linking up with software firms in the United States and

Table 10 <u>U.S. Share of Worldwide Electronics Markets</u>
(1984 and 1987)

	Percent		Worldwide
	<u>1984</u>	<u>1987</u>	<u>Market ($B)</u>
Silicon Wafers	85	22	$>.01
Automatic Test Equip.	75	68	1.2
Semiconductor Mfg. Equip.	62	57	6.5
Microlithography Equip.	47	35	2.0
All Semiconductors	54	41	$38.1
ASICs	60	50	7.3
DRAMs	20	8	3.4
Microprocessors	63	47	1.7
Computers	78	69	$121.0
Personal Computers	75	64	47.2
Laptop Computers	85	57	1.6
Supercomputers	96	77	1.1
Computer Subsystems			
Displays	11	8	8.2
Flat Panel Displays	25	15	2.4
Floppy Drives	35	2	2.5
Hard Drives (up to 300 MB)	73	65	8.2
Hard Drives (up to 40 MB)	70	60	2.3
Dot Matrix Printers	10	8	4.8
Software	70	72	$44.5
Operating Systems	90	90	16.4
Data Base Mgmt. Systems	100	95	2.8
Spreadsheets	100	100	0.9
Telecommunications Equip.	33	32	$88.0
Central Office Switching	30	24	4.8
Fiber Optics	75	50	3.0
Private Branch Exchange	29	26	7.8
Data PBXs	100	36	0.2
Facsimile	30	25	3.1
Key Telephone Systems	28	22	5.7
Voice Mail Systems	100	100	0.6
LANs	100	98	2.4
Data Modems	49	37	3.2
Statistical Multiplexors	94	35	0.5
Instruments	52	46	$48.9
Medical Equip.	35	41	12.3
Photocopiers	40	36	$13.4
Consumer Electronics	19	12	$37.2

Source: Science & Electronics, U.S. Department of Commerce

Europe, while the Japanese Government is revamping Japan's educational system, including closer relationships between industry and academic research.

Singapore and India have targeted software for domestic development. Both benefit from low-cost labor and close ties with U.S. and European firms which, in turn, are transferring technology and serving as major customers. India has a large number of trained software developers available for contract programming. Singapore, committed to becoming the leading center for software and computer services in South East Asia, has expended substantial resources on increasing the technical capabilities of its work force. (The Europeans have always had a sound research base and have demonstrated particular skill in developing custom software. In recent years, they have become more interested in overseas markets.)

Systems integration (SI) can be viewed as a software-based activity, in that SI suppliers generally select computer and telecommunications equipment from a variety of vendors, develop software for specific applications, and sell the complete system directly to the users. These systems can be microcomputer-based, e.g., a personal computer system for doctors or dentists, or very large systems, e.g., an air traffic control system. U.S. firms are currently leaders worldwide in the large systems. The smaller systems often have to be customized for geographic and cultural differences, and, thus, U.S. suppliers frequently compete with domestic suppliers in each country.

Both the Japanese and the Europeans should draw on their strengths in custom software development to make them very competitive with U.S. firms in systems integration. The leading Japanese computer suppliers are also major telecommunications suppliers and can bring to bear a broadly based expertise in competing for large-scale information systems projects.

Telecommunications

Japan, France, West Germany, Sweden, and Canada are the major U.S. competitors in telecommunications. These nations are seriously challenging the U.S. lead in networking equipment. Japan, in particular, has become a primary rival in terminal equipment while Taiwan and South Korea are now the dominant suppliers in certain low-end telecommunications products like telephone handsets. Japanese and European firms have also mounted a significant challenge in the newer fiber optics, satellite, and cellular radiotelephone technologies.

Semiconductors

Japan, the current world leader in DRAM memory chip production, is vying with the United States for the technological lead in all segments of the semiconductor industry, especially in the latest generation of memory devices and application-specific integrated circuits (ASICs). Japan is also making a strong effort to catch up in microprocessors. Other challengers are on the horizon. Most of the major Asian and European players in the electronics equipment market realize the importance of domestic semiconductor production to their long-term strategies of competing more effectively at the systems level and are actively promoting this sector. For example, Korea has made significant strides in DRAM production, while the EC is using its internal rules-of-origin directives to improve its capabilities in semiconductor production. Notable EC R&D efforts in this area are the Joint European Submicron Silicon Initiative (JESSI) and the MEGA Project.

Electronic instruments

In process controls, the Japanese have replaced the Europeans as the major competitor of the United States. The principal Japanese supplier, Yokogawa, rose from obscurity during the 1980s to become one of the world's three major manufacturers in this area. The other two are U.S. companies. A Japanese firm, Advantest, has also become a major challenger in electrical test and measuring instruments, having benefitted significantly from the government-sponsored VLSI research project during the 1970s. In laboratory instruments, which is populated by smaller firms, the market is divided among American, Swiss, West German, British, and Japanese companies. Because the electronic instruments sector is characterized by specialized markets and customized products that are less applicable to low cost or mass production, the newly industrialized countries have made little headway in capturing market share.

Medical electronics

West Germany has historically been the leading U.S. competitor in the medical electronics field and should remain so in the near future. Siemens, the largest German manufacturer, has moved aggressively into the U.S. market by establishing manufacturing plants and purchasing U.S. medical device firms. Siemens is active in pacemakers, lithotripters, hearing aids, and all modes of diagnostic imaging.

Japan has just begun challenging the United States in this industry, but will probably be the leading contender over the long run. Unlike West Germany, Japan has a number of small competitive firms that traditionally have been OEM (original equipment manufacturers) suppliers of components and devices to U.S. and European firms. However, these firms are now marketing their products under their own brand names. Japan has been strong in X-ray apparatus, and ultrasound and CT scanners; it also is becoming very active in low-cost magnetic resonance imaging.

The Foreign Investment Boom

Douglas P. Woodward

A decade ago, international economic policy concerns focused almost entirely on trade. Now, with the rise of direct investment in the United States, foreign firms have brought global competition directly to America, posing a new and significant economic challenge. Foreign ownership of U.S. factories, mines, and real estate more than quadrupled during the 1980s, from $83 billion in 1980 to $401 billion in 1989. Total foreign capital flows, which include portfolio and direct investment, grew from $500 billion to over $2 trillion during the same period.

The term "investment" implies ownership or effective control over an American asset by a foreign-based enterprise. Although effective control is difficult to determine, the standard practice is to define foreign investment as direct when the investor has a stake of ten percent or more in an asset. A position falling below ten percent constitutes portfolio investment, such as foreign purchases of U.S. Treasury bonds or stock market shares. These generally have little influence on the management and day-to-day operations of U.S. businesses.

In all, foreign-owned firms in the United States account for only about 4 percent of gross domestic product.[1] But these aggregate figures mask some important developments. For example, foreign ownership is larger today than at any time in the recent past. It has reached significant levels in important industries: 30 percent of chemical assets, 27 percent of U.S. refining capacity, 23 percent of banking assets, and increasingly dominant positions in semiconductors, biotechnology, and other industries vital to America's economic future. Indeed, as of 1987, foreign-owned firms accounted for more than one-tenth of U.S. manufacturing output.

The response to the rise of direct investment during the late 1980s has

Douglas P. Woodward *is a research economist and Assistant Professor of Economics at the University of South Carolina. He is a member of the Advisory Board of the Economic Strategy Institute.*

varied dramatically. Some see these acquisitions as "deceptively friendly and fraught with danger."[2] Others, including the Bush administration, insist that direct investment "looks innocent" and requires no change in U.S. policy.

Yet the "buying of America" is really neither an external problem nor a non-problem. Instead, it is an internal problem. The foreign investment boom signals the U.S. economy's sluggish (at best) reaction to major changes in the international arena—i.e., its inability to create a strong foundation for home-grown, globally competitive industry. The boom's origins lie in America's short-term business planning horizons, low savings, lack of long-run vestment commitments, slow productivity growth, failure to commercialize in research and development, and mismanagement of international economic policy.

Consequently, foreign rivals have achieved competitive advantages over domestic firms in a growing number of industries. These competitive advantages enable foreign firms to augment their presence in the domestic economy. For tangible evidence, one need only examine the rising share of quality U.S. patents awarded to non-Americans, and foreign firms' ability to turn innovations into marketable products. At the macroeconomic level, foreign firms are attracted primarily to the large and diverse American market, not to America's productive climate.

The dollar's post-1985 decline further spurred takeovers of U.S. companies, as the price of assets acquired by foreign-based competitors fell dramatically. Large foreign acquisitions became more common in the mid-1980s and persisted into the 1990s: Cheeseborough-Pond's (consumer products); Pillsbury (food); Macmillan, Harper & Row, and Doubleday (publishing); Genentech (biotechnology); Firestone and Uniroyal Goodrich (tires); Holiday Inns (hotels); the Farmers Group and Fireman's Fund (insurance); Federated and Allied Department Stores (retail); as well as many other lesser-known companies. But two Japanese deals prompted the greatest reaction: Mitsubishi's interest in Rockefeller Center and Sony's purchase of Columbia Pictures. In the words of two observers, "So much Japanese investment has flowed into the United States in the 1980's, that the nation is in danger of seeing its economic sovereignty washed away in a tide of yen, its history pawned to a foreign power.[3]

But if anything, the problem raised by direct investment is not a plethora of foreign capital, but a dearth of domestic capital. As long as the U.S. savings rate remains below the rates of its major competitors and the nation fails to devote adequate resources to future expansion, America will indeed wind up "selling-out" itself. For example, in absolute terms Japan's capital investment in the home economy has exceeded American domestic investment since 1987. Over a quarter of Japanese gross national product is devoted to capital spending, compared with 10 percent in America. Meanwhile, many technology start-ups in the United States look abroad for financial backing—unable to raise capital from U.S. venture capital funds.

Even those who dismiss the foreign investment "threat" agree that the ascendancy of the foreign ownership poses a challenge.[4] When Europeans faced the challenge of American multinational expansion during the 1960s, they neither dismissed it nor accepted the status quo. Instead, they sought to uncover the "secrets" of U.S. business enterprise—then the world's most advanced and powerful multinational organizations. Today, European and Japanese multinational exhibits increasing strengths both in structure and strategy, yet the nature of this challenge is largely unexplained.

Painting with a broad brush

Most foreign investment analysis to date has been based on broad brush summaries of official government data. But these numbers raise as many questions as they answer.

It is well known, for example, that the sources of total direct investment are changing. The United Kingdom has been the leading investor nation in the United States, with $119.1 billion of U.S. assets in 1989. Investment from continental Europe has flowed mostly from the Netherlands, West Germany, and France. The average annual growth of Dutch investment in America during the 1980s was about 19 percent (compared with 22 percent for Great Britain) and reached $60.4 billion by the end of 1989. Yet the Dutch fell from first to third place among all sources of direct investment during the 1980s. West Germany's direct investment position grew at about the same rate as the Netherlands, ending the decade with a $26.9 billion stake—less than half the size of the Dutch.

Japanese companies have advanced more rapidly than any other source, with an annual growth rate (42 percent) far exceeding all major investor nations during the 1980s. In 1980, Japan held the seventh largest position. By the decade's close it had vaulted to second place, with $69.7 billion of U.S. holdings—17 percent of the total. The gross product of Japanese-affiliated companies in the United States also grew faster than any other nation from 1987-1987, but remained below the United Kingdom and Canada.

Yet other aggregate measures of foreign firm activity paint a different picture. Japan is the largest investor in America when measured by sales of U.S. subsidiaries. Measured in terms of employees, however, Japanese acquisitions rank below those of West Germany, the United Kingdom, and Canada—although once again the Japanese growth rate is the fastest. Japanese investors also rank low (sixth) in research and development expenditures, with West German investors holding the lead.

Aggregate measures of direct investment sources yield different rankings for two principal reasons. First, the composition of investment varies widely among investor countries. Sales by Japanese-affiliated companies tend to be higher than other countries, for example, because these firms have substantially more investment in wholesale trade than companies based elsewhere. According to U.S. statistics, manufacturing affiliates account for only 7.5 percent of Japanese assets in America, while wholesale operations comprise 23 percent of all assets. In contrast, non-Japanese foreign firms in the United States have 28 percent of their assets in manufacturing and just 7 percent in wholesaling.

Second, the aggregate figures largely reflect takeovers of existing U.S. companies. The overwhelmingly preferred mode of foreign entry continues to be acquisition, not new plant investment. Recent data released by the U.S. Bureau of Economic Analysis show that in 1988 about 92 percent of transferred assets came under foreign ownership through corporate buyouts.[5] Large takeovers, like the Grand Metropolitan's buyout of Pillsbury, tend to raise the number of jobs in foreign-owned firms by the tens of thousands in one fell swoop. Yet Japanese investors (until recently) tended to build new plants rather than acquire existing assets.[6] More new jobs are created in this way, but the figures pale in comparison with the overall employment levels of U.S. firms sold to foreign owners.

More serious problems emerge in comparing the aggregate economic activity of foreign-owned firms and domestic firms. Edward M. Graham and Paul R. Krugman, for example, claim that foreign and domestic firms are essentially similar, using value-added per worker figures based on Bureau of Economic Analysis data. Yet the methods and data underlying this inference are suspect. The authors' comparisons of value-added per worker mostly cover foreign acquisitions (more than four-fifths of all direct investment). All the value-added of an acquired firm is simply transferred to the new foreign owners. But the important questions about foreign takeovers concern growing control of specific critical technologies and the impact on U.S. military and economic security, which the authors cannot and do not isolate with government data.[7]

On top of this are the problems inherent in any comparison of foreign firms' gross product data and the separate national income and product accounts (NIPA) for all U.S. companies.   Many members of the "non-problem" school of thought ignore the Bureau of Economic Analysis's own disclaimer on the data: "Because sources of data for affiliates [of foreign companies] and NIPA [U.S. national income and product accounts] estimates differ, differences in timing, valuation, and industry classification, among others, could significantly affect comparisons."[8]

Such problems with the aggregate data render it impossible to reach detailed and reliable conclusions about foreign firms' impact on specific economic sectors. The Bureau of Economic Analysis, for example, provides an industry-by-industry breakdown of value-added for U.S. affiliates of foreign companies and total U.S. value-added. These data show that foreign firms' average value-added per worker (a relative measure of the net contribution to the U.S. economy) was higher that the U.S. average, and higher still for affiliates of Japanese companies. But value-added per worker in wholesale trade, finance, and real estate was significantly higher than any other sector of the economy.[9]

Thus, understanding the composition of investment is critical. If foreign firms invest a significant share of their investment in an industry like wholesale trade, then total aggregate value-added per worker will be high. But the results depend on how one chooses to cut the data. Although Japanese-owned firms lead all investor nations in value-added *per worker*, they in exhibit lowest value-added *per sales* of all major investor nations.

What matters are industry, not aggregate, comparisons. Unfortunately, even the broad industry breakdown of foreign investment statistics released by the Bureau of Economic Analysis is not reliable. Foreign companies only supply information on an "enterprise basis." This means, for instance, that all of a foreign automobile company's operations (or establishments) can all be categorized under one industry group. But many foreign concerns own U.S. establishments spanning several industry classifications.   They may both assemble automobiles and distribute them through a network of wholesale affiliates. A foreign-owned auto assembly plant may be classified under wholesale trade, not manufacturing. Meaningful conclusions about the contribution of foreign firms to the U.S. economy become impossible.

Another unresolved question concerns foreign firms' contribution to U.S.

research and development (R&D). Aggregate data fail to shed much light on this important issue. Promoters of foreign direct investment often point out that foreign firms have invested heavily in research and development. Yet all we can say based on the official data is that when foreign firms acquire R&D-intensive U.S. concerns, they will tend to show significant R&D activity. That is why research and development per worker (or per sales) for Swiss and West German owned firms vastly exceeds totals for Japanese-owned firms. West Germany and Switzerland have invested heavily in chemicals and pharmaceuticals, which require large R&D outlays.

A glaring illustration of the problems that arise in interpreting that official data can be seen in the Canadian direct investment figures for 1981. A naive analyst would conclude that Canadian investors' R&D spending per worker, for example, leaped from $465 to $1,776 between 1980 and 1981. In fact, all that happened was that the Seagram company took a 23 percent stake in Du Pont.

The unfinished agenda

Despite growing concern, major questions remain about foreign direct investment and its role in shaping U.S. competitiveness. Several important issues urgently require serious research.

1. *Critical technologies.* The foreign investment debate in Washington has centered on foreign control of critical technologies and strategic industries such as semiconductors and semiconductor materials, computers, and biotechnology. The questions have little to do with the "stripping" of U.S. technology. Rather, fears have been voiced about the foreign assimilation of U.S. technical advances that could be detrimental to commercial and military development in the United States, and that could even lead to supply disruptions. Some believe that the Japanese have already gained control and leverage over key segments of the nation's defense industrial base.

The problem is that it is impossible to know with any reasonably degree of certainty. A study is needed to identify emerging sectors of commercial and technical importance, and to analyze foreign penetration of those sectors. The study would have to expand beyond the usual definition of direct investment and encompass minority equity stakes in new high-technology start-ups, as well as funding arrangements in U.S. research centers and academic institutions. The study should also examine strategic alliances and joint ventures in critical technologies and their implications for U.S. competitiveness.

2. *Foreign sourcing patterns.* The optimists notwithstanding, it is not possible to say whether certain types of foreign investment are hollowing out the U.S. production base by drawing on offshore supplies. A survey conducted by the author and Norman J. Glickman and reported in *The New Competitors*, indicates that the manufacturing operations of foreign-based firms exhibit a higher tendency than domestic manufacturers to import their inputs for processing and production. But the differences were really not that large, except for high technology inputs.[10] A detailed report is needed to determine input sourcing patterns of U.S. affiliates of foreign companies, including the nation of origin of these inputs and their industrial classification, capital imports (for example, machinery imported for use in U.S. plants), finished goods, semi-finished goods, and raw materials.

A special study of Japanese input sourcing is needed. The aggregate trade numbers reported by the Bureau of Economic Analysis show that Japanese-owned firms import more than five and a half times the products imported by the average foreign direct investors in the United States. The merchandise trade deficit of affiliates of Japanese companies in the United States has been roughly equal to the overall U.S. merchandise trade deficit in recent years—some $50 billion. That figure for Japanese companies operating in the U.S. is also roughly the size of U.S.-Japanese bilateral trade deficit in recent years. So far, this phenomenon has been completely neglected in discussions of the seemingly intractable negative trade balance with Japan, which now accounts for about 45 percent of the overall U.S. trade deficit.

To date, no detailed research on the sourcing patterns for Japanese affiliated production has been conducted. One survey of 62 companies in Australia, however, found that Japanese-owned subsidiaries differ markedly in this respect from American and European subsidiaries. Japanese subsidiaries are "tightly controlled by the parent company," mainly using Japanese inputs.[11]

3. *American Keiretsu.* It is possible, although hard to prove with aggregate numbers, that the Japanese *keiretsu* system of industrial-financial combines is largely responsible for the aggregate trade and input sourcing patterns. But the integrated industrial structure of Japanese operations in the United States remains an unexplored dimension of foreign investment. Japan's distribution network in the United States has the potential to regulate and control trade and production, exports, and U.S.-based production.

What has been largely ignored is that Japanese *keiretsu* groups may be creating key competitive advantages through forward integration—by creating a vast network of distribution arms to market domestic and foreign-produced goods. Japan has apparently created a highly effective and tightly woven distribution network in the United States, quite unlike the patterns found for any other foreign investor nation. New research is called for to understand new forms of firm integration and to explore the relationship among distribution networks and manufacturing assembly and component operations within integrated Japanese companies operating in the United States. This study should focus on determining whether the Japanese *keiretsu* groups and their affiliated companies in the United States create a closed loop that could injure domestic U.S.-owned competitors.

4. *Employment effects*. In a widely read *Harvard Business Review* article, Robert Reich argued that in 1989, foreign-owned manufacturers created more jobs that domestic firms in the United States, yet no data was presented to back the assertion.[12] A detailed study of job creation and displacement resulting from foreign investment, including the quality of employment, is essential. Areas of concentration should include job change through new plants, expansions, cutbacks, acquisitions, and sales of U.S. assets—broken down by industry and region.

In a complete model of the employment effects of foreign investment, one would have to consider how the flow of foreign finds paid to acquire domestic assets is channeled into other enterprises, potentially creating additional jobs. Unfortunately, no one knows how the money paid to acquire American assets filters through the economy. Of course, one must also account for inward investment's potential displacement effects on domestic business. Additional studies are needed on the wage and occupational distribution of foreign-firm employment by industry and region on an establishment-level basis.

5. *Tax revenues from foreign subsidiaries*. As direct investment has grown, the small amount of taxes collected from many foreign-owned businesses has attracted increased attention. Foreign subsidiaries pay a relatively low amount of corporate taxes. Although foreign-owned assets more than tripled during the 1980s, the taxes collected from them by the U.S. Internal Revenue Service (IRS) remained surprisingly constant. More than half of 36,800 foreign owned companies filing U.S. returns in 1986 reported no taxable income to the IRS. Foreign-owned subsidiaries earned $542 billion in gross income that year, yet paid just $3 billion in federal income taxes. Foreign-based multinationals have been widely accused of transfer pricing—a scheme through which companies adjust the books of their subsidiaries to reduce their tax burden. These subsidiaries pay above-market prices to their parent

companies for goods and services in order to decrease their reported domestic earnings. A study of taxation and foreign-owned firms in the United States should be undertaken with comparisons of U.S. firms in similar industries.

Notes

[1] See U.S. Department of Commerce, Bureau of Economic Analysis, *Foreign Direct Investment in the United States: Gross Product of Nonbank U.S. Affiliates of Foreign Companies, 1977-1986, August 23, 1988* (Washington, D.C.: U.S. Department of Commerce, Bureau of Economic Analysis, mimeo).

[2] Martin and Susan Tolchin, *Buying Into America: How Foreign Money is Changing the Face of Our Nation* (New York: Times Books, 1988, p. 142).

[3] Douglas Frantz and Catherine Collins, *Selling Out: How We Are Letting Japan Buy Our Land, Our Industries, Our Financial Institutions, And Our Future* (New York: Contemporary Books, 1989), p. 2.

[4] Bill Emmott, *The Sun Also Sets: The Limits of Japan's Economic Power* (New York: Times Books, 1989), pp. 162-3.

[5] Ellen M. Herr, "U.S. Business Enterprises Acquired or Established by Direct Foreign Investors in 1988," *Survey of Current Business*, May 1989, pp. 22-30.

[6] Norman J. Glickman and Douglas P. Woodward, *The New Competitors: How Foreign Investors Are Changing the U.S. Economy* (New York: Basic Books, 1989).

[7] Edward M. Graham and Paul R. Krugman, *Foreign Direct Investment in the United States* (Washington, D.C.: Institute for International Economics, 1989).

[8] *Foreign Direct Investment in the United States: Gross Product*, op. cit.

[9] Final assembly "screwdriver" plants, then, may also show higher value-added per worker, since relatively little labor is used, while mark-ups and distribution charges would add significant value to the product, thus yielding relatively high value-added per worker.

[10] *The New Competitors*, op. cit.

[11] Mordechai E. Kreinin, "How Closed is the Japanese Market: Additional Evidence," *The World Economy*, vol. 11, no. 4, December 1988, pp. 529-542.

[12] See Robert B. Reich, "Who Is Us?" *Harvard Business Review*, January-February 1990, pp. 53-64.

II

A Strategic World

Troubling as the weakening of America's economy may be, it does not necessarily mean that an overarching national strategy is either essential or even desirable. That depends on the kind of world Americans believe they live in. If this world is thought to be basically safe and even benign, then there is no need to worry about topflight economic performance—especially if the world's new economic leaders are America's friends. But by the same token, there would be no need to worry about security or independence, either.

Even as the Cold War fades, American policy obviously does not believe that our world is benign militarily and politically—that is why we are only shrinking, not eliminating, the armed forces. But U.S. leaders seem to believe in an economically cozy world. Thus U.S. economic policy aims less at preserving freedom of action and Number One status than at another set of goals: common rules for what is seen as an economic game, greater global integration and interdependence, and the greatest prosperity for the world as a whole.

The selections in Part Two argue not that either set of priorities is wrong but that the military and political worlds on the one hand and the economic world on the other cannot be neatly separated. American cannot be militarily strong and in charge of its own fate unless it is economically powerful. And it cannot be economically powerful unless it is militarily strong and politically free. If one sphere is strategic, both are. And in such a world, a comprehensive national economic strategy is imperative.

In David Fromkin's view, academics are largely to blame for U.S. policymakers' neglect of the world's strategic dimensions. Modern Western scholars and the statesmen they have influenced, he writes, have wrongly viewed international politics as being basically similar to domestic politics—a realm that can and should be characterized by law, order, morality, and justice, and one in which reason, good will, and cooperation can settle any dispute. They have overlooked the state of global anarchy that forces nations to seek maximum freedom of action and control over their own destiny.

Secretary of Defense Richard Cheney, for his part, allows that losing the international economic and technological competition even to friends can have unacceptable consequences for the nation, and explains that "markets would be lost, the U.S. industrial base would erode," and dependence on foreign military technologies would reach alarming levels. David P. Calleo and Benjamin M. Rowland assail the Orthodoxy for treating national politics as a one-dimensional quest for short-term earnings. They argue that states cannot and should not simply entrust their futures to market forces, no matter how they affect their national power and their citizens' welfare. And they fault traditional economic thinking for treating individuals simply as consumers, and forgetting that most are also producers.

The next two contributions note that not even international economics, narrowly defined, is as economists have portrayed it. According to Pat Choate and Juyne Linger, unrealistic views about the economies of our trading partners have played havoc with U.S. trade policy. Washington assumes that other countries share its free trading ideals, and thus have followed the world trading system's principles of treating them exactly alike. Far better, say the authors, would be treating each country's exports exactly how that country treats America's.

As Paul R. Krugman explains, however, foreign protectionism isn't the only problem. The nature of many of the world's biggest new industries and technologies confound the notion of "perfect competition"—the traditional economic idea that newcomers to international markets face no built-in obstacles in mounting effective challenges to established producers. Krugman writes that some economists are starting to realize that because preeminence can mean a lasting edge, not only enterprises but countries gain a strong incentive to achieve it—i.e., to act strategically.

Closing the section are two pieces eloquently describing the consequences of falling behind economically in the real world. James Chace evocatively details how America's failure to maintain productivity growth and investment directly affects the quality of our lives—in this case, by turning the world's greatest metropolis into a nightmare for many of its inhabitants. Paul Kennedy draws an eerie parallel between the economic origins of Britain's early 20th century decline from great-power status and travails afflicting the American economy—and threatening America's world position—today.

The Independence of Nations

David Fromkin

In 1939, on the eve of the renewed war, the English historian E.H. Carr published a short book that, though it did not provide a satisfactory answer, asked the question more lucidly than it had ever been asked before. College students of international relations have read it, year after year, and continue to read it today. Carr wrote it at a time when Western leaders, such as Neville Chamberlain, in their quest for peace, had made things worse rather than better. For his time, and for ours. Carr posed the question with which the following chapters will be concerned. Where had they all gone wrong?

. . .[T]he misunderstanding of international politics that has characterized the statements and actions of leaders of opinion and government in the Western world throughout the twentieth century goes back to the aftermath of the 1914-1918 war; and, because the field of international relations was developed in the university, it is a misunderstanding that is rooted in economic theory . . . .

In [American] international relations courses . . . . [t]he current tendency . . . is to avoid the use even of historical examples; one of the most popular of the recent textbooks begins by saying that "no historical background is provided" and that the subject is to be taught instead by the "rigorous development of concepts and theories." What this shows is the intention with which the study of international relations has been developed in the twentieth century. The international politics of the past are not to be emulated, for they are to be fundamentally changed. . . .

. . .[F]rom the time of its origin in the teachings of Plato, political science has avoided dealing with what is fundamental in international relations. Initially, this was because Socrates and Plato discussed politics in terms of an imaginary ideal state. A distinguished classicist has written that

David Fromkin *is an attorney-at-law in New York. Reprinted by permission of Greenwood Publishing Group, Inc., Westport, CT, from* The Independence of Nations *by* David Fromkin. *Copyright © by Praeger Publishers.*

"the sole form of political thought originally recognized by Aristotle was that handed down by Plato, the Utopia"; and, "It is significant that one of his criticisms of Plato's ideal states is that they take no account of foreign affairs." It has remained a characteristic of utopian literature ever since that the ideal state is so situated, on a remote island or so inaccessible, that the rest of the world can be safely ignored. The most famous of modern utopians, Karl Marx, achieved the same theoretical result in a different way: in his vision, the state would dissolve, which in turn would cause interstate relations to disappear. Utopia never has a foreign policy.

Even after political science outgrew utopianism, political science continued to ignore the fundamental reality of international relations, which is that the corporate entities that are its principal actors are independent of higher authority. *This is not a phenomenon that occurs within countries, and so political science does not deal with it.* E.H. Carr failed to see that it was the ignoring of this central reality that had led the theorists of international relations astray. An understanding of the meaning of independence is fundamental to an understanding of international relations. It is that fundamental matter to which we should turn now.

The meaning of independence

Independence is the aspect of freedom that is negative. It means that an entity is not ruled by anybody else, that there is no entity above it, no political superior, no authority it recognizes and obeys. It is a special case: it describes a state of political affairs that is found only in international relations.

In this context, whether or not an entity is independent is a question of fact. The relevant question is whose orders, in case of conflict, are obeyed. If the government of Algeria gives its people an order, and if any other government or political authority gives a contrary order, the people of Algeria will follow the order given by their own leaders; and that is what is meant by saying that Algeria is independent. It does not mean that Algeria is free to do whatever it chooses. Like any other country, it is the prisoner of its circumstances: for example, its geography, its relative power, its relative wealth, the nature and number of its inhabitants, and the disposition of its neighbors. Independence means only the freedom to choose between such alternatives as fate may offer, few and disagreeable though these may be.

This has been a frustrating discovery for many of the poorer countries of Asia, Africa, and the Caribbean, newly liberated from colonial rule, and having won their freedom with high hopes for what it would bring. . . .

Every state is independent. But no human being is—or ever has been. Except for hermits who live and die alone in the desert, the life of every person is lived in the context of a group. This difference between the way individuals live and the way that states live has been a continuing source of misunderstanding in the study of political affairs . . . .

. . .[I]t is important to differentiate relations between people, who as members of a group are bound by a common ethic, and relations between the alien corporate entities that are states. That is something that E.H. Carr in his famous book *The Twenty Year's Crisis* denied. He admitted that the personality of the state was a fiction; but he asserted that it was necessary to postulate it anyway. He argued that it was necessary because only in this way could one clearly express the moral and legal responsibility of states from their actions. It was an argument that betrayed its own error, for states, being independent, do not have legal obligations in the same sense that fellow citizens do, and it was the confusion of the different senses in which the word "law" can be used that had characterized the unrealistic idealism of the 1920s and 1930s which Carr, in his book, undertook to attack. The unrealistic idealists had thought that if Nazi Germany did not live up to its obligations to the world community to behave peacefully, it would find itself in much the same situation that a person would be who broke the laws of a particular country by committing rape or murder. Carr wrote his book in part to explain why these two situations are different. It was a major flaw in his otherwise brilliant performance that he undermined his case by arguing that states should be thought about as though they were persons.

When Carr came to explain the difference between the law that applies to states and the law that applies to persons who live within the same country, he wrote that the former lacks three institutions: "a judicature, an executive, and a legislature." Carr apparently did not see that this adds up to more than just a "lack." These three—the executive, the legislative, and the judiciary—are the three parts of government. It is no accident that states are not subject to them. The aspects of world government do not exist because a world government does not exist.

The most important political fact about individual human beings is that they live in groups and are subject to the government and the laws of their group. Pretending that states are like people enabled Carr and others to imply that states, too, owe allegiance to a higher political authority and owe obedience to a body of laws. This pretense resulted from a fear that is at any rate understandable. The independence of states is so frightening that the natural reaction is to turn away from it. That, I suppose, is why the concept of independence, in the United States for example, is relegated to Fourth of July parades and why it is pretended that independence means freedom from only those restraints that are deplorable (such as the tyranny imposed by colonial empires). But it means more than that: it means freedom from any normative restraint whatsoever.

Dostoyevsky's Ivan Karamazov's assertion was that if human beings were not restrained by a belief in immortality, nothing would be immoral and anything would be permitted, even cannibalism; and that in these circumstances, people ought to act out of self-interest even if it leads them to crime. As a practical matter, that is not true with respect to individual humans; whatever their beliefs may be about immortality, they are restrained by civic loyalties and by the civil authorities. But it is a reasonably true statement about states. At their worst, states are beasts that roam the jungles of world politics, killing when they are hungry, and obeying no laws but those of their own nature. Where they are concerned, Dostoyevky's terrible words ring true: anything is permitted.

But whereas Ivan Karamazov feared what he himself might do if unrestrained, in international relations it is the freedom of others that is most frightening. There is no protection against the others except self-defense. No matter how extreme and unwarranted may be the cruelties that states inflict, there is no context to give either meaning or effect to the notion of punishment. There is justice within our respective states, but there is no justice between the states. In the dark streets and alleyways that the states of the world roam, the least convincing of all cries is the victim's impotent threat that "you can't get away with this!"—for countries, if they are strong enough, can get away with anything.

Of course, there are limits to the freedom of action of independent states, but from the point of view of justice and morality, these limits are irrelevant. They are such morally accidental limitations as relative strength, resources, and geographical location. They do not correspond to the limitations that domestic societies impose upon their members, because they are not imposed by a superior authority, let alone a superior authority who is morally purposeful. They are merely a form of trial by combat, and the results of trial by combat are not necessarily just. Indeed it is one of the attributes of justice—genuine justice—that it does exactly the reverse; that it protects the weak against the strong, and that on appeal, it reverses the results of those of life's trials that are by combat, rather than by reason, in the search for truth, mercy, and fairness.

International affairs are constantly a surprise because our expectations about politics are conditioned by the experience of living within a political entity. Within that entity we expect and to a certain extent obtain physical security and justice, and the benefits of programs to ensure our welfare. There is a tendency to approach international affairs with similar expectations, but the expectations prove to be false. Among states, there is no justice for the weak, no security even for the strong, and often no aid for the needy. World politics do not provide the satisfactions that can be obtained in national politics and that have come to be thought of as mankind's due. It is not because of the wickedness or stupidity of leadership groups that the satisfactions are not obtained; it is because world affairs do not have a unitary political structure.

The world of independent nations is, therefore, most unsatisfactory: its methods, its goals, and its characteristic solutions to problems are not what we would wish them to be. The characteristics of international politics—the lack of a political structure, the lack of justice, the inevitability of wars—are repugnant to civilized values and human ideals. Yet we must recognize them for what they are if we are to function effectively in their domain . . . .

After the Second World War, when the German threat had been replaced by the Soviet one, Hans Morgenthau systematically applied this perception in his textbook to the description of world politics. He portrayed international relations in all times and places as the expression of power politics. His picture of international politics was masterly and realistic, but his explanation of *why* it was so was unconvincing. He wrote that international politics are power politics because *all* politics are power politics. Anyone can see this is untrue in terms of the politics we know best, the politics of our own country. We can see that not all domestic American politics are power politics, that there are other kinds of politics, too. And we can see that in our domestic politics, the justification for playing power politics does not exist.

Within an organized and civilized political community, such as ours, a person ought not to need to have any power. He ought not to need it in order to physically survive, for his government purports to enclose him within a matrix of security. Police and other armed forces are supposed to protect him from harm. The judiciary and the other branches of government are supposed to insure that his interests receive due consideration and are not treated unfairly. Welfare, health, and educational programs provide positive benefits that go far beyond mere protection. One should be able to live, thrive, and be happy without being powerful.

In a democracy, such as our own, it also is not necessary to be powerful in order to have an equal vote in determining who will govern the country. We are enfranchised as of rights. . . . Since it is not necessary to seek power, we are suspicious, and rightly so, of anyone who does seek it . . . .

Moreover, in domestic politics a great deal of what goes on is the pursuit of *influence* rather than the pursuit of power. Washington lobbyists, presidential advisers, television personalities, and newspaper editorialists play an important role even though they hold no official position in the shaping of American national decisions. To influence a decision requires a different ability from that to make a decision, but in internal affairs both are parts of the political process.

It is not so in international affairs. In politics among nations, there is no influence without power. There is also no enfranchisement as of right; there is no entitlement to a voice or a vote in the making of international decisions. A state cannot advance its views except through the use of its power. A state cannot exist unless it has the power to compel other states to recognize its sovereign independence. There is no world government to guarantee and secure the rights of states or the inviolability of their frontiers or even their bare survival.

Thus the first and essential condition that enables an entity to exist and participate in international politics—which is to say, to be an independent state—is the possession of an adequate amount of power. That is the price of independence. What this means is that, in the first instance, all *international* politics necessarily are power politics, for only if a state achieves at least a minimum amount of success in power politics can it go on to engage in any other kind of politics. This condition of existence is what all states have in common with one another. Their response to this condition was described by Hans Morgenthau when he wrote that what states have to do, before they can do anything else, is to attempt to pursue their national interests as defined in terms of power.

The national interest means different things to different governments. Yet Morgenthau's generalized description remains meaningful. It is true that governments define the national interest of their respective states with varying degrees of wisdom and accuracy, and that the measures they take in pursuit of the national interest also vary. At the simplest level, however, there are imperatives that all governments recognize. . . .

Armed force, of course, is only one kind of power. Power can mean many things. Japan is a great industrial Power. Saudi Arabia is a great petroleum Power, and the Soviet Union is a great military Power. All of them are powerful, but in such different ways that perhaps one should not use the same word to describe all three. Power can mean the resources that a nation has at its command: its military forces, the skill of its leadership, its wealth, and such things as these. But it can also refer to the state of affairs that its resources make possible, such as its independence or its influence over domestic or foreign events. Power can be thought of as a means, as an end, or as both. Some make the distinction, too, between the power that a state expresses by successfully asserting and maintaining its own independence, and the kind of power that it seeks when it tries to exercise dominion over others. . . . [I]n large part the confusion of meanings inheres in the English language and is difficult to avoid.

What the concept of the national interest as defined in terms of power enabled Morgenthau to do was to point to the common denominator of international relations. . . . What remained to be done was to explain why this is so—why states pursue power interests and why international politics can most accurately be defined as power politics. As long as international relations were thought of in political-science terms, rather than in their own terms, no satisfactory explanation was possible. Independence makes all the difference. It is *because* states are independent that inter-state relations are power politics; in this and other respects, international politics are not, contrary to what Hans Morgenthau taught, like other kinds of politics: they are unique . . . .

Competition Among Friends

Richard B. Cheney

The overall U.S. lead in technology relative to the rest of the world has eroded over the last 20 years, and the outlook is for even greater technological competition in the future. In the years ahead, the United States will confront new challenges, perhaps from a revitalized and restructured Soviet economy, but almost certainly from a unified and competitive Europe, a dynamic Japanese economy, rapidly developing countries like South Korea and Singapore, and an unstable Third World armed with increasingly sophisticated weapons . . . .

Europe

The highly industrialized nations of Western Europe have become increasingly competitive in advanced technologies over the last 30 years. Their already formidable science and technology base will very likely expand and become even more productive as the region moves toward economic integration in 1992. While in many ways these are positive developments for U.S. security, they also represent a strong challenge to the United States' technology base.

Interestingly, many U.S. allies in Europe make a concerted effort to tie their nation's technology policy to their national security goals—to include the political and economic dimensions, as well as the military dimension. Many provide direct aid to their defense industries, while others provide financial support through their economic policies.

The Pacific Rim

The Pacific Rim presents unique dilemmas for the United States. Japan is both a very important ally of the United States and its most formidable economic competitor. The Republic of Korea is important to U.S. defense

---

Richard B. Cheney *is Secretary of Defense. Excerpted from* Soviet Military Power: Prospects for Change 1989 *(Washington, D.C.: U.S. Department of Defense, 1989).*

strategy in East Asia and the Pacific. Yet as the ROK increases its economic power it is seeking greater independence from U.S. influence. Taiwan, Hong Kong, and Singapore also are increasingly important economic competitors. China has immense political and economic power potential, and can become a regional influence of the first order if it can stabilize its internal situation.

Many of these nations are already strong competitors with the United States in developing and marketing advanced technologies. To the extent that this competition affects U.S. trade and commerce, it affects the health of the U.S. economy and, ultimately, its industrial base as well. Should the United States lose its competitive R&D edge, its ability to sustain those industries critical to defense would be diminished. A corollary issue is the increasing U.S. dependency on foreign sources. The United States already is dependent on Japan for numerous critical weapon systems components that would be essential in the prosecution of any prolonged conflict. There is great concern that this dependence could, in the future, extend to other technologies as well . . . .

The United States

Over the last 20 years the United States has lost much of its lead in many important technology fields. This trend is, in part, a natural phenomenon that stems from the unique conditions that spawned an era of U.S. dominance following World War II. The trend is also the product of a lag in funding for research and development. Furthermore, other factors—such as concentration on short-term gains and adhering to outdated management techniques—also have contributed to the erosion of the American R&D base. At the same time, other Western advanced industrial states have realized substantial benefits from investing in and developing a strong technology base. For example, in 1970 the United States, Germany, and Japan each invested about 1 percent of their gross national product in R&D. Yet by 1989 the Japanese and Germans had increased this rate by 50 percent or more, while U.S. investment remained stagnated at 1 percent. Japan and West Germany also have benefitted from significantly greater capital investments by their business sector than has occurred in the United States. Furthermore, Tokyo and Bonn have invested in specific areas, often building on initial U.S. research breakthroughs and gaining an economic lead in production.

Perhaps the best example of this phenomenon is the U.S. loss of the microchip market to the Japanese. Bell Labs in the United States developed the concept and produced the first products. The Japanese took the basic research finding and spent their money on refining them and securing a sales base with quality products. They were then able—and willing—to increase their investment in that specific area, thereby leap-frogging U.S. technology and establishing themselves as the world leader . . . .

If the United States proves unable to compete effectively in areas of advanced technologies, it would incur the most severe economic and security consequences: markets would be lost, the U.S. industrial base would erode, and the United States would become increasingly dependent upon offshore technologies for its defense at the same time as its economic health weakens. It is somewhat ironic that, although the Soviet Union constitutes the greatest threat to U.S. security, the greatest challenge to the U.S. technology and industrial base will almost certainly come from the United States' own allies. Thus the United States must succeed in this "friendly competition" with advanced Western industrial states if its economic power, and the West's system of collective security, is to endure. Indeed, an essential part of any U.S. R&D effort will seek to take full advantage of potential technological contributions that can be made by the allies on defense-related programs.

Fortunately, the United States is not faced with the need for radical change of the magnitude that the Soviets are experiencing with *perestroika*. It is, however, evident that the United States cannot persist in its current laissez-faire approach to the competition in advanced technologies without incurring major economic and security problems of its own in the future.

Our Economic Policy Blinders

David P. Calleo and Benjamin M. Rowland

There is something fundamentally defective and simple-minded about the classical economist's view of the world as expressed in the principle of comparative advantage. The principle is not "wrong" in its own terms; it is simply an insufficient guide to understanding the modern world. All governments today play a highly active role in shaping the economic environment of their citizenry. Governments are the agents by which people seek to impose their cultural ideas upon their environment. In this respect, we live in a mercantilist and not a liberal world. Undoubtedly economic intercourse among nations brings advantages all around. But when that interdependence begins to threaten the social and political values of society, or impinge seriously upon a government's ability to control its economic environment, then that government is bound to resist if it can. Thus, to push interdependence too far is to run the risk of violent and self-defeating reactions.

From the perspective of politics, such ideas seem self-evident; but less so from the perspectives of economics. . . . [T]hroughout this modern era the political ideal of community has had to contend with the economic ideal of growth. The uneasy relationship, of course, continues to the present day and is clearly reflected in many of the issues raised by trade.

Economic Man versus the General Will

In a hungry world, as Ricardo saw it, the alternative to economic efficiency was mass starvation. The more the state interfered with the market to promote uneconomic ends, the more the society would suffer deprivation.

David P. Calleo *is Dean Acheson Professor and Director of European Studies at the Paul H. Nitze School of Advanced International Studies, Johns Hopkins University.* Benjamin M. Rowland *is Treasurer of the InterAmerican Investment Corporation. Excerpted with permission from* America and the World Political Economy: Atlantic Dreams and National Realities *(Bloomington, In.: Indiana University Press, 1973) by* David P. Calleo *and* Benjamin M. Rowland.

And as we have seen, for Ricardo free trade was the essential element in achieving economic efficiency. Modern trade theory, for all its many refinements, has not moved far from Ricardo's fundamental view. Liberal trade is still believed vital to economic prosperity. While modern trade theories are often impressive intellectual constructions, in their essential points the arguments for international trade liberalization are not complicated, and are roughly analogous to the theory of domestic trade or even village exchange.

Trade began, economists will tell us, with the recognition that any particular person or tool was not equally well suited to perform every task. Specialization was therefore logical, and with specialization came the incentive for the exchange of goods. Trade let men share the benefits of specialization—within the village and region, or even across seas, deserts and mountains.

As specialization put men, machines and materials to work where they were relatively most useful and efficient, productivity increased. The larger the market and the fewer the obstacles between its parts, the greater the possibilities for specialization. Specialization moved an economy closer to its ideal state of *economic efficiency*—defined as that point of specialization where the return to no single factor of production can be increased by putting it to work in any other way.

The concept of ideal economic efficiency was and is, of course, highly theoretical. Realizing it requires a "perfect market" with "perfect competition," itself the product of several utopian conditions. In a perfect market, the unimpeded laws of supply and demand determine costs and prices. Neither suppliers nor buyers of a productive factor can fix its price and no producer or consumer can arbitrarily depress or raise the price of goods produced and consumed. Perfect competition, of course, assumes also that every buyer and seller of a factor or a product possesses perfect knowledge of market supply and demand, and that all factors of production are perfectly mobile and can be can be combined according to the principles of economic efficiency as dictated by the market. Finally, to achieve economic efficiency requires not only all these ideal objective conditions, but also the subjective will to use them as the ideal dictates, in other words, a determination by the actors in this perfect market to guide their behavior by strictly economic criteria of efficiency.

In the actual world, these conditions are elusive. Various distortions, like monopolies and governments, inevitably influence the workings of the market, and hence prevent it from approximating the model. Nevertheless, the model market and its informing principle of economic efficiency stand as ideal constants against which, economists believe, reality should be tested. In a fallen world, if policy must deviate from the optimum of economic efficiency, economists should at least ensure that governments know the costs, and suffer from bad consciences.

The principle use of the model is to show how an economy ought to allocate its factors and determine what they should produce—in other words, how an economy should decide on its inputs and outputs. The object is to employ fully all the factors at a given state of technology and to maximize total production. Normally, there are a variety of product mixes which will employ all the factors.

How, then, does a society decide what to produce? In a free market model, the consumer decides. Consumers may decide to buy more of good A and less of good B—in response to price or taste changes, for example. It is assumed, however, that as a consumer acquires more and more of A, he becomes increasingly loath to accept any more of it in place of B. Indeed, it is assumed that—beyond a certain point—one good can no longer be substituted for another. Thus, no matter how much lower A's price may fall the consumer will not buy any more of it in substitution for B. When consumer demand is satisfied and all available factors of production are employed in the most economically efficient fashion, the economy is then said to be in a state of *output consumption equilibrium*.

So far, we have been speaking, in effect, about a closed economy which contains its own production factors and consumers within itself. What happens when this economy enters into trade with another which is also in an optimum state of economic efficiency? In effect, trade simply creates a larger market. If either production possibility curves or consumption indifference curves are not identical, trade will satisfy consumer demand at a higher level in both economies. In other words, either a difference in consumer preferences or a difference in factor endowments (or in available technology) permits mutually profitable trade between two economies.

In short, trade creates a bigger market; a bigger market allows more specialization; specialization means more production at less cost—in other words: greater economic "efficiency." But for the efficiency to be realized, perfect market conditions must prevail. Ideally, nothing should interfere with the free expression of consumer preferences or with the free movement of productive factors in response to those preferences. Thus, the case for free trade is an extension to an international market of the case for laissez-faire in the domestic market.

The case for freer trade is also, in its essentials, a case for achieving a maximum of consumption. The object of the ideal market mechanism is to organize economic activity so that the consumer gets all that he wants at the lowest possible price. The consumer is sovereign. While the consumer allegedly benefits all the time, a particular producer—and entrepreneur, or a laborer—benefits only so long as he remains competitive. Freer trade, in fact, increases the risk and vulnerability of any particular producer even as it enhances the benefits of consumers in general.

Herein lies a great flaw in classical free-trade theory, a flaw which is both practical and moral. Practically speaking, in Western societies, most consumers are also producers. Most people have to work to consume; the great bulk of consumption is by people who also work. From the perspective of the producer or the producer/consumer, a system which focuses on the welfare of consumers and expects producers to shift for themselves has it priorities backward. From this perspective, a more rational system would orient itself toward production, toward achieving the full and satisfying employment of its labor and capital. Consumption would then take care of itself. If there is thereby some loss in theoretical economic efficiency, if prices are somewhat higher, the corresponding benefits to society as a whole will more than compensate. So it is likely to seem to the producer.

In fact, in modern capitalist countries since the war, producers have more or less had their way. Full employment is at least the stated goal of economic policy for most governments. Neither modern business, labor, nor even capital will in fact submit willingly to the discipline of absolute economic efficiency. Labor's efforts to protect itself against risk are manifest, as are those of farmers and businessmen. For the successful company, limited risk is counterbalanced by general prudence. Thus the corporation attempts to control its environment by manipulating the "sovereign" consumer through advertising or by spreading its risk through diversification. Some liberal theorists still complain about how corporations pass the costs of risk-avoiding along to the consumer. Thus, it is said, the few exploit the many. No doubt, some corporations, either from bad judgement or venality, greatly abuse the consumer. Certainly, the particular interests of unions and corporations lead them to a highly partial view of the general welfare. Nevertheless, the notion that lower prices for the consumer should be the principal value guiding economic policy reflects a view no less partial and simple-minded.

Governments, of course, introduce another set of perspectives about the general welfare and another set of "distortions" into the market. A government charged with the general welfare does not blindly submit the nation's security or independence to the dictates of the consumer's market. Like business corporations, states draw back from the logic of economic efficiency. Free trade is supposed to encourage national economies to specialize for a world market. In practice, rather than grow dependent on alien sources, governments in major industrialized nations prefer to conserve a full range of industries within their national boundaries. The American government furnishes a particularly good example, as the growing number of our restrictive bilateral trade agreements suggests. Even within the Common Market, where integration through trade liberalization might be expected to have proceeded farthest, the great bulk of trade across borders still occurs within groups of products which are produced in nearly all countries, as opposed to between groups produced in only one or two countries. A German, for example, may buy a French car, but both Germany and France make a full range of automobiles.

It is, incidentally, a striking feature of contemporary trade that it grows fastest among countries with similar economies, a phenomenon which suggests doubts about the marginal advantage of a good deal of international trade, even for the consumer. How heavy a price in the disruption of domestic industry and labor should be paid to get that putative consumer advantage?

Deciding among the competing perspectives of various interests, and hence measuring and balancing social costs and gains, is in the end more a problem for philosophy than for economics. And in these matters, classical economics presents a primitive and even dangerous view. In the model world of the classical economist, the consumer is sovereign and that economy is best which is most fluid in response to the consumer's demands. That, after all, is what the economists' optimum state of *free factor mobility* means. But no economy is separable from the society it serves, and economic fluidity thus imperils societal stability. No association or institution is sacred. All must be prepared to be uprooted according to the dictates of the market place.

The moral poverty of such an economic model is apparent. Its basic assumption of consumer sovereignty is not only questionable practically, but morally as well. Most political philosophers would find it difficult to isolate the public welfare either within the "production function" or within the "consumption function." It lies in both and in neither. Nor can the public welfare be found automatically in some simple majority—organized either as consumers or producers. Rousseau, wrestling with this problem, assigns moral sovereignty neither to the will of a governing elite, nor to the "will of all," but to a "general will"—the general welfare as it ought ideally to be conceived.

Rousseau's suggestions for the institutional structure to define the general will doubtless leave much to be desired. In any event, for the reason to which Burke gives classical expression, no simple, let alone universal, constitutional formula can ever be satisfactory. Finding the general will while engaging the citizenry in its formulation and expression will always be the fundamental and continuing business of any democratic political economy. And particular definitions of an ideal good tend naturally to be partial and incomplete in accordance with the particular perspectives of the definer. But in this era, we can really do better at locating the general welfare than equating it with the maximization of consumption. No political community has ever done so, for we continue to live in a fallen world where politics "distorts" economics. And why not? Why, for example, should consumer values necessarily be taken as superior to producer values? In an age of technological abundance, why shouldn't an economic system be set the primary task of providing the individual with a steady and interesting job, as opposed to providing the consumer with the cheapest price? Why isn't unemployment, insecurity or the dehumanization of labor a cost worse than lessened consumption? But neither production nor consumption is, in itself, an adequate standard for economic policy.

The individual, after all, is not only a producer/consumer, but a man and a citizen. Such a role calls for a broader set of values than even the most enlightened economics is likely to provide. To paraphrase Burke, a nation is not a commercial affair, to be taken up and dissolved according to the dictates of the market, but a fundamental human partnership—stretching across the generations—to build a good society. It is this membership in the general community which, according to Rousseau, joins the individual will to the general will. In the ideal society, the general will of the citizen incorporates his particular will as consumer and producer into some broader ideal of a good life, and of a good society for achieving it. Economic prosperity is obviously an essential element in the general welfare, but scarcely the only one. No doubt the market remains one of the basic instruments for expressing and refining the general will, but only after the mechanism has been corrected by what the classical economist would call "distortions" and the rest of us might call equity and morality—in short, civilization.

Obviously, capitalist societies have long ago ceased using the market place as the measure of all things. Indeed, the progress of capitalist civilization over the past hundred years might be described as movement away from laissez-faire toward the "mixed economy" and the welfare state. The welfare state may or may not be economically "efficient." The money spent on social security for the aged would perhaps produce more if spent by IBM or General Motors. But economic efficiency is not the only goal of any modern state. Each seeks, in theory at least, to develop a broadly humanitarian society, not merely an efficient one. The achievement of a high degree of economic efficiency is highly desirable, but by no means a sufficient or exclusive objective for a good society.

In summary, quite apart from its manifest irrelevance because of the innumerable "distortions" which prevent its operation in the real world, economic efficiency is of questionable use, even as an ideal. Two of its basic principles, consumer sovereignty and free factor mobility, would—if they prevailed—mean the collapse of modern civilization.

Similarly, the discipline of economics in today's world derives its public utility not as a special source of prescriptive moral wisdom, but as a highly elaborate form of systems analysis whose concepts provide a means for predicting certain of the consequences of choice among economic options.

Whatever moral pretensions may linger around the ideal of economic efficiency and the free market should be banished to the museum of history. By the same token, free trade should be ejected from the pantheon of unquestioned precepts for the governance of foreign economic policy. The costs and benefits of trade, like those of any other economic activity, must be judged according to the broad criteria which define the general welfare.

Seen in this light, our postwar international economic policies have presented a curious anachronism. While we have been able to imagine, and have made great efforts to create, a humanitarian welfare system domestically, our vision and policy for the international economic environment has been very much dominated by the ideals of laissez-faire. This contrast between domestic and international ideals has become more than an anomaly; it has become a fundamental danger. The international dimension of our economy has been growing to a point where it threatens to encroach upon the achievements of the humanitarian state itself, both in America and abroad. Many of the arguments heard today which contrast the wisdom of liberalism with the perils of protectionism sound curiously like the conventional defense of laissez-faire in the bad old days of undirected nineteenth-century capitalism. Enthusiasts for free trade, perhaps regretting the demise of laissez-faire on the national scale, apparently hope to bring it back on a world scale.

The Real World of Trade

Pat Choate and Juyne Linger

The United States is floundering in the global marketplace, incurring devastating losses in market position, profits, equity, and jobs. The real problem is less with America's products than it is with America's trade policy.... We are operating with an obsolete American trade policy, an artifact of the mid-1940s when the United States and Britain dominated the global economy, tariffs were the principal obstacle to trade, and U.S. supremacy was uncontested in virtually all industries. In the intervening decades, economic circumstances have shifted radically. United States trade policy has not.

Today America's trade policy seems frozen by intellectual and political inflexibility, paralyzed by the relentless conflict between proponents of "free" and "fair" trade. The free traders argue that American markets should be open, and the movement of goods and services across national borders unrestrained. The fair traders assert that access to American markets should be restricted until U.S. businesses are granted equal access to foreign markets. . . . Of course, both are correct: fair trade requires equal access and equal access leads to free trade. The problem is that both sides base their positions on the same two long-held and now outdated premises:

1. Global commerce is conducted under the terms of the General Agreement on Tariffs and Trade (GATT) and dominated by the United States and similar economic systems abroad.
2. Multilateral negotiations are the most effective way to resolve pressing trade issues.

Pat Choate, *an economist, is the author of the forthcoming* Agents of Influence *and several other books.* Juyne Linger *is a policy consultant who collaborated with Mr. Choate on* The High-Flex Society: Shaping America's Economic Future *(1986). Reprinted by permission of* Harvard Business Review. *An excerpt from "Tailored Trade: Dealing With the World As It Is" by* Pat Choate *and* Juyne Linger, *(January/February 1988). Copyright* © *(1988) by the President and Fellows of Harvard College; all rights reserved.*

Both assumptions are wrong. The 40-year-old GATT now covers less than 7% of global commerce and financial flows. More important, world trade is no longer dominated by the free-trade economies. Today, nearly 75% of all world commerce is conducted by economic systems operating with principles at odds with those of the United States. . . .

Five competing economic systems

America's involvement in the global economy has passed through two distinct periods: a development era during which the United States sought industrial self-sufficiency in the eighteenth and nineteenth centuries, and a free-trade era in the early- and middle-twentieth century during which open trade was linked with prosperity. Now America has entered a third, more dangerous era—an age of global economic interdependence. . . .

But. . .American trade policies remain locked in the past. U.S. trade policy still rests on three pillars:

1. Open markets and free trade are the most efficient means to expand global trade and, therefore, should form the economic model that guides world commerce.
2. Multilateral negotiations are the best means to open markets and promote free trade.
3. The United States has a primary responsibility among nations to advance free trade.

There is, however, a fundamental flaw in this thinking: other nations' economies are not like the United States' economy, nor will they be, nor should they be. Economic systems differ in ways both manifest and subtle, reflecting basic differences in history, culture, national aspirations, and politics. Five types of economic systems confront the United States. Four of them are not founded on our free-trade economic model: centrally planned (like the Soviet Union); mixed (France); developing (Mexico); and plan-driven (Japan). Only the Anglo-American system is rooted in a free- and fair-trade approach.

Within this framework, there are, of course, variations. The mixed economy of France differs in many ways from the mixed economy of Sweden; Japan's version of a plan-driven system differs from South Korea's plan-driven economy; and even between America and Canada there are clear distinctions. Yet each model possesses characteristics that are important to the design of future U.S. trade policies. It is possible, for example, to sketch the differences among the five systems by comparing them along four dimensions: the role of government in the economy; the ownership of industry; the relationship between process and results in the system; and how trade is conducted.

In the rule-driven, market-oriented Anglo-American economic model, for instance, government sets the economic backdrop but takes few direct positions on which industries should exist, grow, or decline. In contrast, plan-driven economies, like Japan's, and mixed economies, like Sweden's, skillfully blend the strength of government with the flexibility of the marketplace. Once decisions are made, government backs them with resources and, at strategic moments, with trade protection.

In free-market and plan-driven economies, private ownership of business and industry is the rule. The mixed economies, like France's, are based on a combination of state and private ownership, market and nonmarket decisions. Major industries are either owned by the state or tightly regulated. The major enterprises in the centrally planned economies, of course, are state owned.

The Anglo-American economies are process oriented; once rules are established, market processes dominate. The plan-driven economies are results oriented; business and government shape a national "vision" that often includes targeting certain industries like semiconductors or computers. To guide the economy toward desired results, governments of plan-driven economies will provide special financing, encourage joint research, and offer adjustment assistance like worker retraining. The mixed economies rely on a combination of market processes and government planning. The command economies are dominated by state planning.

The process-oriented Anglo-American economies are heavily influenced by economists and lawyers who make, interpret, and enforce the rules under which market processes operate. Because the plan-driven economies are results oriented, they have far less need for lawyers and economists to make and enforce rules. . . . Instead, politicians and business leaders direct the results-oriented economies. In trade talks, therefore, U.S. and Japanese trade negotiators often have different orientations: the Americans focus on rules that will facilitate market processes while the Japanese focus on measures that can advance their national economic vision. Negotiations are handled differently in the different systems as well. In the Anglo-American economies, trade is conducted mainly by business. In the mixed and planned economies, trade often involves negotiations with both business and government. In the centrally managed economies, the government alone conducts trade. . . .

In fashioning their economic systems, the developing nations have borrowed from each of the other four systems, patching together combinations of public and private sector initiatives. In virtually all these countries, however, government predominates in designing and implementing a national trade strategy.

American policymakers, devoted to free trade and open markets, have ignored the often vast differences between U.S. and foreign economic systems. Rather, they still operate on the free-trade premise that policies that are neutral to the fate of American industries will produce the same market-oriented benefits globally as they do domestically. Consequently, American trade policies are doing enormous harm to U.S. industry.

Even where there is ample evidence of harm—as in the case of consumer electronics—industries have been unable to get relief from predatory foreign practices like dumping, theft of American intellectual property, foreign regulation that forces U.S. companies to move plants and jobs offshore as a condition of market entry, and nontariff barriers that restrict exports of America's most competitive goods and services. Free-trade advocates have exacerbated the problem of gaining legitimate relief by discrediting reciprocal market access as a negotiating strategy. And they mistakenly brand tough negotiating tactics as protectionism.

Multilateral negotiations via the GATT have been unable to bridge the differences among the world's five economic systems. If we continue to depend on these agreements, the United States must resign itself to failure: we will effect no major changes in the global trade system by the end of the 1980s. And by then the cumulative U.S. trade deficit for the decade is likely to exceed $1 trillion.

Despite America's spirited urging of other nations to adopt the U.S. economic model—reliance on market forces, free trade, and deregulation—this system has enjoyed little appeal abroad. It suits us, but it would never fit many other nations—and they know it. Consequently, U.S. trade policy is at a crossroads: we can either continue to urge other nations to adopt our free-trade economic model or we can change U.S. trade policy to deal with other nations as they are, rather than as we wish they would be.

New Thinking about Trade Policy

Paul R. Krugman

[T]heoretical economic analysis is necessary to make sensible evaluations of trade policy. However, the fact that an economist offers a theoretical analysis does not and should not automatically command respect. What is needed is some assurance that the analysis is actually relevant. On this score the standard economic analysis of trade policy has begun to look a little wobbly. . . .

In part this is because the world has changed. . . . [T]he classical case for free trade may have been more in tune with the workings of the economy in 1880 or even 1950 than with the world economy of 1984. In part it is because we have become more sophisticated about the way markets actually work. . . .

Over the last few years the ways in which economists analyze trade have begun to change. . . . We can identify three reasons why . . . . First, the role of trade in the U.S. economy and the role of the United States in the world economy have changed. Second, the character of international trade itself has been shifting, affecting the United States along with other countries. Third, changing views within the field of economics, especially in the analysis of industrial structure and competition, have affected the view of economists dealing with trade policy as well.

The changing position of the United States in the world economy

The most important change in the U.S. position in the world economy over the past generation has been the steadily increasing importance of trade. In a simple quantitative measure, the shares of imports and exports in U.S. manufacturing value-added both more and doubled from 1960 to 1980. But the change was more than a quantitative one—it amounted to a qualitative

Paul R. Krugman *is Professor of Economics at the Massachusetts Institute of Technology. Excerpted with permission from* Strategic Trade Policy and the New International Economics *(Cambridge, Mass.: MIT Press, 1986).*

change in the importance of international considerations to the U.S. economy. In 1960 the typical U.S. manufacturing firm was basically oriented toward selling to U.S. consumers and competing with U.S. rivals. If it exported, this was usually a secondary activity; if it faced foreign competition, this was usually a minor irritant. By contrast, in the 1980s . . . . [m]any, perhaps most, firms either rely heavily on export sales or face important foreign competitors in the U.S. market.

How does this affect our view of trade policy? What it does is to make some issues traditionally viewed as domestic in nature into issues that have a vital trade policy component. . . . Consider first the issue of market power. A traditional concern of U.S. policy has been to limit the ability of firms in concentrated industries to raise prices and earn excessive profits at the expense of consumers. Now that the United States has become so much a trading nation, however, the aim becomes more complicated. Protection of the consumer from exploitation remains an issue. To the extent that high returns remain, however, there is the additional concern of trying to maintain or enlarge the share of these returns that goes to domestic firms. . . . [T]here are reasons to believe either that in concentrated industries trade policy can usefully take on an active role in promoting the interest of domestic firms against their foreign competitors, or that we should at least be concerned about the possibility that foreign governments will use trade policies to promote their firms in these industries.

Turning to innovation and technological change, the traditional concern of U.S. policy here has been with promoting activities, such as basic research, that yield valuable spillovers to the rest of the economy. What makes this a trade policy issue is the fact that the United States is now only one of a number of countries engaging in activities that can be argued to yield such spillovers. This means that trade policy can be an important factor in determining the pace of technological change. For example, foreign "targeting" of high-technology sectors through subsidies or protection of home markets might cause a shrinkage of U.S. industries which, in fact, yields valuable spillovers to the rest of the U.S. economy—a possibility that is at the heart of concern over the international repercussion of industrial policy.

The changing character of trade

The rapid growth in the importance of trade has also highlighted another change that is not as recent but whose significance is only now beginning to be fully appreciated. This is a change in the *character* of trade, which is no longer very much like the kind of exchange envisaged in classical theory and still taught in textbooks.

Traditional theories of international trade view trade as essentially a way for countries to benefit from their differences. Because countries differ in climate, culture, skills, resources, and so on, each country will have a comparative advantage in producing goods for which its particular character suits it. Such a theory leads one to expect to see trade dominated by exchanges that reflect the particular strengths of economies—for instance, exports of manufactures by advance countries and exports of raw materials by underdeveloped countries.

Now it remains true that underlying characteristics of countries shape the pattern of international trade. . . . Since World War II, however, a large and generally growing part of world trade has come to consist of exchanges that cannot be attributed so easily to underlying advantages of the countries that export particular goods. Instead, trade seems to reflect arbitrary or temporary advantages resulting from economies of scale or shifting leads in close technological races. . . .

The reasons for the massive two-way trade in products in which countries have no underlying comparative advantage are not particularly hard to find. They lie in the advantages of large-scale production, which lead to an essentially random division of labor amount countries; in the cumulative advantages of experience, which sometimes perpetuate accidental initial advantages; and in the temporary advantages conveyed by innovation. What is important is that the conventional economic analysis of trade policy is based on a theory of trade that does not allow for these kinds of motives for international specialization. . . . [T]raditional conclusions about trade policy may therefore not be right for the kind of world we live in. . . .

We should also note a related change in international trade. Among the forces that seem to be driving international specialization, an increasingly important one seems to be technology. . . . As we have already noted, however, technological innovation. . .may well generate important spillovers to the rest of the economy. Its growing importance in international trade thus reinforces the need for a rethinking of the analytical basis for trade policy.

New tools for analysis

The final strand in the changing nature of trade policy analysis is the application to international economics of new ideas coming from other fields of economics. In particular, the 1970s were marked by major innovations in the field of industrial organization, with new approaches developed for the analysis of industries in which only small number of firms are competing at any one time—"oligopolies," in the jargon of the economics profession.

Much traditional economic analysis is based on the working assumption that markets are not too far from being "perfectly competitive"—that is, there are many producers, each of whom is too small to attempt to influence prices or the future actions of his competitors. What the changing pattern of trade has done, however, is to make this a clearly unworkable assumption for trade policy. As just noted, a good deal of trade now seems to arise because of the advantages of large-scale production, the advantages of cumulative experience, and transitory advantages resulting from innovation. In industries where these factors are important, we are not going to see the kind of atomistic competition between many small firms that is necessary for "perfect" competition to be a good description of the world. Major U.S. exporters like Boeing or Caterpillar, and many smaller firms as well, are in a different kind of competition from that facing wheat farmers or garment manufacturers. They face a few identifiable rivals, they have some direct ability to affect prices, and they make *strategic* moves designed to affect their rivals' actions. Firms in this situation are described by economists as being in "imperfectly competitive" markets. . . .

Although our understanding is imperfect, it is getting better. Important new work has helped reveal, in particular, how the strategic choices of firms are influenced by and in turn help to determine the structure of industries. This new work was originally intended for thinking about domestic issues such as antitrust, regulation, and innovation policy. As we have seen, however, the distinctions between domestic and international issues have been breaking down. Thanks to the new work on imperfectly competitive industries, international economists are in a position to approach the problems raised by the changing environment with an expanded set of tools.

In summary, then, the rethinking of the analytical basis for trade policy is a response to both a real change in the environment and intellectual progress within the field of economics. . . . But what difference does this make for the conduct of trade policy? . . . When economists call for free trade, this is not a blind prejudice. Rather, it is based on a theoretical framework that is compelling in its logic. Even the new ideas that have begun to change our way of looking at trade amount to a modification rather than a wholesale rejection of this framework.

The case for free trade is of course part of the general case for free markets. . . . The essence of the economist's view is that exporting and importing are basically no different from other economic activities. International trade can be viewed as a productive process, whereby goods that are relatively cheap in our country are in effect converted into relatively expensive goods. And like other activities, foreign trade is likely to be most efficiently carried out if it is left up to a decentralized market mechanism. . . .

It is particularly important to stress one not-so-fine point about this argument. The conventional case for free trade does not break down just because other countries do not themselves have free trade. . . . There is an old economist's analogy, which runs as follows: to say that our government must depart from free trade because other governments are not free traders is like saying that because other countries have rocky coasts, we must block up our own harbors. . . .

But conventional analysis, as we have seen, is under considerable challenge as an appropriate framework for thinking about trade. The next question is, what difference does a modification of that analysis make for economist's views about trade? . . .

Implications of new ideas

Economists have always known that the conclusion that markets are efficient becomes suspect when one abandons some of the idealization of. .. theoretical cases. Yet they have tended to regard the idealized models as giving a basically correct view. . . . This traditional faith in the efficacy of markets partly reflected a judgment about reality; equally it reflected a lack of any ability to describe precisely what difference deviations from perfect markets make.

The combination of a changing character of trade and a growing sophistication of theory undercuts this way of justifying free trade. On one side. . .the industries that account for much of world trade are not at all well described by the supply and demand analysis that lies behind the assertion that markets are best left to themselves. As we have seen, much of trade appears to require an explanation in terms of economies of scale, learning curves, and the dynamics of innovation—all phenomena incompatible with the kind of idealizations under which free trade is always the best policy. Economists refer to such phenomena as "market imperfections," a term that in itself conveys the presumption that these are marginal to a system that approaches ideal performance fairly closely. In reality, however, it may be that imperfections are the rule. . . .

On the other side, the increased sophistication of the analytical toolbox has removed at least part of the reason for clinging to the assumption of perfect markets. Fifteen years ago economists could and did assert that so little was known about the implications of imperfect competition for international trade policy that nothing useful could be said on the matter. There is still considerable uncertainty, but not so much that economists are without useful insights.

What are these insights? The rethinking of the basis of trade policy that is now occurring suggests two ways in which an activist trade policy can benefit a country relative to free trade, perhaps at the expense of its competitors. The first is through the ability of government policies to secure for a nation a larger share of "rent"; the second is through the ability of these policies to get the country more "external economies. . . ."

"Rent," in economic parlance, means "payment to an input higher than what that input could earn in an alternative use." It could mean a higher rate of profit in an industry than is earned in other industries of equivalent riskiness, or higher wages in an industry than equally skilled workers earn in other sectors. If there are important rents in certain sectors, trade policy can raise national income by securing for a country a larger share of the rent-yielding industries.

Now the conventional view is that who gets the rent is not an important issue because in a competitive economy there will be very little rent. If profits for wages are unusually high in an industry, capital or labor will come in and quickly eliminate the unusual returns.

If, however, the new view of trade is right, important trading sectors are also sectors in which rent may not be so easily competed away. If there are important advantages to large-scale production or a steep learning curve, for example, new entry into an industry may look unprofitable even though existing firms are making exceptionally high profits, paying unusually high wages, or both.

Once we begin to believe that substantial amounts of rent are really out there, it becomes possible at least in principle for trade policy to be used as a way to secure more rent for a country. Suppose, for example, that the nature of the world market for some products is such that it can support two highly profitable producers but addition of a third would eliminate the profits. In this case what we will end up with is two firms earning considerable rent, without any way for that rent to be competed away. Clearly a country would like one of its firms to be one of the lucky pair. Common sense suggests, and mathematical theorizing confirms, that subsidies or protection can in fact be used to increase a country's share of rent in a way that raises national income at other countries' expense.

External economies present a different justification for activist trade policies. By an "external economy" economists mean a benefit from some activity that accrues to other individuals or firms than those engaging in the activity. The most plausible example is the diffusion of knowledge generated in one area to other firms and other sectors. Although external economies are different conceptually from rents, they likewise provide a reason to favor particular sectors. This time the point is not that capital and labor in the sector will themselves earn exceptionally high returns; rather, they will yield high returns to society because in addition to their own earning they provide benefits to capital and labor employed elsewhere.

The reason why external economies have become more of a trade issue is that, as noted earlier, the reassessment of trade gives technological innovation an enlarged role. Innovation, because it involves the generation of knowledge, is particularly likely also to generate valuable spillovers. So there is now good reason to suspect that trade policy can be used to encourage external-economy-producing activities. . . .

Traditional trade analysis and the new wave of analysis share certain important features. Both take the view that trade is not a zero-sum game, that it offers an opportunity for mutual gains by all trading nations. Also the new analysis has not lost sight of the crucial point that industries within a country compete with each other for limited supplies of labor and capital, as well as competing with their opposite numbers in other countries for markets. This means that an attempt to promote or protect some particular sector within our country means promoting or protecting that sector at the expense of other sectors. . . .

The difference in the new analysis is on the question of whether changes in the allocation of resources matter. For example, if foreign trade policies cause some U.S. sectors to contract and other to expand, can this lower U.S. national income? Alternatively, can the United States raise its national income by actively favoring certain key sectors?

The answer to these questions depends on whether it is possible to identify some sectors that at the margin are more valuable than others. Are there "strategic" activities in the economy, where labor and capital either directly receive a higher return than they could elsewhere or generate special benefits for the rest of the economy? This is the question on which old and new thinking about trade differs.

What the conventional view argues is that there are no "strategic" sectors. Competition, it is argued, eliminates any large deviations between what equivalent qualities of labor or capital can earn in different sectors. Market prices, which guide the allocation of resources, are good indicators of social return, so that basically producers are paid what their output is worth.

The new approaches open up the possibility that there may be "strategic" sectors after all. Because of the important roles now being given to economies of scale, advantages of experience, and innovation as explanations of trading patterns, it seems more likely that rent will not be fully competed away—that is, that labor or capital will sometimes earn significantly higher returns in some industries than in others. Because of the increased role of technological competition, it has become more plausible to argue that certain sectors yield important external economies, so producers are not in fact paid the full social value of their production.

What all this means is that the extreme pro-free-trade position—that markets work so well that they cannot be improved on—has become untenable. In this sense the new approaches to international trade provide a potential rationale for a turn by the United States toward a more activist trade policy. There is, however, a large gap between showing that free trade is not perfect and arguing for any particular alternative. . . .

Becoming Insolvent

James Chace

At times I think I live in a ruined city. Here, some are protected and some are not. Those like me, who seem safe, have sought out apartments and houses like barracks. Safe from bad surprises. The lines of demarcation between "us" and "them" are drawn, as they have always been, but they are no longer clear. We had to be taught where the lines begin and end and how to maneuver alongside them. Now we are always alert, wired, so to speak, against trouble.

Statistics that show more crime a century or so ago than today distort the way we live now. Violence has grown random since the war, and we are all on our guard. No longer are there nineteenth-century ghettos like Hell's Kitchen, where an outsider could choose to enter or not at his peril. Then the risk was real and known. Now trouble can come from anywhere. Not just physical assault. Most of us—if the means, however modest, are available—have found ways of coping with that. What seems to have happened is that society at large, both at home and abroad, has grown disorderly. In searching for some kind of order that goes beyond the self, I am haunted by the possibility of a world where laws are not obeyed, where the state is predatory or disintegrating, where terrorism has replaced large-scale warfare and the balance of power among nations has broken down with nothing to replace it.

In the South Bronx, less than a fifteen-minute drive from where I live on Central Park West in Manhattan, the buildings are burned out and still burning for miles on end. Just yesterday, I saw an old man carrying blackened logs to a fire he was feeding on a street corner. Nearby, Christmas ornaments hung from a chain-fence bazaar. In front of the fence, there is a

---

James Chace, *author of numerous books on U.S. foreign policy and former managing editor of* Foreign Affairs, *is the director of the program in International Affairs and the Media at Columbia University's School of International and Public Affairs.* Excerpted from *Solvency: The Price of Survival* by James Chace. Copyright © 1981 by James Chace. Reprinted by permission of Random House Inc.

newspaper stand. The bold headlines read: "Iran Terrorists Slay American." Beyond the auto hulks, the Garden of Eden Pentecostal Church blossoms like a floating island.

Is it just a question of "the metropolis"? Should we then abandon it and try to find the civic virtues of the community in smaller cities? Should I?

Not so long ago, I returned to the place where I was born and reared, the Massachusetts mill town of Fall River, which I remembered as comprehensible, but bleak and without promise. Because the collapse of the textile industry had come a full ten years before the Great Depression of the 1930s, the city of about 100,000 had long suffered from an endemic form of despair. Irresponsibility on the part of the mill barons, who reaped large profits during the boom years of World War I but who put nothing aside for capital improvements, combined with the overweening demands of the unions, helped quickly drive the textile industry south where, after all, the cotton grew.

I remember reciting the numbers as a schoolboy: in 1875, with 42 mills, Fall River was the largest cotton-manufacturing city in America; in 1911, it surpassed Manchester, England as the greatest cotton-spinning city in the world; in 1929, there were 101 textile mills; in 1940, 28 textile mills. Today, none. The mill buildings are therefore changed after thirty years. They no longer contain looms that weave cotton cloth, and from the outside, at least, they no longer seem the dark, satanic emblems of the industrial revolution, but rather antique, ivied-over. They have become romantic ruins.

Where I grew up the streets were not mean or hostile; but as you passed the city hall toward the south end, known as the Globe, the streets were ravaged by potholes and garbage. As in the other mill towns of Massachusetts, these ghettos built for the cotton workers always seemed built after the ugliest design that could be devised—blue and pink and brown tenements that sagged against one another. It was as though the cultivated New England landscape had been punished for its luck—the taste of the Georgian and Federal periods—that made possible elsewhere those village greens with their Puritan-white churches and shingled cottages.

Now, a generation later, the exteriors of the three- and four-story tenements are deceiving. There are no gaping windows, no pocked walls, no graffiti; even the pillars supporting the tiers of porches seem not to buckle severely. Since the outsides are rarely painted but are, rather, covered over by a colored sandpaper-like asphalt shingle, the deterioration doesn't seem so marked. But the decay is there even so: the hallways bare of plaster, outhouses in the back, cold-water flats, walls stripped bare. Outside one such neighborhood there is a small park. It was empty, swings broken, cement cracked in a hundred places. The baseball batting cage had long since been torn down. Trees that had once lined the streets had somehow disappeared—ripped by the hurricane of 1944 and never replaced, or withered by disease. A former high city official said to me without joy or sadness: "We should let Fall River fall into ruin and build a new city in the country." What happened to Fall River—the abuse of capital, the failure to maintain productivity, the price of labor, the flight of industry—should have been a warning to the country at large, but it went unheeded.

Back in New York six of us gather for dinner. The apartment is well appointed. Even the most casual pieces have been chosen with care. The furnishings—the wine-red walls in the dining room and the dusky bookcases behind the piano draped with an embroidered cloth—all reflect the European heritage of the owners. Their fathers had come to America and sought their fortunes; their children, one an anthropologist, the other a reporter, are articulate, contentious, committed to those liberal, humane values that define Western civilization. Even the masks from New Guinea that hang from the ceiling derive from the pursuit of these values commonly identified with freedom and self-fulfillment. The room is closed in, a safe and private place.

Outside the snow has been falling and the dark spaces above the rooftops of the reconverted town houses are rimmed with white. Walking home after dinner, I buy a newspaper. The prediction is for five inches. If the report holds, the park will be filled with toboggans and sleds, and the eroded grass will be concealed, broken fences and broken bottles skinned over by healing snow. At this moment the park seems a repository of the common good—workable, usable, enhancing the life of the city. Or at least until the snow melts, and the neglected landscape is laid bare. The physical wrongdoing, so it seems, betrays a deeper disorder. It is the state itself, unable to respond to the demands made upon it, that like the late Roman metropole has lost all control over the "vast machine."

We are certainly a rich country. Our gross national product, as we enter the decade of the 1980s, is over a trillion dollars. We are told our standard of living is the highest among the great powers. Yet we can't afford a lot of things we once could and even those who are better off than their parents expect to be worse off in the future. The South Bronx was a functioning community when we were less rich. Most of us assume that the reason for this is that nowadays we use the money for something else. But if so, for what? There are those who would answer that question by citing the military budget running at well over $100 billion a year. The Carter administration was even prepared in 1980 to consider spending $30 billion on a new system of movable MX missiles as part of a continuing arms race with the Soviet Union. Yet, with all this expenditure, we are hard put to maintain a large standing army in Europe, and, in the parlance of military planners, we are prepared to fight only one and one-half wars—a doubtful figure, at best. In the early 1960s, however, we not only kept up a large army in Europe but claimed we were able to fight two and one-half wars. Our commitments have not significantly lessened, yet we are supposed to support about the same degree of potential involvement with smaller conventional forces.

Then is the money going for public services? Evidently not. In New York and in other cities garbage is collected spasmodically, the police are undermanned and neighborhoods unsafe. Subways are such an assault on the senses that to descend into one seems a punishment. And even the best of our railroads are hard put to maintain their roadbeds, their schedules, their coaches, their debt service.

If the public services are in decay and the conventional military forces reduced to the degree that many believe may be inadequate for our national security, then maybe the answer is to levy greater taxes on the people. But the tax burden is already so severe that American citizens are reluctant to bear greater taxes for new schools, for better health care, for improving the quality of the very life they deplore.

How, then, did we get into this messy state? Felix Rohatyn, who was instrumental in devising ways of preventing New York City from going bankrupt in the mid-1970s, compares America now to New York then. "Like New York," he says, "America finds herself with increasing debts, both internal and external. In seeking to pay off debts, New York relied on short-term notes, the United States printed money. They neglected capital formation in other areas. Thus, when physical plants began to deteriorate, there was no financial plan already thought out to maintain or improve them. There was no financial plan either to cover greater and greater liabilities incurred by private and public pensions or social security. And jobs in the private sector were driven out by high taxes and low productivity."

One of the ways out of this dilemma other than reduced consumption of television sets, electric typewriters and Adidas running shoes—what we call our standard of living—would be to increase America's productivity. What this would mean is investing our income in new machinery, working harder and consuming less than we produce. To do this would require some personal sacrifice, and no one seems willing to curb his or her appetite for consumption when the rewards for such sacrifice appear random. But if we did increase our productivity, this would allow us to sell more and buy more—both at home and abroad. Instead, we are going in quite the opposite direction. Growth in productivity has gone down from an average rate per year of about three percent for the thirty years after World War II to about half that rate in the late 1970s. Business investment in the United States, as a share of our gross national product as we enter the 1980s, is already two-thirds the rate in West Germany, less than half the rate in Japan.

Moreover, throughout this decline in productivity we have been profligate. We have continued to buy abroad, most dramatically by increasing our imports of foreign oil, allowing them to rise a staggering forty-two percent between 1973 and 1978, until they ran to about fifty percent of our needs at the end of the decade. Partly as a result of our oil dependence, America's visible overseas trade, which was in surplus from 1893 to the 1970s, was running in 1978 at a deficit of about $30 billion a year, just about the amount initially estimated to build the MX missiles. To finance the deficit, the government simply created more credit—IOUs that become worth less and less to whoever holds them, as our deficits increase and we go on printing more money to cover them. We go on printing money and importing oil and running shoes because the alternative—to live within our diminished means—seems unthinkable. Thus, inflation becomes not an aberration within an otherwise healthy economy but the definition of the economy itself.

For a time, America's declining productivity and the consequent weakening of the dollar could be concealed by the fact that the dollar was the main currency used by all nations to settle their accounts among themselves. It was, in a sense, world money, and thus the United States could finance it external deficit by simply issuing more dollars. What General de Gaulle once called our "exorbitant privilege," however, became an enormous disadvantage when foreigners began to lose confidence in America's ability to manage her economy. This meant that we had to pay more and more dollars for the goods *they* produced and we imported. They also paid less and less for the goods *we* produced and they imported. In short, when dollars were scarce overseas in the 1950s, foreign goods we imported were cheap because we held dollars that foreigners wanted; by the 1970s, when this dollar shortage no longer existed and indeed foreigners held more dollars than they wanted, our goods became cheaper for them. Rather than importing foreign goods at high prices, the American consumer should have been able to spend his money on cheaper domestic products, which would have reduced the flow of dollars aborad. However, domestic producers often simply raised their prices to compete with foreign imports that were taxed or otherwise restricted from entering the home market, thus aggravating inflation.

As we enter the 1980s, U.S. administrations, reacting to the passions of the electorate, remain reluctant to forgo printing money. To suggest otherwise would be to ask the voters to give up their privileged position to import whatever they want with an ever-devaluating currency. Yet, like it or not, we may be facing a long-term decline in our freedom to consume. With the dollar no longer so desirable as the key currency to provide liquidity or world money to finance global trade, a world of several key currency blocs is beginning to emerge that will share this function with the dollar. The Japanese yen and the German mark—and perhaps, in time, a European currency unit—already rival the dollar as favorable currencies to hold in reserve or to exchange for goods and services. The reason for holding such currencies is simply that people believe the economies that produce them are better managed than ours, and thus a holder of marks or yen gets more goods for his money than he would with dollars. Moreover, the size of the world economy has grown so great that the U.S. economy—even at its most powerful—is no longer able to underwrite all the world money needed for trade and investment.

If confidence in the American economy falls so low that investment in dollar-denominated securities is scorned except at very high interest rates, then America will find it even more costly to buy what it needs abroad—petroleum, for example. Already, the OPEC cartel of oil-producing nations, fearful that its dollar reserves will be worth less and less as inflation undermines the value of the dollar, has entered the decade by proposing to use a number of currencies as its reserves, and, finally, by buying gold as a last defense against the collapse of the Western economies.

As Rohaytn has pointed out, the forces that had earlier been driving New York City toward bankruptcy were doing the same to the United States, though literal bankruptcy is not really possible for America "since the Treasury can, and does, always print money." In reality, "America's debts are continually stretched out, to be repaid in the future with currency worth less and less." This is what economists call inflation and what Rohaytn calls "a polite word for gradual bankruptcy." The question for America, then, is how to conform her rate of consumption to her diminished productivity before a collapse of confidence in the American economy results in a collapse of confidence not only in the international monetary system, but in the United States itself.

For there is no way to insulate the American economy from the world economy. To erect high barriers to protect our uncompetitive goods would most likely create a hostile world of retaliatory protectionist restrictions; to start a cycle of competitive devaluations among nations to gain export advantages or competitive interest rates to attract investors—both of which we have done—could produce beggar-thy-neighbor policies in the monetary and balance-of-payments fields. And for Washington to impose controls over foreign exchange transactions to conceal the effect of inflationary domestic policies would mean the end of the dollar's convertibility and leave those holding dollar reserves with currency that would lose its value to such a degree that the result would be international chaos. Even in 1980, the American economy is enormous—three and a half times as big as West Germany's—and, like a leviathan's, its collapse would help to pull down others around it.

A more optimistic projection, but a difficult one to attain, would be for Americans to produce more while at the same time accepting, at least temporarily, a reduced standard of living. During such a time, the public and private sectors would join together to rebuild America's industrial base and to upgrade her transportation system, to develop new sources of energy while consuming less, to increase basic research and development, to construct modern factories and provide them with the most efficient machinery that technology offers, with the high costs of American labor offset by greater efficiency leading to greater productivity. Such a program could lead to bigger exports, low inflation, a more stable dollar and, in the long term, a higher standard of living.

To rebuild America in this way or to accept gradual bankruptcy—these are the choices before us. But the political difficulties standing in the way of such rational choices are severe. It is hard indeed to imagine their being made at all until a great crisis is upon us—and is perceived as such—which it is not.

How Great Powers Come and Go

Paul M. Kennedy

I want to talk this evening about a Great Power in trouble. The world is in flux, and the power in question faces challenges across the globe. Many countries abroad resent its position as number one and all the cultural, economic, and political advantages that go with it. In more favorable times, the power in question had assumed an array of obligations on various continents. Now there is increasing doubt about its ability to fulfill them all. Only a few years ago, a colonial campaign that had lasted much longer and cost far more than originally anticipated brought home the difficulties of engaging in a war overseas. Public opinion, certainly, is not eager for another such entanglement. That war distorted the economy and exposed the armed services' weaknesses. Now the armed forces are grappling with a dreadful upward spiral in the cost of weaponry, which presses hard upon their budgets. They have so many things to plan for, so many potential theaters of war. In particular, they have to keep their eyes on their most powerful rival, the world's largest land power, possessor of the second largest naval force. Not only is this country a potential threat to the balance of power in Europe, but it has also extended its influence into the Arab world, Africa, the Far East, and even the South Pacific.

All these military problems facing Number One are compounded by the frightening erosion of its economic and industrial ascendancy. Forty years earlier, it was in a class of its own so far as manufacturing output, per capita productivity, high-technology goods, and average personal incomes were concerned. Now a number of other nations have overtaken it in all of those areas. Imports of foreign manufactures are soaring. Exports, apart from certain specialized fields like armaments, have languished. In area after area, from simple consumer goods to advanced technology, its companies are

Paul M. Kennedy, *J. Richardson Dilworth Professor of History at Yale University, is the author of* The Rise and Fall of the Great Powers: Economic Change and Military Conflict from 1500 to 2000 *(1988), among other works. Excerpted from* Lessons from the Fall and Rise of Nations: The Future for America, *(Washington, D.C.: Woodrow Wilson International Center for Scholars, 1987).*

struggling for survival. Year by year the calls for a return to protectionism are rising. As the industrial base erodes, the economy turns to services, a shift which may be profitable but which, strategically, is very worrying.

For some decades now, the country's overall growth rate has lagged behind that of its chief rivals. At the same time, the social problems of its inner cities—poor housing, inadequate education, substandard health conditions for an entire underclass of millions—are the object of increasing concern. A vast sum of money is needed to mend the nation's social fabric, but where can it come from? By diverting funds from a dangerously overstretched military? By short-changing critically important investment in research and development? By reducing personal consumption, that is, by increasing taxes, in a political culture which thinks that the government's share of the national income is already too large?

These problems are making it hard for thoughtful decision-makers to sleep at night. Being number one is a source of pride, but it also has its disadvantages, especially in a period of relative decline.

Now I'm sure all of you know the country I'm referring to. No, it is *not* the U.S.A. in 1987. It is Edwardian Britain, about, say, 1903. At that time Britain was also a number-one power facing problems. Its industry was far less competitive than it had been four decades earlier; its rivals were overtaking it in this or that sector of manufacturing. Strategically it was overextended across the globe. The recent, horrendously expensive Boer War (not the Vietnam War, which some of you may have thought I was referring to) had shown up its military deficiencies. The rising German navy was challenging its domination of the seas. The cost of weaponry, and the overall defense budget, had been going up year by year, but without bringing any marked increase in security. A number of studies had revealed the widespread poverty among the lowest one-quarter of the British population. Money was badly needed for guns, for butter, for long-term investment, but it was now difficult to satisfy all those demands when the nation's share of world manufacturing, its share of global wealth, it per capita income, were declining relative to faster-growing societies. Edwardian Britain, in the words of the politician who became most alarmed at these trends, the colonial secretary Joseph Chamberlain, was now a "weary Titan, staggering under the too-vast orb of its own fate." Slogans of time, like "competitiveness" and "national efficiency," could not conceal—indeed they revealed—widespread angst about the country's decline.

III

Composition Counts

Traditional economics teaches that all economic activity naturally works out for the best. Therefore it is no surprise that traditional economics insists that exactly what economies produce is unimportant. As long as they produce enough of anything that can be sold, they can earn enough to buy whatever else they need. Thus no kind of economic activity is inherently more or less valuable than any other. To quote a well-worn adage, it's just as good for a country to make potato chips as computer chips.

In an ideal, non-strategic world where states have no interests, where power means nothing, where all countries practice free trade, and where countries can move effectively into new industries and technologies practically at will, the composition of a nation's economy would indeed not count. But as indicated by the readings in Part Four, in a strategic world where military, economic, and technological prowess are tightly linked, indifference to composition—to the make-up of a country's industrial mix—can endanger not only prosperity, but security and independence as well.

The security and independence arguments are widely understood. Countries with second-class technology tend to make second-class weapon, and to depend on the mercies of their superiors—whether friendly or unfriendly. Obviously, countries that make computer-aided missiles will be stronger and freer than countries making simply rifles and jeeps.

But the right composition is also a key to the ability to create wealth over the long term. Not just any haphazardly arranged economy can make computer chips well—either for military or civilian markets. The chip companies themselves need the financial strength to compete globally. This strength, in turn, depends in large part on a host of vigorous supporting industries (e.g., chip-making equipment) and on healthy chip consuming industries (e.g., consumer electronics) that provide valuable and demanding markets for their products. It depends as well on a critical mass of related industries whose spillover effects will continually spur innovations by the chip makers and by everyone else. Without this mutually reenforcing structure, moreover, an economy will not only fall behind militarily and technologically, but in terms of wealth-creating ability as well. And those who fall behind in today's world of rapid and often costly innovation tend to stay behind, and find themselves forced to rely on foreigners for the latest in civilian as well as military products.

Joseph Schumpeter, one of this century's leading economic thinkers, was one of the first economists to stress the special role played by certain "leading industries," which spearheaded growth and technological advance. These industries were the leading agents of what Schumpeter called "creative destruction"—the ruthless competition among firms and industries by which capitalism fosters progress. Indeed, Schumpeter viewed this process as the essence of capitalism.

Stephen S. Cohen and John Zysman translate many of Schumpeter's insights into an analysis of the modern American economy. Contending that "manufacturing matters," the authors challenge the argument that the United States can watch its manufacturing capacity wither away and become a service economy. In the first place, they argue, too many services are too intimately linked with manufacturing to be able to survive in an economic vacuum. Second, technological innovation itself will be jeopardized in America unless U.S. firms keep control of the production of high tech goods.

Using the telecommunications industry as an example, Robert G. Harris provides a useful two-part definition of a strategic industry: It must be important to national security; and it must be research-intensive—and thus a source of new technology.

Finally, Miyohei Shinohara, an architect of Japan's post-World War II economic miracle, details how the determination to shape that country's industrial structure has been central to its phenomenal economic performance. Shinohara's analysis reveals the remarkable extent to which Japan's planners have studied how and how much individual industries have contributed to long-term prosperity.

Creative Destruction

Joseph A. Schumpeter

The theories of monopolistic and oligopolistic competition and their popular variants may in two ways be made to serve the view that capitalist reality is unfavorable to maximum performance in production. One may hold that it always has been so and that all along output has been expanding in spite of the secular sabotage perpetrated by the managing bourgeoisie. Advocates of this proposition would have to produce evidence to the effect that the observed rate of increase can be accounted for by a sequence of favorable circumstances unconnected with the mechanism of private enterprise and strong enough to overcome the latter's resistance. . . . However, those who espouse this variant at least avoid the trouble about historical fact that the advocates of the alternative proposition have to face. This avers that capitalist reality once tended to favor maximum productive performance so considerable as to constitute a major element in any serious appraisal of the system; but that the later spread of monopolist structures, killing competition, has by now reversed that tendency.

First, this involves the creation of an entirely imaginary golden age of perfect competition that at some time somehow metamorphosed itself into the monopolistic age, whereas it is quite clear that perfect competition has at no time been more of a reality than it is at present. Secondly, it is necessary to point out that the rate of increase in output did not decrease from the [1890s] from which, I suppose, the prevalence of the largest-size concerns, at least in manufacturing industry, would have to be dated; that there is nothing in the behavior of the time series of total output to suggest a "break in trend"; and, most important of all, that the modern standard of life of the masses evolved during the period of relatively unfettered "big business." If we list the items that enter the modern workman's budget and from 1899 on observe the course of their prices not in terms of money but in terms of the hours of labor that will buy them—i.e., each year's money prices divided by each year's hourly wage rates—we cannot fail to be struck by the rate of the advance which, considering the spectacular improvement in qualities, seems to have been greater and not smaller than it ever was before. If we economists were given less to wishful thinking and more to the observation of facts, doubts would immediately arise as to the realistic virtues of a theory that would have led us to expect a very different result. Nor is this all. As soon as we go into details and inquire into the individual items in which progress was most conspicuous, the trail leads not to the doors of those firms that work under conditions of comparatively free competition but precisely to the doors of the large concerns—which, as in the case of agricultural machinery, also account for much of the progress in the competitive sector—and a shocking suspicion dawns upon us that big business may have had more to do with creating that standard of life than with keeping it down.

. . . . Both economists and popular writers have once more run away with some fragments of reality they happened to grasp. These fragments themselves were mostly developed correctly. But no conclusions about capitalist reality as a whole follow from such fragmentary analyses. If we draw them nevertheless, we can be right only by accident. That has been done. And the lucky accident did not happen.

The essential point to grasp is that in dealing with capitalism we are dealing with an evolutionary process. It may seem strange that anyone can fail to see so obvious a fact which moreover was long ago emphasized by Karl Marx. Yet that fragmentary analysis which yields the bulk of our propositions about the functioning of modern capitalism persistently neglects it. Let us restate the point and see how it bears upon our problem.

Capitalism, then, is by nature a form or method of economic change and not only never is but never can be stationary. And this evolutionary character of the capitalist process is not merely due to the fact that economic life goes on in a social and natural environment which changes and by its change alters the data of economic action; this fact is important and these changes (wars, revolutions and so on) often condition industrial change, but they are not its prime movers. Nor is this evolutionary character due to a quasi-automatic increase in population and capital or to the vagaries of monetary systems of which exactly the same thing holds true. The fundamental impulse that sets and keeps the capitalist engine in motion comes from the new consumers' goods, the new methods of production or transportation, the new markets, the new forms of industrial organization that capitalist enterprise creates.

As we have seen in the preceding chapter, the contents of the laborer's budget, say from 1760 to 1940, did not simply grow on unchanging lines but they underwent a process of qualitative change. Similarly, the history of the productive apparatus of a typical farm, from the beginnings of the rationalization of crop rotation, plowing and fattening to the mechanized thing of today—linking up with elevators and railroads—is a history of revolutions. So is the history of the productive apparatus of the iron and steel industry from the charcoal furnace to our own type of furnace, or the history of the apparatus of power production from the overshot water wheel to the modern power plant, or the history of transportation from the mailcoach to the airplane. The opening up of new markets, foreign or domestic, and the organizational development from the craft shop and factory to such concerns as U.S. Steel illustrate the same process of industrial mutation—if I may use that biological term—that incessantly revolutionizes the economic structure *from within*, incessantly destroying the old one, incessantly creating a new one. This process of Creative Destruction is the essential fact about capitalism. It is what capitalism consists in and what every capitalist concern has got to live in. This fact bears upon our problem in two ways.

First, since we are dealing with a process whose every element takes considerable time in revealing its true features and ultimate effects, there is no point in appraising the performance of that process *ex visu* of a given point of time; we must judge its performance over time, as it unfolds through decades or centuries. A system—any system, economic or other—that at *every* given point of time fully utilizes its possibilities to the best advantage may yet in the long run be inferior to a system that does so at *no* given point in time, because the latter's failure to do so may be a condition for the level or speed of long-run performance.

Second, since we are dealing with an organic process, analysis of what happens in any particular part of it—say, in an individual concern or industry—may indeed clarify details of mechanism but is inconclusive beyond that. Every piece of business strategy acquires its true significance only against the background of that process and within the situation created by it. It must be seen in its role in the perennial gale of creative destruction; it cannot be understood irrespective of it or, in fact, on the hypothesis that there is a perennial lull.

But economists who, *ex visu* of a point of time, look for example at the behavior of an oligopolist industry—an industry which consists of a few big firms—and observe the well-known moves and countermoves within it that seem to aim at nothing but high prices and restrictions of output are making precisely that hypothesis. They accept the data of the momentary situation as if there were no past or future to it and think that they have understood what there is to understand if they interpret the behavior of those firms by means of the principle of maximizing profits with reference to those data. The usual theorist's paper and the usual government commission's report practically never try to see that behavior, on the one hand, as a result of a piece of past history and, on the other hand, as an attempt to deal with a situation that is sure to change presently—as an attempt by those firms to keep on their feet, on ground that is slipping away from under them. In other words, the problem that is usually being visualized is how capitalism administers existing structures, whereas the relevant problem is how it creates and destroys them. As long as this is not recognized, the investigator does a meaningless job. As soon as it is recognized, his outlook on capitalist practice and its social results changes considerably.

The first thing to go is the traditional conception of the *modus operandi* of competition. Economists are at long last emerging from the stage in which price competition was all they saw. As soon as quality competition and sales effort are admitted into the sacred precincts of theory, the price variable is ousted from its dominant position. However, it is still competition within a rigid pattern of invariant conditions, methods of production and forms of industrial organization in particular, that practically monopolizes attention. But in capitalist reality as distinguished from its textbook picture, it is not that kind of competition which counts but the competition from the new commodity, the new technology, the new source of supply, the new type of organization (the largest-scale unit of control for instance)—competition which commands a decisive cost or quality advantage and which strikes not at the margins of the profits and the outputs of the existing firms but at their foundations and their very lives. This kind of competition is as much more effective than the other as a bombardment is in comparison with forcing a door, and so much more important that it becomes a matter of comparative indifference whether competition in the ordinary sense functions more or less promptly; the powerful lever that in the long run expands output and brings down prices is in any case made of other stuff.

It is hardly necessary to point out that competition of the kind we now have in mind acts not only when in being but also when it is merely an ever-present threat. It disciplines before it attacks. The businessman feels himself to be in a competitive situation even if he is alone in his field or if, though not alone, he holds a position such that investigating government experts fail to see any effective competition between him and any other firms in the same or a neighboring field and in consequence conclude that his talk, under examination, about his competitive sorrows is all make-believe. In many cases, though not in all, this will in the long run enforce behavior very similar to the perfectly competitive pattern.

Many theorists take the opposite view which is best conveyed by an example. Let us assume that there is a certain number of retailers in a neighborhood who try to improve their relative position by service and "atmosphere" but avoid price competition and stick as to methods to the local tradition—a picture of stagnating routine. As others drift into the trade that quasi-equilibrium is indeed upset, but in a manner that does not benefit their customers. The economic space around each of the shops having been narrowed, their owners will no longer be able to make a living and they will try to mend the case by raising prices in tacit agreement. This will further reduce their sales and so, by successive pyramiding, a situation will evolve in which increasing potential supply will be attended by increasing instead of decreasing prices and by decreasing instead of increasing sales.

Such cases do occur, and it is right and proper to work them out. But as the practical instances usually given show, they are fringe-end cases to be found mainly in the sectors furthest removed from all that is most characteristic of capitalist activity. Moreover, they are transient by nature. In the case of retail trade the competition that matters arises not from additional shops of the same type, but from the department store, the chain store, the mail-order house and the supermarket which are bound to destroy those pyramids sooner or later. Now a theoretical construction which neglects this essential element of the case neglects all that is most typically capitalist about it; even if correct in logic as well as in fact, it is like *Hamlet* without the Danish prince.

Manufacturing Matters

Stephen S. Cohen and John Zysman

Manufacturing matters mightily to the wealth and power of the United States and to our ability to sustain the kind of open society we have come to take for granted. If we want to stay on top—or even high up—we can't just shift out of manufacturing and up into services, as some would have it. Nor can we establish a long-term preserve around traditional blue-collar jobs and outmoded plants. . . . We must reorganize production, not abandon it. In a catch phrase, if the United States is to remain a wealthy and powerful economy, American manufacturing must automate, not emigrate. . . . There is absolutely no way we can lose control and mastery of manufacturing and expect to hold onto the high-wage service jobs that we are constantly told will replace manufacturing. At the heart of our argument is a notion we call "direct linkage": a substantial core of service employment is tightly tied to manufacturing. It is a complement and not, as the dominant view would have it, a substitute or successor for manufacturing. Lose manufacturing and you will lose—not develop—those high-wage services.

Despite all the upbeat talk to the contrary, the United States cannot hope to let manufacturing go and reconstruct a strong international trade position in services. Exports of services are simply too small to offset the staggering deficits we are running in industrial goods. They will remain so over the foreseeable future. Furthermore, a decisive band of high-wage service exports are linked to mastery and control of manufacturing. . . .

These contentions should be obvious, and are taken as solid premises in policy debates abroad. . . . But in American policy and academic debates they constitute a distinctly minority—and often suspect—view. In part this is

Stephen S. Cohen, *Professor of City and Regional Planning at the University of California at Berkeley, is Co-director of the Berkeley Roundtable on the International Economy.* John Zysman *is Professor of Economics at the University of California at Berkeley.* Excerpted from Manufacturing Matters: The Myth of the Post-Industrial Economy, *by* Stephen Cohen *and* John Zysman. *Copyright* © *1987 by Basic Books, Inc. Excerpted by permission of Basic Books, Inc., Publishers, New York.*

due to the intellectual, political, and ideological power of a central tenet of American economic thought: the composition of national product should be a matter of indifference to policy. (Defense is exempted on noneconomic grounds.) This conventional view is supported in books, in the journals, the op-ed pages and in expert testimony by easily marshaled data. The data show a relentless decline in manufacturing employment, from about 50 percent of all jobs in 1950 down to about 20 percent now, and an irresistible increase in service jobs, up to about 70 percent of all jobs. The data underwrite the basic view that economic development is an ongoing and never-ending process of shifting out of activities of the past and up into the newer, higher-value-added activities of the future. . . . The policy point is clear: keep hands off. Things are going as they should. . . . A substantial capacity in steel or in semiconductors is no more an economic necessity than one in buggy whips or oats. . . .

The strength of this dominant view—that the American economic future is assured by a smooth shift into services—is based on data that although overwhelming in their seeming consistency and scope to a large extent reflect a statistical muddle. That muddle derives from the particular ways in which economic data are organized; it is not without consequence. For example, in the data that economists and policy makers use to shape theories and guide policy, tight linkages of the sort that inextricably tie the crop duster (a service firm) to the farm (agriculture) are indistinguishable from the linkages which loosely and indifferently tie an advertising firm to GM (domestic production) or to Toyota (imports). This leads to policy based on a notion of industrial succession—up out of one sector and into another.

For example, in a recent report to Congress on trade agreements, the president of the United States sets out the following framework for understanding what many take to be a troubling trade situation. "The move from an industrial society toward a 'postindustrial' service economy has been one of the greatest changes to affect the developed world since the Industrial Revolution. The progression of an economy such as America's from agriculture to manufacturing to services is a natural change."

The New York Stock Exchange, in a recent report on trade, industrial change, and jobs, put it more pointedly: "A strong manufacturing sector is not a requisite for a prosperous economy. . . ."

In this view agriculture is the first stage, industry is the second, and services—especially knowledge-based services—is the third, and for the moment the ultimate stage. From this view comes a comforting interpretation (which dominates policy debate) of America's present economic difficulties. Aside from difficulties caused by exchange rate and interest rate differentials which are due to incorrect macroeconomic policies (inherently a bothersome, but temporary, problem amenable to tough, but conventional, treatment), the loss of market share and employment in such industries as textiles, steel, apparel, autos, consumer electronics, machine tools, random-access memories, computer peripherals, and circuit boards, to name but a few, is neither a surprise nor a "bad thing." We should take no special measures to halt or reverse it. It is not a sign of failure but a part of the price of success. . . . It is part of an ever-evolving and ever-developing international division of labor from which we all benefit.

The ideas and the basic vision behind the dominant positions are not new . . . . But since they first gained currency, a lot of evidence has accumulated that clouds the picture and complicates the core notion of development through industrial succession. . . .

Shift out of manufacturing and it is more likely that you will find that you have shifted *out of* such services as product and process engineering, than *into* those services. This is true of a large number of high-level service activities, the very services that are supposed to drive the argument for development by sectoral succession—out of industry and up into services. . . . The wages generated in services that are tightly linked to manufacturing exert an enormous effect on wage levels in services quite independent of manufacturing, activities as distant as teaching, government work, hairdressing, and banking. . . .

High tech

Along with services, high tech is held out as the successor to manufacturing. It is not always clear what people mean when they say "high tech." For most, it is a list of processes and products that they find particularly exotic or complicated and new—microelectronics, biotechnologies, new materials—and their applications—robotics, computers, lasers, magnetic imaging. For our official statistics it is a list of industries with a high proportion of R&D expenditures or a high proportion of employees with advanced or scientific degrees. Though a bit more sophisticated than a simple listing of the new but arcane, it, like the manufacturing/services classification scheme, creates more problems and blind spots than it helps to solve. Many industries—including such big ones as farming, textiles, and insurance—do not perform their own R&D. But they are the users of R&D performed in supplying industries and at specialized nonindustry research centers. It is the historical development of the industry, its relations with its suppliers, and its competitive and institutional structures, not necessarily the nature of the product, that determines whether or where R&D will be performed. . . .

High tech is not defined only by the nature of the product; a better definition would include the way the product is produced. Within a relatively short time, the U.S. economy will have only high-tech industry—whether it be producing computers, trousers, or tennis balls. The others will have long gone offshore.

But the relationship between high tech and manufacturing, like that between services and manufacturing, is not a simple case of evolutionary succession. High tech, however defined, must be understood as intimately tied to manufacturing, and not as a free-floating laboratory activity. . . . First, despite the popularity of home computers and burglar alarms, most high-tech products are producer goods, not consumer goods. They are bought to be used either in the products of other industries (like microprocessors in autos) or in the production process (like robots, computers, and lasers across the range of manufacturing and services) or both. If not American producers of autos, machine tools, telephones and trousers, who is going to buy a bag of American silicon chips? The answers, like the interdependencies of real-world production processes, are. . .anything but simple.

The second tie to manufacturing is even tighter. If high tech is to sustain a scale of activity sufficient to matter to the prosperity of our economy and not shrink down to a marginal research activity, America must control the production of those high-tech products it invents and designs—and it must do so in a direct and hands-on way. There are several reasons for this. First, as we shall see, production is where the lion's share of the value added is realized. It is where the "rent on innovation" is captured. And given the dependence of American high-tech firms on a private capital market, this is where the returns needed to finance the next round of research and development are generated. Second, and most important in the overwhelming majority of cases, unless R&D is tightly tied to the manufacturing of the product—and the permanent process of innovation in production now required for competitiveness in manufacturing—R&D will fall behind the cutting edge of incremental innovation. For example, by abandoning the production of televisions, the U.S. electronics industry quickly lost the know-how to design, develop, refine, and competitively produce the next generation of that product, the VCR. As a result, we make no VCRs in this country, and we are likely to lose whatever positions we still maintain in research and development of products that derive from mastery of that product and production technology. High tech gravitates toward the state-of-the-art producers.

Statistical categories and economic realities

The conventional analytic categories that provide the basis for an image of economic development, distinguishing a movement up a succession of industries defined by the nature of their final product, do not work. Those categories—agriculture, manufacturing, services, high tech—organize employment, output, and profit data in ways that are easy to collect and count. They satisfy a popular understanding of how an economy works and ought to work; it is simply clear as a bell that a country that does brain surgery and computer programming is, in a fundamental way, ahead of a country that doesn't and can't. But it is a slippery path from that hard truth to a model of development—and worse, a policy for development—based on those categories which now become analytic categories though they embody no real theory, though they do not square with the realities of economic organization and linkages, and which, like the Brand X candies in the M&M's ads, melt in your hand when you try to use them.

The demarcations between *services* that find their finality in the production of a product (such as product design, process engineering, and the repair of automated equipment, as well as accounting, dispatching, and billing) and *production* tasks (such as the monitoring of automated equipment, the regulation of an on-time inventory system, testing, quality control, and systems integration) are generally the results of statistical categories and institutional arrangements external to the logics and realities of actual economic activity. These statistical categories tend to become analytic categories. This is especially true when both the evidence and the very vocabulary of analysis must be drawn from those same statistics.

Even when these initial doubts about the viability of the categories are pushed aside and the employment data are studied closely within their own framework, the statistics reveal what is, at best, a mixed message. . . . Though many of the figures, such as increases in programmers, systems integrators, designers, and bioengineers, are positive signs of development, the overwhelming preponderance of service jobs created in the past fifteen, ten, or even five years are not futuristic . . . . They are not especially knowledge-based, "advanced," high-paid or difficult to emulate abroad or to import. Instead, in every way except the best ways, they are very traditional: wholesale and retail sales, routine office work, restaurant work. . .security, and so on. Overwhelmingly, they are simple, low-skill, hands-on, part-time, low-wage, dead-end jobs.

But a simple dismissal of this sectoral-succession view would be wrong, or at least premature, whether based on the obvious inadequacies of its division of the economy by final product or on the ambiguous statistical relationship of increased service employment to any notion of progressive development, or both . . . . It would also flaunt common sense and casual observation: we are, after all, overwhelmingly a service economy. And so are the French, the Dutch, the Swiss, and the Germans. We are quite prosperous and consider ourselves to be as "advanced" as anyone . . . . It is a big and rich argument, and it calls for a big and rich discussion, rooted in a sympathetic understanding. . . .

Tight linkages between services and manufacturing

If we turn from agriculture to industry—where the conventional base of direct employment is not 3 million but 21 million jobs—even a remotely similar "direct linkage rate" would radically change the meaning of most interpretations of the place of manufacturing in our economy. And it would radically change the drift of policy suggestions . . . . Manufacturing employment would not be discussed, as it now is in conventional economic presentations as something that was about one-third of all jobs in 1953 and is now down to one-fifth and doomed to continue down that trend line. Instead, we would have to say that the particular organizational structure of manufacturing production in the United States (and probably in most other highly advanced economies) makes the employment of perhaps 40 or 50 or even 60 million Americans, half or two-thirds or even three-quarters of whom are conventionally counted as service workers, depend directly upon manufacturing production.

If this tight-linkage argument has anything at all going for it, we must recast our national discussion of the place of manufacturing in the economy . . . . The proportion of jobs in the economy classified as manufacturing or services must be dropped as a defining and operational concept. In its place we must substitute: (1) an analysis of the ways economic activities are linked to one another, something completely absent from the current stock of ideas from which conventional economics draws to set the terms for policy making, and (2) an analysis of how a declining proportion of manufacturing jobs brought about the loss of offshoring of the production process would compare, in its overall impacts, with a declining proportion brought about by maintaining production while substituting capital, technology, and indirect labor for direct labor. It is our strong suspicion that in the aggregate, onshore development extends the chains of linkages that are the generators of development; offshoring weakens and ultimately unlinks the hauberk; it generates decline . . . .

Clearly, what is needed is a major reworking (or rather development) of the notion of linkages from the perspective of economic development and decline.   Analytically, linkages must be categorized by the degree of dependence—tight, medium, weak—and by the direction of dependence. These must be crossed against the causes and principles of linkage. In the simple and clear illustrations used in this text, the tight linkages are determined by technology; their principle is physical propinquity.   There are also other causes of tight and medium linkages and other principles affecting their operation, including market forces, social and communal structures and mores, cultural concerns, and political rules and uncertainties. Finally, quantitative work must be undertaken so that we have a body of theory and information that can inform policy. . . .

If the United States loses control and mastery of manufacturing production, it is not simply that we will not be able to replace the jobs lost in industry (narrowly defined) by service jobs; nor simply that those service jobs will pay less; nor that the scale and speed of adjustment will shock the society—and the polity—in potentially dangerous ways . . . . It is that if we lose mastery and control of manufacturing, the high-paying service jobs that are directly linked to manufacturing will, in a few short rounds of product and process innovation, seem to wither away (only to sprout up offshore, where the manufacturing went) . . . . It is the high-value-added service roles tied directly to manufacturing (whether they are located in service or manufacturing categories) that we must hold and develop if we are to remain a powerful economy. It is not manufacturing jobs per se . . . .

Linkages and wealth

Most, though certainly not all, of the service jobs that are likely to be tightly linked to manufacturing are upstream (backward linkages). The great battalions of service jobs downstream from manufacturing, such as wholesaling and retailing, would not be directly affected if manufacturing were ceded to offshore producers; the same sales effort is involved in selling a Toyota as in selling a Buick. Nor would there by any *direct* negative impact on services such as health or education, or fire insurance or sanitation, or hairdressing or dry cleaning. These constitute the great bulk of service employment, and they have no direct linkages to manufacturing, tight or loose . . . .

Rather, direct linkage is concentrated in the relatively narrow band of services to manufacturing businesses and (awkward though it sounds) in services to services to manufacturers. Examples of such closely linked activities include design and engineering services for product and process; payroll, inventory, and accounting services; financing and insuring; repair and maintenance of plant and machinery; training and recruiting; testing services and labs . . . .

Two questions pose themselves immediately; many more follow. The first involves scale: How important are these upstream services to manufacturing? Do they constitute a scale of employment and value added sufficient to justify a new set of concerns . . .? The second concerns the nature of the linkages between these upstream services and manufacturing: What are their concrete relationships to manufacturing? How can we go about determining how many of those jobs would vanish from the U.S. economy if U.S. producers lost control and mastery of manufacturing and U.S. markets were sourced from offshore? . . .

The *Report of the President on the Trade Agreements Program* [1983] provides an approximate answer for the first question. It is staggeringly large: "25% of U.S. GNP originates in services used as inputs by goods-producing industries—more than the value added to GNP by the manufacturing sector."

. . . . [I]f it is even close to accurate it compels us to stop and immediately reconsider the treatment of manufacturing by conventional economics categories.   After all, manufacturing plus services sold to manufacturing firms equal half the economy. Talk of shifting out of it is not something that should be complacently contemplated . . . .

These numbers are a rough estimate of an upper limit of upstream service employment. They are not at all an estimate of tightly linked jobs. Many of these upstream services, such as advertising (150,000 jobs), would do quite as well with foreign or offshore manufacturers . . . .

Charting just how the different pieces of that upstream service employment are linked to manufacturing . . . . should be right at the top of the economics research agenda, so that it can get to the top of the policy debate. For, unless it can be shown that the overwhelming bulk of those services are very weakly linked to manufacturing (so weakly linked as to be indifferent to whether manufacturing stays or moves offshore), we must quickly reformulate the terms of that policy debate. . . .

Some upstream service jobs are so tightly linked into manufacturing that they are best understood as direct extensions of that employment base. These would include, for example, truckers (and those who service them) who specialize in interplant shipments of raw materials, components, and semifinished goods . . . . The same is obviously true for those who repair and service the machinery used in manufacturing: in almost all cases, they have to be located close to the machines that will need servicing. . . . Whatever the scale and location of those who collect the funds for venture investments, those who place those funds, and hand hold and monitor the ventures, and decide whether to go further to second-round financing or just write off the grubstake must operate in tight propinquity with the start-up companies. If "the action" in high-tech start-ups moves from the United States to Korea or Spain or Japan—regardless of whether the pension funds that collect the venture cash remain in New York, Paris, and Zurich—the venture industry will find itself slouching toward Seoul or Madrid or Tokyo. . . .

Given the reality of these tight linkages—the complementary rather than the substitutability of service jobs and manufacturing jobs—the critical questions emerge: How big are they? How many jobs are involved? How much income? Those questions can be answered only after careful empirical study. But asking them, and getting the questions to be taken seriously, may define a good first step . . . .

Sometimes new notions capture our fancy, resonate to some element of our experience, and color the way we see the world. The concept of a post-industrial society is just such a notion. It gives voice to our experience of big changes, shapes our perceptions of their tone and texture, and organizes our understanding of their direction. But the notion obscures the precise location of those changes and their meanings.

Things, of course, have changed. Production work has changed. People go home cleaner; more and more of them leave offices rather than assembly lines. Service activities have proliferated. The sociology of work and the organization of society have changed along with the technologies of product and production . . . . But the key generator of wealth for this vastly expanded and differentiated division of labor remains mastery and control of production. We are shifting not out of industry into services, but from one kind of industrial economy to another.

Telecommunications as a Strategic Industry

Robert G. Harris

. . . . [I]n going to Europe and Japan to study recent changes and developments in their telecommunications industries and in their public policies towards telecommunications, I tried to follow that advice both to learn lessons from those countries and also to learn about what the consequences of their policies would be for the U.S. and vice versa.

The first major difference that I learned is that those countries—France, the U.K., Japan, and now Germany, view telecommunications as a strategic industry and they know what they mean by "strategic industry."

We don't think in terms of strategic industries in this country; in public policies we typically don't think of strategies at all, and so the first point I'd like to cover today is to explain what a strategic industry is and why I consider telecommunications to be one of those industries. Referring to telecommunications as a strategic industry, is not just to say that it matters, all industries matter. I want to distinguish between industries that are important and that contribute to economic welfare from industries which can truly be shown to be strategic and, hence, deserving of special treatment.

Secondly, I want to review why the Japanese have designated telecommunications as a strategic industry and what the consequences have been in terms of their public policy toward telecommunications. In particular, I want to emphasize the very stark differences between their approach and that of the U.S.

Third, drawing on my experience in Japan, but frankly many of the same lessons could be drawn as well from the U.K. and France, I want to talk about the lessons for the U.S. Given what Japan has done and is doing, what does

---

Robert G. Harris *is president of EconomInc and Associate Professor at the University of California at Berkeley's School of Business Administration. Reprinted, with the author's permission, as published in* Vital Speeches of the Day, *April 1, 1989.*

it imply for what we should be doing in the U.S.?

Now in discussing these issues I want to make one point clear—telecommunications is not now a failure in the U.S. The system works. It works extremely well. Costs are going down. Prices are going down. Technology, new technology, in many cases, the best technologies are being introduced. But people, when I start this talk, typically say, so what is the problem? The problem is not failure on one side, success on the other, it is differential rates of change. We're on one trajectory, a trajectory that is limited in growth, in rate of improvement, and technological adoption by inappropriate, often antiquated public policies.

Japan, France, the U.K., probably now Germany, major competitors in global markets, are on a faster trajectory. We should have all learned by now the consequences of differential rates of growth from Japan over the last 20 years. You remember what "Made in Japan" used to mean just 20 years ago? We now see what a few additional points in productivity rates, in economic growth rates, means for the long run performance of an economy.

What is a strategic industry? Traditionally, there were three main aspects to an industry being identified as a strategic industry. First, it was important to national security or had military consequences. There's no doubt that telecommunications is absolutely essential to national security interests, but alone this hardly provides an adequate basis for public policy making.

It is interesting to note, however, that it is really only this argument that has typically served as a sufficient rationale for giving the industry special treatment. All of the kinds of arguments I'm going to make about telecommunications have been made about military expenditures for years, the space program, all the spillover effects, the side benefits, and filter down effects, justify spending. But this is not the reason I think we should give telecommunications special treatment. And I certainly don't think we should give it the kind of special treatment we've given the defense contractors.

Secondly, the industry is research-intensive. Hence, it's an important source of new technology. Again, there's no doubt about telecommunications being a research-intensive industry. Overall, the industry composite expenditures on R&D in the U.S. in 1986 were 3.5 percent. Telecommunications equipment is at a 50 percent higher rate than R&D expenditures, which are 5.1 percent. Computers, also part of this generic class of information technologies are 8.3 percent of total industry expenditures revenues spent on R&D. Software is 7.7 percent. The learning by doing, the knowledge base, that's increased by these kinds of investments are one important reason why telecommunications has been seen as a strategic industry in other countries.

The most important class, though, comes from what might be called spillovers, or in the more formal economic jargon, positive externalities. By that we mean that the value of the outputs of a given industry greatly exceed the cost of the inputs into that industry, resulting in a huge net surplus which can be felt throughout the economy. By investing in one area, services and benefits are provided to lots of industries. Lots of people are better off—and not only the people who buy the products that resulted from the research.

That's the sense in which the term externality is used. Others, even people who aren't buying those products nevertheless directly realize some of the benefits. Telecommunications has a multiplier effect of increasing efficiency. As our telecommunication system has become more efficient, so too has all of our industries which depend on it.

Think about the provisioning of financial services today. It is markedly different from only a few years ago and would have been impossible without advances in telecommunications technology. Think about the introduction of electronic data exchange in manufacturing. A vital source of efficiency gains in all the manufacturing industries and not possible without telecommunications.

In government services, we have both experienced such efficiency gains and discovered many, many other potential gains to be had for the seeking. Further benefits have been made in education, in research and in development. A stunning development in the way research is now conducted is the use of electronic mail that ties researchers together. Talk to people who are doing superconductivity research today. They will tell you that a principle cause of the rate of breakthroughs being made on superconductivity is the immediate transmission of research results from one research point to another.

What used to take a year or more to go through the journal review, editing, printing and mailing process, now happens simultaneously. There's tremendous net benefits and it's not just what researchers spend on that electronic mail system that measures the social benefits of their subscription charges.

The second type of spillover is that the developments in telecommunications services induce the demand for new technology. So, as that first class of benefits are on the users looking downstream from tele-communication services, there's also an important set of upstream spillover benefits.

As we invest in new technologies for providing telecommunications services, we provide the market and hence the economic incentive for equipment manufacturers, system manufacturers and software producers to produce new and better technology in order to compete for the sale of equipment and software to the telephone companies, the inter-exchange carriers and the like.

And finally, a third major class of spillovers is that the research done in communications has tremendous spillover benefits into other industries. Think of the transistor. Where did it come from? It came from Bell Labs. Why was the money spent developing the transistor? Because it produced better telephone service. Who has benefitted?—name me a product today that doesn't have transistors or its successor, integrated circuits, another discovery that also came out of basic telecommunications research.

Other countries have recognized this spillover advantage and are beginning to deliberately exploit some of the possibilities I've already discussed. Now there's a fourth class of benefits associated with tele-communications. And even though historically these haven't been used to justify a strategic industry, it seems to be a new class of benefits.

I know it's very much in the minds of policy makers in Tokyo, and I suspect it's in your minds as well. Telecommunications, the wider applicability and range of services in telecommunications, has tremendous possibilities for improving the quality of life, in both urban and rural areas.

On the one hand, as we use telemarketing, teleshopping, tele-conferencing, telecommuting and all the other tele's of the world, we can reduce congestion, pollution, and capacity constraints and pressures on the transportation infrastructure in our large urban areas. Likewise for the rural areas, we can remotely deliver many services like education, health care and so on, at a far lower cost by using telecommunications than we can in more traditional ways.

For these reasons, Japan, through a national, public, discussion and debate beginning in the late 1970s and into the early 1980s, has designated telecommunications as the key strategic industry for the 21st century. They have invented a word for it. It's called informatization.

I will try not to use that word frequently in my presentation. But the word is used frequently in Japan. So much so that the annual white paper on communications and informations now literally counts up the quantity of information, total information, from all sources that is created, transmitted and received in the Japanese economy.

Now to tell you the real truth, I could not for the life of me figure out how they actually acquire that figure. But they do it and they publish that number and take it to be a measure of economic welfare and progress in the same way we view the GNP statistics—this should give you some idea of the importance to which they attach telecommunications.

Now let's put this discussion of Japan's policy towards telecommunications in context. We all know that the thrust of the Japanese economy during the 50s, 60s and 70s, was an export driven economic policy . . . .

In order to promote their export driven economy, they targeted strategic industries—automobiles, steel, ship buildings, and computers. In targeting those industries they gave them favorable treatment in taxation, in R&D subsidies, in export licensing and financing, in capital allocation for new investment and in regulatory treatment by the government.

These policies were, with only a very few exceptions, remarkably successful . . . . Even so by this time, by the late 1970s, it became increasingly clear that the strategy, based as it was in the manufacturing sector, had certain limits.

First of all, the yen was going to start catching up with them. The bigger their trade balance, the faster the yen would rise in value. Secondly, even at that time there were the next generation of rapidly developing countries following closely on Japan's heels as the newly industrialized countries, the so-called Asian Tigers, pursuing much the same line of public policy, were rapidly catching up with the Japanese, at least in certain basic industries like steel, shipbuilding and automobiles as well as consumer electronics.

In recognition of this, Japan began, in that time period, about ten years ago, a major process of industrial restructuring. The main elements of which were to bring further product gains in these basic industries in order to remain competitive. We've all been astonished at how little the price of Japanese products has risen, given that the yen has gone from 260 to the dollar to 120. That is absolutely unimaginable to us. How they could have done that so fast? But they have.

Secondly, they identified and rationalized declining industries . . . .
Third, and most importantly with regard to telecommunications, the Japanese
shifted the emphasis from the manufacturing sector to the service sector.

As they observed the European economies and the U.S. economy during
that time period, it became increasingly clear that, while manufacturing
continued to be an always will be important, an increasingly large share of the
value added in advanced economies is in the service sector. The service
sectors are uniformly heavily dependent on information technologies and
communication services.

And finally, they recognized that given the politics of trade, an export
driven policy, even with reduced costs, with rationalized industries and with
an increasing emphasis on services, could not succeed over the long run.
Sooner or later, probably sooner, a reaction sets in. Congress, the president,
whomever, starts demanding that the trade surplus be reduced.

So the fourth key element of this industrial restructuring, the most
recent added element of it in just the past few years, was to promote domestic
investment and consumption as a further spur to the demand for the
production of products and services in Japan.

In that context, their policy identified: a) a belief in information and the
Information Age—not as a cliche, as a fundamental premise of public policy.
And b) part of industrial restructuring, Japan undertook to fundamentally
restructure its telecommunications industry and its telecommunications policy.
It did so by doing the following:

First, they privatized NTT, long a nationally-owned enterprise. They've
done it gradually, stepwise; now about 40 percent of the shares have been
sold. The government continues to own about 60 percent. The sale of NTT
shares (NTT by the way has a market evaluation of $240 billion today, which
makes it in terms of market valuation far and away the largest company in the
world), the sale of those shares has brought in revenues that as of last year
constituted nearly 9 percent of the total central government budget. So in
selling off NTT they've done a number of things, one of which was to help
reduce their own budget deficit.

Secondly, they opened markets to entry and they're actually using public
policy to affirmatively promote competition in the provision of long distance
services, local services and value-added services. This policy, which was
signed into law on December 25th of 1984 and went into effect on April 1,

1985, has already witnessed the emergence of five strong new national carriers and 25 regional carriers, using a combination of microwave, satellite and optical fiber distribution systems.

There are also more than 500 new companies and joint ventures involved in the provision of value added network services over the basic telecommunications infrastructure, many of them involving American companies. Many of them involve joint ventures, including joint ventures between IBM and NTT and between AT&T and NTT. Can one imagine a joint venture between IBM and a regional holding company cutting mustard in this country? I suspect not—companies will have to go to Japan to do what they're not allowed to do at home.

Third, this policy removed virtually all restraints on NTT, including its employment and staffing policies, which have enabled it to rationalize operations by cutting employment within the traditionally defined telephone business. But because NTT is also allowed to enter any new line of business it chooses, and it's done so by forming more than 100 new subsidiaries in the past three years, it has transferred its employees from one task, one set of responsibilities, to another. This was a major condition that, if you will, reduced the objections of labor unions to this policy reform package. And also in terms of restraints being removed, few additional restraints have been imposed even in the face of competition.

Instead of formalizing, having a very heavy handed regulatory policy, imposing all kinds of terms and conditions on the relations between NTT and the NCCs as they call them, the new common carriers, basically the MPT provides a forum in which people can voluntarily negotiate, workout in terms of a managerial and technical point of view, the best kind of arrangements, interconnections and the like. They are standing ready to step in and resolve disputes only when the parties are unable to reach agreement. Doesn't exactly sound like the American way does it?

The fourth major element of their policy was large-scale experimentation with new information technologies. What we're now beginning to read about in the newspapers in the U.S., the Japanese started doing five years ago. The experiments are over; the results are in, it's time to get on with the real thing. If we would take the time and effort to learn from Japanese experiments, maybe we could cut down the length of time we need to spend experimenting ourselves.

The sixth element was large scale public financing of information technology R&D. I explained that the government has been selling off the shares of NTT piece by piece. All of the dividend income which runs into the hundreds of millions of dollars from NTT stock the government continues to hold, is channelled directly by the Minister of Finance into what are called the Japanese Key Technology Centers—a large share of which goes to the advanced telecommunications research institute. This is above and beyond what companies are spending themselves. We have no equivalent in the U.S.

Moreover, in a comparison I did in some earlier work, the Japanese companies are already spending more than their U.S. counterparts. So when you add the public funding on top of that, you get a very significant margin of difference.

And finally, there was a decision made at this time, a national commitment to the next generation of the telecommunications infrastructure. We're talking fully digital, full broadband, fully optical, from home to home, from business to business. Not just for high density, highly concentrated traffic areas as we're seeing in New York City or across the Atlantic but the whole system. A $150 billion investment will obviously accelerate the development of broadband services.

And the Japanese also make certain that not just the large intensive users of telecommunications have those services, but that everyone in the Japanese society will have them. They are determined not to have an information-rich, information-poor society, which I fear we will have if we don't change our direction.

Now when people in this country ask, why don't we have optical fiber to the home? The response is, there aren't enough services to justify it. The Japanese have it right. They put in the capacity and expected the services to quickly follow and the demand for those services to quickly pay for the investment. We seem to have lost our will on this count. There's no way one could justify the investment in the interstate highway system by the volume of inner city auto traffic at that time. The numbers weren't there.

There's no way that you could have justified the national investment in the airport and air traffic control system we now have on the basis of the traffic we then had. To some degree this requires an act of faith and we seemed to have lost that faith.

What are the lessons for the U.S.? We keep reading about it in the newspapers and we all can say the words. We even think we mean them when we say them. It's a global economy. We have global competition. We have to fully appreciate what that means—it means that we can no longer, in making public policy choices, look at the effects of that decision, of one policy alternative compared to another, in terms of the effects they have at home. This is an advanced and rapidly advancing technology. If, however well we're doing, someone is doing better, we're not doing well enough.

Not only is the U.S. competing with Japan and Europe, New York City is competing with London, with Tokyo, with Hong Kong. Will that transaction be made here, and the people who make it live in New York City? Or will it be made in Tokyo? And the people who are employed there-in live in Tokyo? That requires making telecommunications a national commitment and a state commitment . . . .

The Japanese View

Miyohei Shinohara

Since the war, the Ministry of International Trade and Industry has devoted major efforts to fostering and developing key industries such as steel, petrochemicals. . . . The development of such key industries did much to induce the expansion of many affiliated and processing industries such as automobiles, machinery, plastics, synthetic rubber, and synthetic fibers through the so-called forward linkage effect. And the demand-induced expansion of the processing industries and the parallel development of the key industries combined in turn to strengthen markedly the international competitive position of these sectors.

Now this created an unforeseen situation: despite the heavy emphasis which the Ministry of International Trade and Industry had placed up to 1970 on the development of capital-intensive key industries, the less capital-intensive processing sectors, which had required little in the way of incentives and protection, outperformed the key industries . . . .

It was in 1967 that I first pointed out this empirical tendency. Subsequently, the Economic Survey released by the Economic Planning Agency took note of this tendency, and *The Basic Direction of Trade and Industrial Policy in the 1970s*, a position paper released in 1971 by the Council on Industrial Structure, called it the tendency towards a "knowledge-intensive industrial structure." . . . . [T]he term "knowledge-intensive industry," by definition, covers the R&D-intensive industries (as typified by computers), the assembling industries (automobiles), and the fashion goods industry. . . .

In my opinion, the issued can be viewed from the dual standpoints of supply and demand. From the demand side, it may be observed that as

Miyohei Shinohara, *Professor of Economics at the Tokyo International University, served as director of the Economic Research Institute of the Economic Planning Agency from 1970 to 1973. Excerpted with permission of the University of Tokyo Press from* Industrial Growth, Trade, and Dynamic Patterns in the Japanese Economy *(Tokyo: University of Tokyo Press, 1982).*

society becomes increasingly affluent, demand inevitably becomes diversified, calling for a matching diversification and sophistication of the nation's industrial structure. This necessarily increases the importance of the processing sectors relative to the basic sectors.

When viewed from the supply side, successive technological breakthroughs enable an industry to cut down the materials input required for producing a unit of output, and this, in turn, reduces the weight of the "materials" or basic industry relative to the processing industry. A case in point is in electronics, where the replacement of the electric desk-calculator by the electronic desk-computer has brought about substantial savings in materials used, and the use of integrated circuits (IC) and large-scale integration (LSI) further cut down on raw materials requirements and, at the same time, boosted the efficiency of the calculator. What is more, the increased value-added per unit of product generated through the development of a processing-oriented industrial structure was accompanied by a gradual but perceptible shift in the mode of production from one of a manual labor- and energy-intensive nature to one of a knowledge- and information-intensive nature based on scientific and technological innovation. This, in turn, created a tendency to move from more to less material consumption, from a production system based on single-item demand to one based on systems demand. This entailed a dramatic increase in the number of component parts, from a 10^3 level to, say, a 10^4 to 10^6 level; witness the technological breakthroughs from vacuum tube to IC, from IC to LSI, and from LSI to hybrid integrated circuits.

Technical advances are not confined merely to electronics; similar dramatic breakthroughs were achieved in other areas of technology, and these have combined to intensify the drive toward an ever higher degree of processing. In this context, an increasing sophistication of processing is unthinkable in the absence of continual technological innovation.

However, the development toward a higher degree of processing has two important implications. One is the tendency toward the development of technology-intensive industries, which leads to the production of increasingly sophisticated goods. The other is the increasing emphasis on the "soft" aspects of products, as typified by the growing consumer preference for "fashion goods.". . . Thus one perceives a clear tilt in the Japanese industrial structure toward higher degrees of processing. . . .

The late Kaname Akamatsu published before World War II an article substantiating his theory of the "flying geese pattern" of industrial development—the successive pattern of imports-increased domestic production-exports. According to Akamatsu, a newly imported industry induces the development of associated domestic demand, thus stimulating the growth of domestic production of the same goods; and once the domestic industry expands enough, it will reduce its unit production cost, thus facilitating the expansion of exports. The product cycle theory advanced by Raymond Vernon also outlines a sequential pattern of "domestic production—exports—overseas investment." I shall synthesize these two theories into a pattern of "imports—domestic production—exports—overseas investment." My feeling is that the development pattern of industry in postwar Japan provides a typical example of the Akamatsu-Vernon cycle.

Because exports grew at a faster pace than domestic production in many growth industries, the shares of different industry groups in the nation's total exports have drastically changed . . . . [T]he export share or textiles decreased sharply from 30.2% in 1960 to 4.8% in 1979, while that of machin- eries (including autos and ships) rose dramatically from 25.5% in 1960 (it was as low as 13.7% in 1955) to 71.3% in 1979. In no other country have the exports of machineries accounted for as much as 60% of the total value of exports. . . . Japan's brilliant success in machinery exports was due to a great capacity to transform in the highly income-elastic automobile industry . . . .

[E]ven though Japan had actively tried to expand its heavy and chemical industries in the 1950s, their share in the nation's total exports remained far smaller than in the Western industrial nations. In the 1960s and 1970s, however, the export shares of the heavy and chemical industries increased sharply, to the point where they accounted for as much as 85.8%. This is a very substantial increase compared with the 38% share for these industries in 1955. In such a manner, the export structure has become heavily transformed toward the heavy and chemical industries—rather, I would say, toward the machinery industry—at a pace much faster than that of the industrial structure as a whole . . . .

As noted earlier, the share of the machinery industry in the nation's total exports has exceeded 60%, the largest in the world. Can the Japanese machinery industry maintain its relatively superior position in the world? MITI has established a Machinery Information Industry Bureau, and this suggests that the machinery industry has entered the stage where hardware and software are of equal importance. More than half of the watches and clocks being produced in Japan are electronically driven, but 15 years ago electronic watches and clocks were unknown to Japanese makers. Electronics technology became available not only to the watch industry but also to other sectors of the machinery industry. Now the electronicization of machinery is spreading rapidly to other industry groups. Indeed, systematic sharing of advanced technologies among related industries will become a task of central importance for Japanese industry.

In the second half of the 1950s, the development of the machinery industry, particularly the automobile industry, was one of the highest priorities of MITI. With this in mind, MITI pushed through the Diet a Special Measures Law for the Promotion of the Machinery Industry (the Machinery Development Law, for short). As the 1970s advanced, the development of the computer industry has taken on growing importance, and MITI pushed through the Diet a similar law for the promotion of the computer industry known (for short) as the Machinery and Computer Promotion Law. This indicates that MITI attaches an importance to the computer industry comparable to that of the automobile industry. . . .

In modern economics it has been considered that in an economy of abundant labor and scarce capital, the development of labor-intensive production methods would naturally bring about a rational allocation of resources.

On the other hand, in an economy with abundant capital and a shortage of labor, it has been taken for granted that capital-intensive industries would grow by becoming export industries. It has also been assumed that any measures taken contrary to this theorem would be going against economic principles, thus distorting resource allocation.

If this reasoning is correct, the industrial policies adopted by MITI in the mid-1950s were wrong. Ironically, however, Japan's industrial policies achieved unprecedented success by going against modern economic theory. Whether it was steel, petrochemicals, or other industries, dissenting voices were raised claiming that the development of capital-intensive industries was irrational. The cost of international steel products was then comparatively high, and the industry was highly capital-intensive. In terms of classical comparative cost theory, such industries as textiles, apparel, and shipbuilding were in comparatively advantageous positions during the 1950s. However, the government tried to introduce protective measures in industries which appeared to have potential for achieving an advantageous position over the next decade, despite a comparatively disadvantageous position at the time. The policy achieved remarkable results in the case of the steel industry, which has grown into the strongest in the world.

The problem of classical thinking undeniably lies in the fact that it is essentially "static" and does not take into account the possibility of a dynamic change in the comparative advantage or disadvantage of industries over a coming 10- or 20-year period. To take the place of such a traditional theory, a new policy concept needs to be developed to deal with the possibility of intertemporal dynamic development. The two basic criteria to which the industrial structure policies adopted by MITI conformed, therefore, were an "income elasticity criterion" and a "comparative technical progress criterion."...

The "income elasticity criterion" provides a suggestion that an industry whose elasticity of export demand with respect to world real income as a whole is comparatively high should be developed as an export industry. Under this criterion, as long as the income elasticity of textile products is higher than that of agricultural commodities, and the elasticities of automobiles and electronic products are higher than those of textile goods, automobiles are obviously preferable to textiles as export products, and textiles are more advantageous than agricultural products.

The "comparative technical progress criterion" pays more attention to the possibility of placing a particular industry in a more advantageous position in the future through a comparatively greater degree of technical progress, even if the cost of the products is relatively high at this stage. This could be termed the "dynamized comparative cost doctrine."

It must be pointed out that there are sufficient grounds for the government to foster industries which have a comparatively high growth rate on the demand side while displaying a comparatively high rate of technical progress on the supply side. In this particular regard, the industrial policy concept adopted by MITI, which tried to take into account potential intertemporal dynamic developments rather than automatically applying the ready-made static theory of international economics, proved to be a wise choice. . . .

[O]n the one hand, MITI's industrial policies were expected to foster the industries whose demand growth and technical progress were comparatively high. At the same time, they proved successful in strengthening some key industries which took a "backward linkage" position in relation to the processing industries. From the standpoint of inter-industry structure, the "industrial block" often found in advanced countries was formed, in which such machinery-linked industries as automobiles, industrial machinery, and electrical machinery are closely related to such basic metal sectors as iron and steel and non-ferrous metals. . . .

The goal of "building up international competitiveness," an unchanging industrial policy objective in Japan since the end of World War II, finally had to be abandoned in the 1970s . . . . The long period when the exchange rate was fixed at ¥360 was replaced by the "managed float." Many modern industries reached the levels of the advanced nations, both in the levels of production and technology. Therefore, it became necessary not to chase after a single visible goal of strengthening international competitiveness, but to seek various diversified national objectives.

At the end of 1970, the Minister of MITI called on the Industrial Structure Council to study "The Basic Direction of Trade and Industry in the 1970s.". . . Specifically the report called for a shift of the fundamental attitudes concerning economic management from "growth pursuit" to "growth utilization." It mentioned the "knowledge-intensive industrial structure" as the industrial structure vision of the 1970s, and stated that it would attach importance to industrial structure policies which emphasized such industries as:

1) Research and development-intensive industries (computer, aircraft, industrial robots, atomic power-related industries, large-scale integrated circuits, fine chemicals, ocean development, etc.);

2) High processing industries (office communication equipment, numerical counted machine tools, pollution prevention machinery, industrial housing production, high-quality printing, automated warehousing, educational equipment, etc.);

3) Fashion industries (high-quality clothing and furniture, electronic musical instruments, etc.);

4) Knowledge industries (information management services, information supplying services, education-related industries such as video, software, systems engineering, consulting, etc.) . . . .

MITI made public its "Trade and Industiral Policies for the 1980s" in March 1980, as a report of the Industrial Structure Council. . . . [I]t recognizes the 1980s as a period of preparation for energy security and of departure from an oil-oriented society in order to overcome resource limitations. At the same time, it advocates exploring ways of establishing highly sophisticated technologies putting particular emphasis on technology based upon new-type materials, large-scale system technology, and social system technology. . . .

The following four points are considered important for the evolution of a creative industrial structure: (1) the establishment of dynamic comparative advantages, (2) the fulfillment of the needs of the people, (3) the promotion of energy and resource saving, and (4) the maintenance of security. . . .

[T]he aim is to promote a highly sophisticated and diversified industrial structure, but this target is to be realized within as framework which will maintain economic security as a whole, enhance the quality of life, promote local economic societies, and also develop dynamic and unique small and medium-sized enterprises.

IV

Thinking Strategically: An American Tradition

If thinking strategically about economics was something completely foreign to the American experience, the case made by the Economic Strategy Institute for a comprehensive economic strategy today would be, in effect, dead in the water. The urgent need for a strategy would be irrelevant if history provided no reason to consider Americans capable of developing one. Similarly, all the favorable historical evidence in the world would mean nothing if some built-in obstacle made formulating a strategy impossible for the country today.

The Orthodoxy makes both arguments against a strategic approach. The American tradition is supposed to be wholly individualistic—we prospered because lone workers and entrepreneurs and families and enterprises were free to act in their own self-interest. Thus the magic of the marketplace was able to produce the best possible outcome for the country as a whole. In addition, whatever history does or does not teach, American society today is widely considered incapable of acting coherently, much less strategically. There are too many special interests. We are too fragmented, too diverse, too selfish.

But ample evidence indicates that the United States has a long, rich tradition of acting strategically economically as well as militarily, and that wise, farsighted government policies were instrumental in achieving national economic success. In fact, Part Four shows that strategic thinking is as American as apple pie.

The classic work of economic strategy in America is surely Alexander Hamilton's "Report on Manufactures." Submitted to Congress nearly two centuries ago (1791), Hamilton's study not only insisted that the United States could not keep its hard-won independence—much less reach its potential—without strong industries. In an uncanny preview of today's emerging economic debate, Hamilton disputed those who insisted that agriculture was man's most productive activity, and that any government effort to direct economic activity—specifically, to promote manufacturing—would only upset the natural order and waste precious resources.

Hamilton's arguments were shaped by the difficult straits in which the young American economy found itself. He advocated flat out protection until infant American industries could compete effectively against established foreign counterparts. And he emphasized the importance of developing domestic sources of militarily critical goods, to avoid dependence on potential adversaries. But more important than his specific policy prescriptions was Hamilton's belief in the need for long-term economic strength, and for a comprehensive, government-assisted program for achieving it.

Robert Cohen demonstrates that strategic American economic policies were hardly confined to the 18th century. From radio to aircraft and communications satellites to the integrated circuit that opened the modern computer age, America's 20th century economic, technological, and military predominance has been nurtured and even originated by Washington. U.S. leaders have consistently recognized the imperative of world leadership on these fronts, and worried that the private sector could not assume all the costs and risks of development.

One of the most compelling calls for active federal promotion of scientific progress was made at the end of World War II by Vannevar Bush, a pioneer in American computer science and then Director of the Office of Scientific Research and Development, the U.S. agency that mobilized civilian science during the conflict. Commissioned by President Franklin D. Roosevelt to outline a federal science policy for the post-war period, Bush submitted Science - The Endless Frontier to President Harry S Truman in July 1945. Its key recommendation was the creation of a "focal point" in the public sector for assisting American scientific research activities outside the government. As a result of Bush's report, the National Science Foundation was created in 1950.

Report on Manufactures

Alexander Hamilton

The expediency of encouraging manufactures in the United States, which was not long since deemed very questionable, appears at this time to be pretty generally admitted. The embarrassments which have obstructed the progress of our external trade, have led to serious reflections on the necessity of enlarging the sphere of our domestic commerce. The restrictive regulations, which, in foreign markets, abridge the vent of the increasing surplus of our agricultural produce, serve to beget an earnest desire that a more extensive demand for that surplus may be created at home; and the complete success which has rewarded manufacturing enterprise in some valuable branches, conspiring with the promising symptoms which attend some less mature essays in others, justify a hope that the obstacles to the growth of this species of industry are less formidable than they were apprehended to be, and that it is not difficult to find, in its further extension, a full indemnification for any external disadvantages, which are or may be experienced, as well as an accession of resources, favorable to national independence and safety.

There are still, nevertheless, respectable patrons of opinions unfriendly to the encouragement of manufactures. The following are, substantially, the arguments by which these opinions are defended:

"In every country. . .agriculture is the most beneficial and productive object of human industry. This position, generally if not universally true, applies with peculiar emphasis to the United States, on account of their immense tracts of fertile territory, uninhabited and unimproved. . . .

"To endeavor, by the extraordinary patronage of government, to accelerate the growth of manufactures, is, in fact, to endeavor, by force and art, to transfer the natural current of industry from a more to a less beneficial channel. . . . [I]t can hardly ever be wise in a government to attempt to give

---

Excerpted from "Report on Manufactures," *Samuel McKee, ed.,* Papers on Public Credit, Commerce, and Finance by Alexander Hamilton *(New York, 1934).*

a direction to the industry of its citizens. This, under the quick-sighted guidance of private interest, will, if left to itself, infallibly find its own way to the most profitable employment; and it by such employment, that the public prosperity will be most effectually promoted. . . .

"If. . .an unseasonable and premature spring can be given to certain fabrics, by heavy duties, prohibitions, bounties, or by other forced expedients, this will only be to sacrifice the interests of the community to those of particular classes. . . .

In order to an accurate judgement how far that which has been just stated ought to be deemed liable to a similar imputation, it is necessary to advert carefully to the considerations which plead in favor of manufactures, and which appear to recommend the special and positive encouragement of them in certain cases and under certain reasonable limitations. . . .

Some essays. . .render it probable that there are various branches of manufactures, in which a given capital will yield a greater total product, and a considerably greater net product, than an equal capital invested in the purchase and improvement of lands; and that there are also some branches, in which both the gross and the net product will exceed that of the agricultural industry, according to a compound ratio of capital and labor. . . .

It is now proper to. . .enumerate the principal circumstances from which it may be inferred that manufacturing establishments not only occasion a positive augmentation of the produce and revenue of the society, but that they contribute essentially to rendering them greater than they could possibly be without such establishments. . . .

As to the division of labor

It has justly been observed, that there is scarcely any thing of greater moment in the economy of a nation than the proper division of labor. The separation of occupations causes each to be carried to a much greater perfection than it could possibly acquire if they were blended. This arises principally from three circumstances:

1st. The greater skill and dexterity naturally resulting from a constant and undivided application to a single object. . . .

2d. The economy of time, by avoiding the loss of it, incident to a frequent transition from one operation to another of a different nature. . . .

3d. An extension of the use of machinery. A man occupied on a single object will have it more in his power, and will be more naturally led to exert his imagination, in devising methods to facilitate and abridge labor, than if he were perplexed by a variety of independent and dissimilar operations. Besides this the fabrication of machines, in numerous instances, becoming itself a distinct trade, the artist who follows it has all the advantages which have been enumerated, for improvement in his particular art; and, in both ways, the invention and application of machinery are extended. . . .

As to an extension of the use of machinery, a point which, though partly anticipated, requires to be placed in one or two additional lights

The employment of machinery forms an item of great importance in the general mass of national industry. It is an artificial force brought in aid of the natural force of man; and, to all the purposes of labor, is an increase of hands, an accession of strength, unencumbered too by the expense of maintaining the laborer. May it not, therefore, be fairly inferred, that those occupations which give greatest scope to the use of this auxiliary, contribute most to the general stock of industrious effort, and, in consequence, to the general product of industry?

It shall be taken for granted, and the truth of the position referred to observation, that manufacturing pursuits are susceptible, in a greater degree, of the application of machinery, than those of agriculture. If so, all the difference is lost to a community which, instead of manufacturing for itself, procures the fabrics requisite to its supply from other countries. The substitution of foreign for domestic manufactures is a transfer to foreign nations of the advantages accruing from the employment of machinery, in the modes in which it is capable of being employed with most utility and to the greatest extent. . . .

As to the furnishing greater scope for the diversity of talents and dispositions, which discriminate men from each other

This is a much more powerful means of augmenting the fund of national industry, than may at first sight appear. It is a just observation, that minds of the strongest and most active powers for their proper objects, fall below mediocrity, and labor without effect, if confined to uncongenial pursuits. And it is thence to be inferred, that the results of human exertion may be immensely increased by diversifying its objects. When all the different kinds of industry obtain in a community, each individual can find his proper element, and can call into activity the whole vigor of his nature. And the community is benefitted by the services of its respective members, in the manner in which each can serve it with most effect.

If there be any thing in a remark often to be met with, namely, that there is, in the genius of the people of this country, a peculiar aptitude for mechanic improvements, it would operate as a forcible reason for giving opportunities to the exercise of that species of talent, by the propagation of manufactures. . . .

As to the affording a more ample and various field for enterprise

. . . . The spirit of enterprise, useful and prolific as it is, must necessarily be contracted or expanded, in proportion to the simplicity or variety of the occupations and productions which are to be found in a society. It must be less in a nation of mere cultivators, than in a nation of cultivators and merchants; less in a nation of cultivators and merchants, than in a nation of cultivators, artificers, and merchants. . . .

It merits particular observation, that the multiplication of manufactories not only furnishes a market for those articles which have been accustomed to be produced in abundance in a country, but it likewise creates a demand for such as were either unknown or produced in inconsiderable quantities. The bowels as well as the surface of the earth are ransacked for articles which were before neglected. Animals, plants, and minerals acquire a utility and a value which were before unexplored. . . .

If the system of perfect liberty of industry and commerce were the prevailing system of nations, the arguments which dissuade a country, in the predicament of the United States, from the zealous pursuit of manufactures, would doubtless have great force. It will not be affirmed that they might not be permitted, with few exceptions, to serve as a rule of national conduct. In such a state of things, each country would have the full benefit of its peculiar advantages to compensate for its deficiencies or disadvantages. If one nation were in a condition to supply manufactured articles on better terms than another, that other might find an abundant indemnification in a superior capacity to furnish the produce of the soil. And a free exchange, mutually beneficial, of the commodities which each was able to supply, on the best terms, might be carried on between them, supporting, in full vigor, the industry of each. . . .

But the system which has been mentioned is far from characterizing the general policy of nations. The prevalent one has been regulated by an opposite spirit. The consequence of it is, that the United States, are, to a certain extent, in the situation of a country precluded from foreign commerce. . . .

In such a position of things, the United States cannot exchange with Europe on equal terms and the want of reciprocity would render them the victim of a system which should induce them to confine their views to agriculture, and refrain from manufactures. A constant and increasing necessity, on their part, for the commodities of Europe, and only a partial and occasional demand for their own, in return, could not but expose them to a state of impoverishment, compared with the opulence to which their political and natural advantages authorize them to aspire.

Remarks of this kind are not made in the spirit of complaint. It is for the nations whose regulations are alluded to, to judge for themselves, whether, by aiming at too much, they do not lose more than they gain. It is for the United States to consider by what means they can render themselves least dependent on the combinations, right or wrong, of foreign policy. . . .

The remaining objections to a particular encouragement of manufactures in the United States now require to be examined.

One of these turns on the proposition, that industry, if left to itself, will naturally find its way to the most useful and profitable employment. Whence it is inferred that manufactures, without the aid of government, will grow up as soon and as fast as the natural state of things and the interest of the community may require.

Against the solidity of this hypothesis, in the full latitude of the terms, very cogent reasons may be offered. These have relation to the strong influence of habit and the spirit of imitation; the fear of want of success in untried enterprises; the intrinsic difficulties incident to first essays towards a competition with those who have previously attained to perfection in the business to be attempted: the bounties, premiums, and other artificial encouragements with which foreign nations second the exertions of their own citizens, in the branches in which they are to be rivalled.

Experience teaches, that men are often so much governed by what they are accustomed to see and practice, that the simplest and most obvious improvements, in the most ordinary occupations, are adopted with hesitation, reluctance, and by slow gradations. The spontaneous transition to new pursuits, in a community long habituated to different ones, may be expected to be attended with proportionally greater difficulty. . . . [T]hese changes would be likely to be more tardy than might consist with the interest either of individuals or of the society. In many cases they would not happen . . . . To produce the desirable changes as early as may be expedient may therefore require the incitement and patronage of government.

The apprehension of failing in new attempts is, perhaps, a more serious impediment. There are dispositions apt to be attracted by the mere novelty of an undertaking; but these are not always the best calculated to give it success. To this it is of importance that the confidence of cautious, sagacious capitalists, both citizens and foreigners, should be excited. And to inspire this description of persons with confidence, it is essential that they should be made to see in any project which is new—and for that reason alone, if for no other, precarious—the prospect of such a degree of countenance and support from governments, as may be capable of overcoming the obstacles inseparable from first experiments.

The superiority antecedently enjoyed by nations who have preoccupied and perfected a branch of industry, constitutes a more formidable obstacle than either of those which have been mentioned, to the introduction of the same branch into a country in which it did not before exist. To maintain, between the recent establishments of one country, and the long-matured establishments of another country, a competition upon equal terms, both as to quality and price, is, in most cases, impracticable. The disparity, in the one, or in the other, or in both, must necessarily be so considerable, as to forbid a successful rivalship, without the extraordinary aid and protection of government.

But the greatest obstacle of all to the successful prosecution of a new branch of industry in a country in which it was before unknown, consists, as far as the instances apply, in the bounties, premiums, and other aids which are granted, in a variety of cases, by the nations in which the establishments to be imitated are previously introduced. It is well known (and particular examples, in the course of this report, will be cited) that certain nations grant bounties on the exportation of particular commodities, to enable their own workmen to undersell and supplant all competitors in the countries to which those commodities are sent. Hence the undertakers of a new manufacture have to contend, not only with the natural disadvantages of a new undertaking, but with the gratuities and remunerations which other governments bestow. To be enabled to contend with success, it is evident that the interference and aid of their own governments are indispensable. . . .

Whatever room there may be for an expectation that the industry of a people, under the direction of private interest, will, upon equal terms, find out the most beneficial employment for itself, there is none for a reliance that it will struggle against the force of unequal terms, or will, of itself, surmount all the adventitious barriers to a successful competition which may have been erected, either by the advantages naturally acquired from practice and previous possession of the ground, or by those which may have sprung from positive regulations and an artificial policy. This general reflection might alone suffice as an answer to the objection under examination, exclusively of the weighty considerations which have been particularly urged. . . .

There remains to be noticed an objection to the encouragement of manufacturers . . . . derived from its supposed tendency to give a monopoly of advantages to particular classes, at the expense of the rest of the community, who, it is affirmed, would be able to procure the requisite supplies of manufactured articles on better terms from foreigners. . .and who, it is alleged, are reduced to the necessity of paying an enhanced price for whatever they want, by every measure which obstructs the free competition of foreign commodities. . . .

But, though it were true that the immediate and certain effect of regulations controlling the competition of foreign with domestic fabrics was an increase of price, it is universally true that the contrary is the ultimate effect with every successful manufacture. When a domestic manufacture has attained to perfection, and has engaged in the prosecution of it a certain number of persons, it invariably becomes cheaper. Being free from the heavy charges which attend the importation of foreign commodities, it can be afforded, and accordingly seldom or never fails to be sold, cheaper in process of time, than was the foreign article for which it is a substitute The internal competition which takes place soon does away with every thing like monopoly, and by degrees reduces the price of the article to the minimum of reasonable profit . . . . Whence it follows, that it is the interest of a community, with a view to eventual and permanent economy, to encourage the growth of manufactures. In national view, a temporary enhancement of price must always be well compensated by a permanent reduction of it. . . .

Not only the wealth but the independence and security of a country appear to be materially connected with the prosperity of manufactures. Every nation, with a view to those great objects, ought to endeavor to possess within itself, all the essentials of national supply. These comprise the means of subsistence, habitation, clothing, and defence.

The possession of these is necessary to the perfection of the body politic; to the safety as well as to the welfare of the society. The want of either is the want of an important organ of political life and motion; and in the various crises which await a state, it must severely feel the effects of any such deficiency. The extreme embarrassments of the United States during the late war, from an incapacity of supplying themselves, are still matter of keen recollection; a future war might be expected again to exemplify the mischiefs and dangers of a situation to which that incapacity is still, in too great a degree, applicable, unless changed by timely and vigorous exertion. To effect this change, as fast as shall be prudent, merits all the attention and all the zeal of our public councils: 'tis the next great work to be accomplished. . . .

A full view having now been taken of the inducements to the promotion of manufactures in the United States, accompanied with an examination of the principal objections which are commonly urged in opposition, it is proper in the next place, to consider the means by which it may be affected. . . .

Pecuniary bounties

This has been found one of the most efficacious means of encouraging manufactures, and is, in some views, the best. Though it has not yet been practiced upon by the Government of the United States. . .and though it is less favored by public opinion than some other modes, its advantages are these. . . .

It is a species of encouragement more positive and direct than any other, and for that very reason, has a more immediate tendency to stimulate and uphold new enterprises, increasing the chances of profit, and diminishing the risks of loss, in the first attempts. . . .

It avoids the inconvenience of a temporary augmentation of price, which is incident to some other modes; or it produces it to a less degree, either by making no addition to the charges on the rival foreign article, as in the case of protecting duties, or by making a smaller addition. . . .

Bounties have not, like high protecting duties, a tendency to produce scarcity. An increase of price is not always the immediate, though, where the progress of a domestic manufacturer does not counteract a rise, it is commonly, the ultimate, effect of an additional duty. . . .

The encouragement of new inventions and discoveries at home, and of the introduction into the United States of such as they may have been made

in other countries; particularly those which relate to machinery.

This is among the most useful and unexceptionable of the aids which can be given to manufactures. The usual means of that encouragement are pecuniary rewards, and, for a time, exclusive privileges. . . . For the last, so far as respects "authors and inventors," provision has been made by law. But it is desirable, in regard to improvements, and secrets of extraordinary value, to be able to extend the same benefit to introducers, as well as authors and inventors; a policy which has been practiced with advantage in other countries. Here, however, as in some other cases, there is cause to regret that the competency of the authority of the National Government to the good which might be done, is not without a question. Many aids might be given to industry, many internal improvements of primary magnitude might be promoted, by an authority operating throughout the Union, which cannot be effected as well, if at all, by an authority confined within the limits of a single State. . . .

It is customary with manufacturing nations to prohibit, under severe penalties, the exportation of implements and machines which they have either invented or improved. There are already objects for a similar regulation in the United States; and others may be expected to occur from time to time. The adoption of it seems to be dictated by the principle of reciprocity. Greater liberality, in such respects, might better comport with the general spirit of the country; but a selfish exclusive policy, in other quarters, will not always permit the free indulgence of a spirit which would place us upon an unequal footing. As far as prohibitions tend to prevent foreign competitors from deriving the benefit of the improvements made at home, they tend to increase the advantages of those by whom they may have been introduced, and operate as an encouragement to exertion. . . .

The facilitating of the transportation of commodities

Improvements favoring this object intimately concern all the domestic interests of a community; but they may, without impropriety, be mentioned as having an important relation to manufactures. There is perhaps, scarcely anything which has been better calculated to assist the manufacturers of Great Britain than the melioration of the public roads of that kingdom, and the great progress which has been of late made in opening canals. Of the former, the United States stand much in need; for the latter, they present uncommon facilities. . . .

Picking Winners: The Historical Record

Robert Cohen

Mainstream economists have turned the thought of industrial policy into a political anathema. However, the U.S. has a long history of promoting industries as a means to assure our nation's economic and social well-being. Indeed, during the era of deregulation and free market dominance that we have just traversed, major institutions derived from the long history of U.S. government involvement in industries ranging from agriculture to housing and education have remained in place. Our economy still relies heavily upon such interventions in the marketplace as: federally-chartered financing entities for housing, farms and student loans; government-backed consortia, such as SEMATECH in semiconductor manufacturing equipment; COMSAT, the communications satellite corporation established by President Kennedy and Congress in the early 1960s; and scores of government laboratories that have an increasing mandate to spread their innovations to industry.

In addition, as we move into a new economic framework for the international economy, U.S. policymakers, faced with the end of the cold war as a source of political conflict, will need to reconsider what forces provide the engine for U.S. economic growth and stability. Most glaring in this reevaluation will be the decline of U.S. competitiveness in the technology-based industries where we once were world leaders. . . .

The major efforts in Europe and Japan should force us to question how the U.S. will be able to compete in the future. In the face of concerted efforts to promote key industries in other nations, it will be increasingly difficult for us to assume that our technology industries will develop strategies

Robert Cohen *is Senior Fellow at the Economic Policy Institute in Washington and a consultant to the National Advisory Committee on Semiconductors. This piece is part of a longer study on U.S. and Japanese policies to promote emerging industries that will be published by the Economic Policy Institute.*

that will reverse the current pattern of decline. . . . However, while the memory of some failed efforts remains fresh in the minds of some policymakers, including the [synthetic fuels] venture, a whole range of more successful efforts has been forgotten. . . .

The National Advisory Committee on Aeronautics (NACA)

Soon after the Wright brothers flight, the federal government established a number of policies to encourage the growth of the nascent aircraft industry. By the end of the First World War, policies made funding R&D and purchases of new planes a top priority. Large scale purchases of fighters and surveillance aircraft were made by the War Department.

In this climate, the National Advisory Committee on Aeronautics (NACA) was formed to support basic research. NACA operated test facilities, such as Langley Field, where wind tunnels were used for testing by the government and aircraft producers.[1] Other parts of the government, especially under Secretary of Commerce Herbert Hoover, provided funds to establish ground bases and navigational facilities.

This meant that NACA played a very specific role in promoting the development of new aeronautical technologies. Its main objective was the identification, development, and validation of new technologies. NACA supported technology development at its most risky stage, where it was unlikely to receive much financial support from private industry.[2]

The history of NACA is one of the best examples of how a government agency can play a constructive role in the early stages of validating the commercial potential of new technologies. This role was fulfilled in exemplary fashion by NACA and may have served as a guide for the federal government's approach to the computer and electronic device industries when they emerged after World War II.

Today, the concept of government as a validating agent for new technologies is still widespread in efforts by Japan. But it is only carried out in America in the joint government-industry effort at SEMATECH.

The Radio Corporation of America

The role of the U.S. government in the establishment of the Radio Corporation of America is one of the most obvious successes of government attempts to promote a new industry. In addition, the foundation of RCA gave

In the RCA case, the U.S. Navy played the role of stockholder and was a key investor in the new radio technology. Its commitment to the expansion of radio and its ability to work closely with the other firms that were pioneers in technologies that were needed for radio opened the opportunity for the creation of RCA. It also provided critical sources of capital . . . . This type of patient capital—the Navy held shares in RCA for over five years—is one element that proved critical in the early success of RCA. The commitment of the government to radiotelegraphy as a technology that was necessary for national security made a major difference to corporations that were somewhat reluctant to make the capital investments needed to exploit the technologies they had begun to develop.

Computers and integrated circuits

When computers and integrated circuits were first developed there was little interest in commercial applications. Thus, not only did the technologies require validation to prove their effectiveness, they also needed support over the early, especially risky phase when funds were difficult to obtain and mistakes might put a fledgling firm out of business. Thus, the role played by the Navy in purchasing and finding important functions for early computers to perform and by the Air Force in funding the first transistorized computer and its non-transistorized twin was especially critical. Without the . . . military, commercial development would have been delayed significantly.

Several types of research that were supported by the military contributed to the development of the first computers. Differential analyzers were used to solve certain types of differential equations. . . . Much of this work was funded by the War Department and the Army installed an analyzer at Aberdeen Proving Grounds in Maryland in order to [devise] artillery firing tables prior to the war. Another government-sponsored research effort in radar also proved to be a key to the creation of electronic components that were used to modulate, or change, high-speed, high-frequency electronic pulses. Since digital computers also relied on electrical pulses, very fast computing speeds could be achieved using components that were originally developed for radar.[6]

The Navy's central role in the development of computing grew out of its involvement with cryptology. Because radio communications were the only way to offer contact between a vast fleet and such communications could be intercepted, the Navy had begun a substantial effort in crytography in 1921.

The Navy's highly secretive Communications Security Group initiated much of the early American work on digital computers. Its aim was to manage the security of naval communications and attach foreign codes. In the early 1930s the Navy began to mechanize its work on cryptanalysis, installing IBM punch card machines to process code traffic. However, when the Navy approached Vannevar Bush, the vice president and dean of engineering at MIT and key participant in the work on differential analyzers, he recommended that special machines that were at least 10 and possibly 100 times faster than punched card equipment be developed. "A small, secret research group was formed at MIT and developed a machine . . . . By the end of the war, at least seven copies of this particular machine had been built and were instrumental in breaking Japanese codes."[7]

The Navy also funded a third line of work, on servomechanisms, which resulted in the development of analog computers for fire control at MIT, RCA, and Bell Labs. This line of innovation led to digital computers. Together with the differential analyzer. . .and the Navy's cryptanalysis work, this work provided the three main paths by which the U.S. entered the computer age.[8]

While some of the more innovative computers were built during the war, the Navy and Air Force played an interesting role immediately after the war in stimulating the further development of computers that facilitated their commercialization. In the Navy's case, interest in computers remained high because of the need to decode messages. But in its efforts to assist wartime experts in the creation of the next generation of computers, several highly intelligent steps were taken in the development process. In the case of the Atlas computer's development—the first digital computer—which was given top priority by the Navy, two interesting features characterized the design and development process: 1) engineers from Engineering Research Associates (ERA), the firm responsible for the Atlas, were given access to reports on computer work on other government projects; and 2) one year after delivery of the first machine to the Navy, ERA received permission to market a commercial version of Atlas. Subsequently, ERA produced twenty machines, the first to be in large-scale production, and accounted for 80 percent of the dollar value of machines sold in the U.S. through 1952.[9]

Another interesting characteristic of the early computer development was the willingness to share designs among a host of centers that built early machines. In the case of the Selectron memory device developed by [John] Von Neumann and a group at the Institute for Advanced Study [(IAS)] at Princeton with funding from RCA, the Army and the Navy, preliminary designs for the IAS computer greatly influenced the design of the IBM 700 and 7000 series computers.[10]

The outbreak of the Korean War increased the urgency of developing an air defense system for the Air Force, which became the largest supporter of computer development at MIT primarily to create an air defense system. The development of ferrite core memories. . .for fast primary memories from the mid-1950s to the 1970s was the major contribution of this effort. The MIT machine was also much faster than other machines of the day and had a major influence on other computer projects.[11]

When integrated circuits were first developed at Texas Instruments in 1958, there were few sources to support the next stages of innovation. In mid-1959, the Air Force awarded TI $1.15 million to develop various integrated circuit devices (ICs) over the next two and one half years. This was followed in 1960 with funds to support the development of production processes and the special equipment needed for the mass production of ICs. When strong doubts about the value of ICs persisted in the commercial and scientific communities in 1961, the Air Force sponsored the creation of two identical digital computers, one built with tubes and another with transistors, as a means of reducing concern about the useful role that ICs could play. The tube model had 9000 individual components, while the transistor model had 587 integrated circuits and much higher reliability. The space program, especially the guidance computers for Apollo, was the main market for sales, with the government purchasing 95% of all monolithic ICs produced in 1963 and 75% of those produced in 1965, when the price had dropped from $50 to below $9.[12]

The Department of Defense and NACA supported the early development of ICs by serving as "creative first users.". . . [Their] support had two effects: 1) it accelerated the pace of [UC] technological development and provided a source of encouragement; and 2) it had the unintended effect of supporting the creation of a unique group of "merchant" producers who specialized in IC production, but did not produce the equipment that they were used in.   This latter group was the one that kept the pace of technological innovation and diffusion alive in commercial markets, long after the military had achieved its objectives.[13]

The Communications Satellite Corporation (COMSAT)

COMSAT is one of the clearest success stories among the efforts by the U.S. government to support the growth of new industries.   It was established in 1962 as a quasi-government entity to encourage the development of U.S. communications satellites. Its charter, described in the Communications Satellite Act of 1962, gave COMSAT the right to act on behalf of the U.S. government in negotiations to establish INTELSAT, the International Telecommunications Satellite Organization, which was to establish standards and set orbital slots.

Congress provided the authority for COMSAT after the Kennedy administration was concerned that legislation to promote commercial communications satellites might enable AT&T to gain a near monopoly. The COMSAT Act created an independent, profit-making firm that would place limits on the amount of influence AT&T would have in this arena. This was accomplished by restricting the amount of stock in COMSAT that could be held by other communications carriers. The legislation called for NASA to offer COMSAT satellite launching and other services, and gave the Federal Communications Commission wide powers to regulate both COMSAT and other communications carriers to assure the greatest amount of competition and efficiency.

Clearly, the motivation to create COMSAT was different from many of the other reasons for promoting innovative technology industries. However, there was a concern that the economic benefits of communications satellite systems be disseminated as widely as possible. AT&T had already launched the Telstar satellite and there was concern in the Kennedy administration that it would establish a system of its own that might not necessarily reflect the aim of maintaining U.S. leadership in this strategic technology. Fortunately, the communications satellite industry grew rapidly in the early 1960s and many of its goals were attained very [soon].

COMSAT is presently a $500 million corporation with three main lines of business: 1) providing communications satellite services to U.S. international service providers and the shipping industry; 2) carrying out research and development and providing consulting on satellite communications, in addition to providing communications services and systems to the Department of Defense and other parts of the government; and 3) offering specialized communications networks and services to corporations and governments.[14] Thus, COMSAT has fulfilled the aims of its original legislation while overcoming many of the risks that it faced in the early days of commercial satellite development. . . .

Notes

[1] Mowery and Rosenberg, "Commercial Aircraft Industry," in Richard Nelson, ed., *Government and Technical Progress: A Cross-Industry Analysis* (1982), pp. 101-141.

[2] Center for Space and Advanced Technology, "An Analysis of Mechanisms to Encourage Private Sector Investment in Space Infrastructure and Advance Space Technologies," August 1989, pp. 11-12.

[3] Richard J. Solomon, "Origins of RCA," MIT Media Lab, undated mimeograph, p. 1.

[4] Solomon, p. 1.

[5] Solomon, p. 2.

[6] Kenneth Flamm, *Creating the Computer* (Washington: Brookings Institution, 1988), pp. 32-33.

[7] Flamm, pp. 35-36.

[8] Flamm, p. 35.

[9] Flamm, pp. 45-46.

[10] Flamm, pp. 52-53.

[11] Flamm, pp. 55-58.

[12] Norman Asher and Leland Strom, *The Role of the Department of Defense in the Development of Integrated Circuits* (Arlington, VA: Institute for Defense Analyses, 1977), p. 17, as cited in Michael Borrus, James Millstein, and John Zysman, *International Competition in Advanced Industrial Sectors: Trade and Development in the Semiconductor Industry*, Congress of the United States, Joint Economic Committee, 1982, pp. 19-20.

[13] Borrus et al., pp. 20-21.

[14] Communications Satellite Corporation, Form 10-K filing with the Securities and Exchange Commission, December 31, 1987.

Science—The Endless Frontier

Vannevar Bush

We all know how much the new drug, penicillin, has meant to our grievously wounded men on the grim battlefronts of this war—the countless lives it has saved—the incalculable suffering which its use has prevented. Science and the great practical genius of this Nation made this achievement possible.

Some of us know the vital role which radar has played in bringing the Allied Nations to victory over Nazi Germany and in driving the Japanese steadily back from their island bastions. Again it was painstaking scientific research over many years that made radar possible.

What we often forget are the millions of pay envelopes on a peacetime Saturday night which are filled because new products and new industries have provided jobs for countless Americans. Science made that possible, too.

In 1939 millions of people were employed in industries which did not even exist at the close of the last war—radio, air conditioning, rayon and other synthetic fibers, and plastics are examples of the products of these industries. But these things do not mark the end of progress—they are but the beginning if we make full use of our scientific resources. New manufacturing industries can be started and many older industries greatly strengthened and expanded if we continue to study nature's laws and apply new knowledge to practical purposes.

Great advances in agriculture are also based on scientific research. Plants which are more resistant to disease and are adapted to short growing seasons, the prevention and cure of livestock diseases, the control of our insect enemies, better fertilizers, and improved agricultural practices, all stem from painstaking scientific research.

Excerpted from Science: The Endless Frontier *(Washington, D.C.: National Science Foundation, 1990).*

Advances in science when put to practical use mean more jobs, higher wages, shorter hours, more abundant crops, more leisure for recreation, for study, for learning how to live without the deadening drudgery which has been the burden of the common man for ages past. Advances in science will also bring higher standards of living, will lead to the prevention or cure of diseases, will promote conservation of our limited national resources, and will assure means of defense against aggression. But to achieve these objectives—to secure a high level of employment, to maintain a position of world leadership—the flow of new scientific knowledge must be both continuous and substantial . . . .

Science, by itself, provides no panacea for individual, social, and economic ills. It can be effective in the national welfare only as a member of a team, whether the conditions be peace or war. But without scientific progress no amount of achievement in other directions can insure our health, prosperity, and security as a nation in the modern world.

Science is a proper concern of government

It has been basic United States policy that Government should foster the opening of new frontiers. It opened the seas to clipper ships and furnished land for pioneers. Although these frontiers have more or less disappeared, the frontier of science remains. It is in keeping with the American tradition—one which has made the United States great—that new frontiers shall be made accessible for development by all American citizens.

Moreover, since health, well-being, and security are proper concerns of Government, scientific progress is, and must be, of vital interest to Government. Without scientific progress the national health would deteriorate; without scientific progress we could not hope for improvement in our standard of living or for an increased number of jobs for our citizens; and without scientific progress we could not have maintained our liberties against tyranny . . . .

Science and jobs

One of our hopes is that after the war there will be full employment, and that the production of goods and services will serve to raise our standard of living. We do not yet know how we shall reach that goal, but it is certain that it can be achieved only by releasing the full creative and productive energies of the American people.

Surely we will not get there by standing still, merely by making the same things we made before and selling them at the same or higher prices. We will not get ahead in international trade unless we offer new and more attractive and cheaper products.

Where will these new products come from? How will we find ways to make better products at lower costs? The answer is clear. There must be a stream of new scientific knowledge to turn the wheels of private and public enterprise. There must be plenty of men and women trained in science and technology for upon them depend both the creation of new knowledge and its application to practical purposes.

More and better scientific research is essential to the achievement of our goal of full employment.

The importance of basic research

Basic research is performed without thought of practical ends. It results in general knowledge and an understanding of nature and its laws. This general knowledge provides the means of answering a large number of important practical problems, though it mat not give a complete specific answer to any one of them. The function of applied research is to provide such complete answers. The function of applied research is to provide such complete answers. The scientist doing basic research may not be at all interested in the practical applications of his work, yet the further progress of industrial development would eventually stagnate if basic scientific research were long neglected.

One of the peculiarities of basic science is the variety of paths which lead to productive advance. Many of the most important discoveries have come as a result of experiments undertaken with very different purposes in mind. Statistically it is certain that important and highly useful discoveries will result from some fraction of the undertakings in basic science; but the results of any one particular investigation cannot be predicted with accuracy.

Basic research leads to new knowledge. It provides scientific capital. It creates the fund from which the practical applications of knowledge must be drawn. New products and new processes do not appear full-grown. They are founded on new principles and new conceptions, which in turn are painstakingly developed by research in the purest realms of science.

Today, it is truer than ever that basic research is the pacemaker of technological progress.   In the nineteenth century, Yankee mechanical ingenuity, building largely upon the basic discoveries of European scientists, could greatly advance the technical arts.   Now the situation is different.

A nation which depends upon others for its new basic scientific knowledge will be slow in its industrial progress and weak in its competitive position in world trade, regardless of its mechanical skill . . . .

Industrial research

The simplest and most effective way in which the Government can strengthen industrial research is to support basic research and to develop scientific talent.

The benefits of basic research do not reach all industries equally or at the same speed.   Some small enterprises never receive any of the benefits. It has been suggested that the benefits might be better utilized if "research clinics" for such enterprises were to be established.   Businessmen would thus be able to make more use of research than they now do.   This proposal is certainly worthy of further study.

One of the most important factors affecting the amount of industrial research is the income-tax law.   Government action in respect to this subject will affect the rate of technical progress in industry.   Uncertainties as to the attitude of the Bureau of Internal Revenue regarding the deduction of research and development expenses are a deterrent to research expenditure. These uncertainties arise from lack of clarity of the tax law as to the proper treatment of such costs.

The Internal Revenue Code should be amended to remove present uncertainties in regard to the deductibility of research and development expenditures as current charges against net income.

Research is also affected by the patent laws.   They stimulate new invention and they make it possible for new industries to be built around new devices or new processes.   These industries generate new jobs and new products, all of which contributes to the welfare and the strength of the country.

Yet, uncertainties in the operation of the patent laws have impaired the ability of small industries to translate new ideas into processes and products of value to the Nation.   These uncertainties are, in part, attributable to the difficulties and expense incident to the operation of the patent system as it presently exists. These uncertainties are also attributable to the existence of certain abuses which have appeared in the use of patents. The abuses should be corrected. They have led to extravagantly critical attacks which tend to discredit a basically sound system.

It is important that the patent system continue to serve the country in the manner intended by the Constitution, for it has been a vital element in the industrial vigor which has distinguished this Nation.

The National Patent Planning Commission has reported on this subject. In addition, a detailed study, with recommendations concerning the extent to which modifications should be made in our patent laws is currently being made under the leadership of the Secretary of Commerce. It is recommended, therefore, that specific action with regard to the patent laws be withheld pending the submission of the report devoted exclusively to that subject . . . .

The special need for federal support

We can no longer count on ravaged Europe as a source of fundamental knowledge. In the past we have devoted much of our best efforts to the application of such knowledge which has been discovered abroad. In the future we must pay increased attention to discovering this knowledge for ourselves particularly since the scientific applications of the future will be more than ever dependent upon such basic knowledge.

New impetus must be given to research in our country. Such new impetus can come promptly only from the Government. Expenditures for research in the colleges, universities, and research institutes will otherwise not be able to meet the additional demands of increased public need for research.

Further, we cannot expect industry adequately to fill the gap. Industry will fully rise to the challenge of applying new knowledge to new products. The commercial incentive can be relied upon for that. But basic research is essentially noncommercial in nature. It will not receive the attention it requires if left to industry.

For many years the Government has wisely supported research in the agricultural colleges and the benefits have been great. The time has come when such support should be extended to other fields.

In providing Government support, however, we must endeavor to preserve as far as possible the private support of research in both industry and the colleges, universities, and research institutes. These private sources should continue to carry their share of the financial burden . . . .

New responsibilities for government

. . . . The Federal Government should accept new responsibilities for promoting the creation of new scientific knowledge and the development of scientific talent in our youth . . . .

In discharging these responsibilities Federal funds should be made available. We have given much thought to the question of how plans for the use of Federal funds may be arranged so that such funds will not drive out of the picture funds from local governments, foundations, and private donors. We believe that our proposals will minimize that effect, but we do not think that it can be completely avoided. We submit, however, that the Nation's need for more and better scientific research is such that the risk must be accepted.

It is also clear that the effective discharge of these responsibilities will require the full attention of some over-all agency devoted to that purpose. There should be a focal point within the Government for a concerted program of assisting scientific research conducted outside of Government. Such an agency should furnish the funds needed to support basic research in the colleges and universities, should coordinate where possible research programs on matters of utmost importance to the national welfare, should formulate a national policy for the Government toward science, should sponsor the interchange of scientific information among scientists and laboratories both in this country and abroad, and should ensure that the incentives to research in industry and the universities are maintained . . . .

Economic Strategy: Foreign Approaches

As suggested earlier, a principal reason for devising an American economic strategy is that America's leading competitors think strategically about economic policy. In fact, the actions of foreign governments to protect their home markets and, more important, promote innovation and productivity, are largely responsible for making the world a strategic place. The challenge for America is how to take comparable measure and still preserve the institutions and values that we so rightly cherish.

In line with its non-interventionist bent, the economic Orthodoxy argues that foreign economic strategies are no reason for America to reciprocate. Quite the contrary. If foreign governments foolishly subsidize their export industries for example, to enable them to undersell American companies in the U.S. market, America and its consumers can only benefit.

The selections in Part Five, however, argue that in a strategic world of power, protectionism, and imperfect competition, indifference to or ignorance of foreign economic strategies can lead straight to the poorhouse. Indeed, the current administration understands this as well—thus its efforts in 1990 to change Japan's economic strategy through the so-called Structural Impediments Initiative. But this policy shows the persistent geopolitical approach that we take in such situations: We try to make others act less strategically—to force our ways on them—rather than act more strategically ourselves.

In the view of Murray Sayle, achieving such changes will be difficult at best. He writes that the economic strategies of Japan and Germany are rooted in powerful historical drives to assume their rightful places in the sun in what they have considered an Anglo-Saxon dominated world. And the success that these state-directed economies have had in outperforming liberal capitalist economies like America's makes change on their part even less likely.

As Chalmers Johnson explains, Japan's strategy has also involved reinventing "the institutions of capitalism in. . .ways that neither Adam Smith nor Marx would recognize or understand." In addition, concludes Johnson, Japan's production-oriented economic structures show that Tokyo "takes its responsibilities in the economic sphere more seriously than do most other democratic governments."

For its part, the European Community (EC) clearly is taking a leaf from Japan's book. Speeding toward a year-end 1992 deadline for substantial economic integration, the Community has launched a sweeping drive aimed explicitly at challenging Japanese and U.S. producers in international markets. The EC report Research and Technological Development Policy *reveals that the cornerstone of this effort is high technology. It makes clear that the Community has not hesitated to identify those industries likeliest to create economic power in the 21st century. The specificity of the European game plan also shows how completely America's trade partners realize that "composition counts."*

Axis, Ltd.

Murray Sayle

It's odd, any way you look at it. Only yesterday, historically speaking, Germany and Japan were at war with the rest of the world. Both started well, and it took the combined strength of the United States, the British Empire ("English-American devils" in the Japanese phrase), and an unexpected late entry out East, the Soviet Union, to pound them into ruins. Well, we all thought, there's two problems out of the way.

Forty-four years on, the winning combination is in trouble. In Moscow the shops are bare, the minorities mutinous. The United States lives on credit. One resolute grocer's daughter is, according to her admirers, all that stands between Great Britain and catastrophe brought on by decades of free medicine. In all the once United Nations the story is the same: social unrest, fading industries, burgeoning trade deficits, incipient inflation, governments that can no longer pay their way.

What a contrast with the two great exemplars of national economic virtue. They run large trade surpluses, enabling them to buy up everyone else's corporations, resources, and real estate. They have huge gold reserves. Their inflation rates are negligible, their currencies diamond-hard. One is the economic heart of an emerging European coalition, the other heads an ominous gang-up of Asian nations. This formidable pair are—two guesses—(West) Germany and Japan. . . .

[I]t is . . . no accident that Japan and West Germany stand apart from all other economies. The historic conditions that produced the Axis have never gone away, nor has the fundamental philosophic dispute between the former members of the Old Fascist Firm and the rest of us ever been resolved. It is, in fact, up for heated discussion right now. . . .

Germans and Japanese cannot both be the master race. So what else,

Murray Sayle *is a freelance journalist. Excerpted with permission from "Axis, Ltd.,"* The New Republic, *June 5, 1989.*

we need to know, do they have in common?

For a start both Germany and Japan were, in Axis times, new industrial nations, latecomers among the world powers. The combination of Prussian generals, Austrian dreamers, and Rhineland engineers the Fuhrer threw against the world only began to take shape with the unification of Germany in 1870. Japan in its modern form dates from only two years earlier, 1868, when Emperor Meiji moved to Tokyo as the front-god for a clique of fire-eating young samurai bent on expelling the foreign, mostly English-speaking devils from their country and winning Japan's true place in the sun.

Kaiser Wilhelm's Germany was in most things the model for Meiji's Japan, with a powerful bureaucracy manipulating a figurehead emperor, a parliament of yes-men, an education system given to military-style uniforms copied from Prussia, and a state-directed drive toward industrialization with a single overriding aim—to catch up with the arrogant Anglos who seemed to rule the world.

The similarity in national pasts and styles that led the Japanese to discover Germany as a political model has often been commented on. For centuries the Japanese looked enviously into the Chinese Empire, but were never part of it, just as the Germans did with Rome. Both developed an immense, even exaggerated respect for book-learning, but neither ever lost their preference for the warrior values of will and endurance, obedience and loyalty. Neither Japan nor Germany, the perpetual outsiders, ever adopted the notion of the free citizen and the sovereign individual, or ever gave up the tribal certainty that anyone who disagreed with the group or the nation had to be wrong.

One day, tribal solidarity was going to have unexpected economic advantages. It's great for zero-defect manufacturing, for instance—no one wants to be the odd man out who bolted the headlights on upside-down. It is also a remedy for wage inflation—if we're all exporting together for national survival and glory. It's easy to keep wage demands in step with gains in productivity, and brother does your currency get hard.

But these were not fashionable ideas in the 1870s when newly united Germany and revitalized Japan studied the international economic system they planned to join. Neither liked the political and moral shape of the world then, and neither has much liked it since, although things started to look up for Germany in 1917 and for both in 1942, only to fade again at Midway and Stalingrad. What was wrong with the planet was that the wrong people with the wrong ideas were running it the wrong way. For the roots of these—complaints—or our case against the Axis, if you prefer—we must look back not one century but two, to when the English speakers first established the lead the others have been trying to close ever since.

1776 is a good date for the breakaway. In that year Britain exchanged a prospective super-Vietnam for a useful trading partner, the firm of James Watt and Matthew Boulton went into the steam engine game in Birmingham, England, and, most important, Professor Adam Smith of the University of Glasgow published *An Enquiry into the Nature and Causes of the Wealth of Nations*, the least understood and (*Das Kapital* excepted) least read great book ever written. . . .

Everyone, said Smith, should be free—free to trade, free to make money, free to tell the government to mind its own business. If only the whole world followed these attractive principles everyone would get rich, Smith promised. He did not add that the British, with their industrial head start, ships, and trading empire, were likely on the Smith plan to get rich quicker than anyone else.

The future adornment of a million neckties is usually taken as the patron saint of capitalism, and for good reason—he and his followers had discovered the second-fastest system of economic growth ever stumbled on by man. . . . The novel ethic behind it, that if every individual tried his hardest to become rich an invisible hand would make sure that everyone benefitted, made the pursuit of wealth a virtue, not a vice, and worried many clergymen. Merchants, manufacturers, and bankers, hearing that they were now the key members of the human race, loved it. There is, indeed, a wonderful lack of vile self-interest in letting the impersonal marketplace decide—especially if you're reasonably sure it will decide in your favor.

The revolting American colonists, fearing that the marketplace would decide for Britain, allowed their West Indian Scot, Alexander Hamilton, to build them a good stout wall of tariffs to protect their infant industries. It was not, in fact, until the early 20th century that the United States, by then the world's lowest cost economy, took up the free trade cause . . . .

This did not stop Americans from aping the exploits of the British of the 19th century, in which free-trading English speakers snapped up most of the remaining resource-rich temperate parts of the planet (the Russians, prophetically, got the rest), completed the world trading system, a.k.a. liberal capitalism (the historic task assigned to us by no less than Karl Marx), opened up the unwilling East, and made fractured English the world's first truly international business language.

All this went down poorly with the stay-at-home Germans and Japanese, longing from afar to get in on the action. Although their institutions were based on the Germans', the Japanese prudently decided to go along, at first, with the Anglos, who successfully used gunboat salesmanship to pry open Japanese markets. Germany viewed the Anglo-Saxon octopus with dismay and the philosophy behind it with distaste. The Tübingen economist Friedrich List had personally witnessed the Yankees grubbing money in Pennsylvania (and himself grubbed a bundle in coal) and later wrote that he could never understand why it was virtuous for an individual to seek wealth but wrong for a nation to do so. No mainstream German or Japanese has ever since seen why, either.

Characteristically, Japan got into the Axis by imitation. No one pondered the German collapse of 1918 more deeply than the Japanese . . . . The Japanese military, subject to little civilian control, drew two lessons from 1918: the first, false, was that the right war would bring big gains for little pain; the second, true, was that if an advanced continental power like Germany could be blockaded into defeat, the resourceless islands of Japan stood no chance of winning a new-style total war.

In Japan between the wars, what the military wanted it usually got. In 1927, in return for a temporary troop cut of four divisions, the army minister got approval for the setting up of a Cabinet Resources Bureau, modeled directly on Rathenau's *Kriegrohstoff-Abteilung*, to begin putting Japanese industry on a potential war footing. In 1933 the army set up a Japanese puppet state, "Manchukuo," in the Chinese province of Manchuria with the aim of building a blockade-proof heavy industrial base on the Asian mainland. This was still not enough; in 1937 they pushed on into China south of the Wall, and into full-scale war. Ironically, the deeper the Japanese went into China in search of autarchy, the more dependent they became on imports, particularly from America, of oil, scrap iron, and strategic minerals. Something had to give. It soon did.

In November 1936 Japan and Germany were the founder members of the Anti-Comintern Pact, a declaration of ideological solidarity in the global crusade against communism that has still, a half century on, never taken place. The pact was also an advertisement that Japan's geographical position threatening Russia, the basis of all its alliances, was available to parties other than Britain and the United States. In September 1940 Japan joined

Germany and Italy's Pact of Steel, the idea being that this would deter the United States form applying economic sanctions against the faltering Japanese war on China.

The munitions for the China war were mostly made in China—that is, in the Manchukuo puppet state. The Japanese military had originally hoped that international capitalists would assist them in developing Manchukuo, but none showed interest. Deciding that if they were to wait for the invisible hand they might wait forever, the army summoned a group of young bureaucrats from the Finance Ministry in Tokyo, who in turn persuaded a bankrupt textile concern from Osaka, Nissan, to try its luck under army protection in the new colony.

In Manchuria, Nissan, the bureaucrats, and their army backers devised a new form of economics, capitalism without capital, based on bank credit and a market share guaranteed by the only customer, the army, which eliminated all risk. This system was brought back to Japan itself by Gen. Hideki Tojo, chief of the army in Manchukuo, and his economic sidekick Nobosuke Kishi, who became his munitions minister. The Americans had tried cutting off strategic exports to compel Japan to abandon the war against China; the Japanese responded by lunging for replacements, especially oil, in Southeast Asia, after first having a go at eliminating the U.S. Pacific Fleet, inconveniently based in Hawaii, and doing even better against the British base at Singapore.

As munitions minister, Kishi (prime minister after the war and, according to Lyndon B. Johnson, "one of the finest leaders the Free World has produced") found all the legal and bureaucratic machinery already in place for a duplication of the Manchurian system in Japan, where it achieved extraordinary feats of wartime production. When the war ended Kishi was arrested as a war criminal but never tried, while his Munitions Ministry changed its name back to the Ministry of Commerce and Industry, with the same bureaucrats in the same offices using the same battered telephones, and with much the same aim—national survival, this time through harmless exports.

In 1949, under the misguided guidance of the American Occupation, the MCI merged with the Board of Trade to become the Ministry of International Trade and Industry, the dreaded MITI, supplying the missing administrative link to bring the coordination of domestic industry *and* foreign trade under the same authority. Throw in close relations with the Ministry of Finance and its executive arm, the Bank of Japan, and we have Japan Inc., an export economy on steroids, a structure with no parallel in the non-communist world—except in West Germany, where the Bundesbank and the Wirtschaftsministerium have much the same powers (not surprising, as both systems trace back to Imperial Germany's efforts to stand off the world 75 years ago).

The marks of the century-long search for autarchy can be seen by any visitor to Japan. The magnificently equipped factories, mostly with the big industrial names of the war years (Nissan, for example), are seldom more than a few kilometers from handsomely appointed docks where purpose-built ships wait to haul away the exports. The import side, descended from the black market of the Occupation, is by contrast a barely tolerated cottage industry that operates at the other end of a sclerotic distribution system, endlessly paying "squeeze" to local politicians and rapacious tiers of middlemen. Naturally, given these social arrangements, the money rolls in and a lot less trickles out, with huge trade surpluses the result.

The rival philosophies can be seen behind the current dispute between the United States and Japan over microchips, specifically large-scale integrated circuits. Japan leads the world in these key devices because MITI decided back in 1957 that consumer electronics, with few raw material requirements and excellent export prospects, would be Japan's core industry. The fact that U.S. industry led the world in those days only showed that there was a big, rich market waiting to be penetrated.

The MITI men took "strategic measures to foster the industry"—that is, they called meetings of prospective manufacturers, allotted tasks, awarded market shares, and arranged finance. The industries gladly cooperated, as anyone would with a bureaucracy able to protect them from foreign competition, and after a while the security of the leash and the food bowl become indispensable—and with the MITI men often coming from the industry they are supervising, everybody knows *everybody*. MITI showed particular concern not with the finished electronic gadgets but with the components. As the (MITI-sponsored) Electronic Industries Association of Japan explains, "A competitive electronics industry needs competitive components"—the autarchic, us-against-the-world approach to manufacturing anything. . . .

In fact, the world marketplace, meaning you and I, has decided that liberal capitalism is not the recipe for the fastest economic growth, because export-led, centrally coordinated illiberal capitalism is. The proof is that, when the chips were down, so to speak, we adopted much the same systems ourselves. Far from waiting for the invisible hand to equip us to fight the Axis, we used war production boards, compulsory market sharing, resource allocation, dollar-a-year bureaucrats, and even company songs. When the danger passed, we couldn't get back to our what's-in-it-for-me ways quick enough--what else were we fighting for?

The one-time Axis powers, particularly Japan, behave like creatures from another economic world because they *are* from another world and they did not exactly ask to join ours in the first place. However, they're here now, and we must either adapt to their economics or persuade them to take up ours. The first thing we should do is review our understanding of Adam Smith. Leaving everything to the invisible hand was fine for seafaring people who were safe behind salt water, who had a long lead in technology, and who could buy up the world for beads and blankets. The despised mercantilists *needed* all that bullion to equip armies, hire mercenaries, increase their tax base, and find their rightful place in the sun. Their modern successors who have found a peaceful way of doing the same thing will be happy to let the marketplace decide—as long as it decides for them.

Japan's Strategic Structures

Chalmers Johnson

. . .[A]ll the social sciences have taken too long to recognize that although Japan is an advanced capitalist democracy, the institutions of capitalism that it has built through its industrial policies differ fundamentally from those encountered in American capitalism.

Institutions in Japan. . .may have the same names in Japanese that we use in English, but they none the less function in quite different ways. Japanese unions are company unions, and organized labor in Japan has *no* role or voice in politics. Joint stock companies may be "owned" by shareholders, but at least 70 per cent of the shares of Japans's most important companies are owned by competing companies and are never traded, regardless of price. Japan's banking system is the primary means whereby the Japanese transfer savings to industry, instead of using capital markets. These are *fundamental* differences.

We are only beginning to recognize that Japan has invented and put together the institutions of capitalism in new ways, ways that neither Adam Smith nor Marx would recognize or understand. This is not due to some mystical difference known as Japanese culture or Japanese social character. Nor does Japanese capitalism work according to different economic or political theories from those that pertain in the West. It is rather that the common capitalist and democratic theory is realized in Japan through different institutions from those in the West—and with markedly different trade-offs, above all, greater and more rational economic performance, but with considerably less popular participation in economic policy-making. Institutions are the key variables. This understanding leads to two related

Chalmers Johnson *is Rohr Professor of Pacific International Relations at the Graduate School of International Relations and Pacific Studies at the University of California, San Diego. His books include* MITI and the Japanese Miracle *(1982). He is a member of the Advisory Board of the Economic Strategy Institute. Excerpted with permission from Kegan Paul International, from* Japanese Models of Conflict Resolution, *eds., S.N. Eisenstadt and Eyal Ben-Ari (New York: Kegan Paul International, 1990).*

axioms. First, capitalist economic theory is an utterly abstract and even utopian body of thought until it is translated into action through concrete institutions. Second, any set of institutions that ignores economic theory will eventually bankrupt a nation in which it is established, other things being equal. . . .

Let me try to illustrate some of these ideas about Japan by briefly describing some ten institutions that are intrinsic to the Japanese economy but virtually unknown in the United States. It should be stressed that each of these institutions is the product of quite recent Japanese history and of conscious innovation. None of them has existed unchanged for more than a few decades, and none of them can be traced to traditional organizations (with the possible exception of the official state bureaucracy, which clearly has its roots in the old samurai class). These institutions are not the product of Japan's unique culture, although they obviously do not clash with that culture. . . . The theory that Japan's institutions are to be explained by its culture is essentially an ideological way of avoiding the competitive implications of Japan's institutional innovations. . . .

The first set of institutions. . .is crucial. . . . This is the Japanese financial system. Instead of relying on a highly developed capital market, such as the New York Stock Exchange, Japan transfers its savings to industry through its banking system. Japan has a stock market, the Tokyo Stock Exchange, but it has never even come close to equalling bank loans or corporate bonds as a source of external funds for Japanese economies. Even though Japan's banking system is starting to undergo deregulation and internationalization, there is not the slightest chance that it will come to look like that of the United States until well into the next century (if ever). Moreover, some of the core elements of the Japanese system, such as the government-owned Japanese Development Bank, are exempt from deregulation.

Japan's choice of different institutions from those in the United States to finance its industries has many implications. I shall discuss four of them. First, through its system, Japan avoids the short-term bias inherent in the American stock market. No manager or chief executive officer of a Japanese corporation begins the morning looking at his company's stock quotations. Such information is irrelevant to him because it is irrelevant to the bankers who have lent his firm its capital. What the bankers are concerned about is the company's market share and its ability to repay its loans over the long term, and these depend upon how well the company is doing in developing new products, controlling costs and quality, and preparing its work-force for the future. These are the criteria of good management in Japan. They are utterly different from those in the United States because the American institutions of industrial financing impose short-term incentives on managers.

Second, Japan avoids the waste of capital and talent inherent in the "paper entrepreneurialism" (in Robert Reich's apt phrase) that the American system generates. There is no shortage of capital in the United States, but in recent years a good part of it has been mobilized for hostile takeover bids... and all the other devices of price manipulation inherent in the capital market. These things do not happen in Tokyo, even in firms that are highly capitalized, for the simple reason (as Rodney Clark. . .puts it) that "unlike Western institutional shareholders, which invest largely for dividends and capital appreciation, Japanese institutional shareholders tend to be the company's business partners and associates: shareholding is a mere expression of their relationship, not the relationship itself." In other words, the concept of "ownership" has become irrelevant to Japanese capitalism, where the managerial revolution has been carried to greater lengths than it has in competing systems.

Third, neo-classical economists argue that even though Japan may not have to contend with some of the unintended consequences of a capital market, it none the less loses the benefits of such a market, above all the *information* that a capital market generates about which new technologies have real commercial potential and which ones do not. This proposition is true, but the Japanese have invented quite effective substitutes for the information-supplying function of a capital market. These substitutes include: Japan's elaborate apparatus of industrial policy within MITI; several dozen forums for public-private consultation; the most effective organization of the private sector of any capitalist country, namely, Keidanren, or the Federation of Economic Organizations; thousands of semi-official trade organizations; and the information collecting, processing, and dissemination capabilities of the general trading companies and JETRO. Taken together, these institutions are more than adequate to signal investors about promising new prospects. In the United States, venture capital to finance new products is supplied through the market, and theorists tell us that it could not possibly be supplied as efficiently in any other way. In Japan, a good part of venture capital is supplied by the Japan Development Bank (*Japan Economic Journal*, July 19, 1983; Nihon Kaihatsu Ginko, 1984).

Fourth, despite the growing internationalism of Japan's financial system, the cost of capital is still significantly lower for Japanese industry than it is for Japan's competitors. This is because many interest rates are still officially administered in Japan, because different industries and enterprises have different degrees of access to the Japanese financial system, because of the ease with which Japanese industrial policy authorities can "guide" capital, and because of the continuing undervaluation of the yen despite the existence of "floating" exchange rates for more than a decade. Any industrialist understands what a competitive advantage his Japanese counterpart enjoys in significantly cheaper prices of capital. . . .

A second set of unusual institutions in Japan is the "industrial groups," known in pre-war Japan as *zaibatsu* (financial cliques) and in post-war Japan as *keiretsu* (lineages) or *kigyo shudan* (enterprise groups). The most famous of them are the Mitsubishi, Mitsui, Sumitomo, Hitachi, Yasuda, and similar groups. They are perhaps most accurately called "developmental conglomerates," because they concentrate huge amounts of capital and then use it along with their well-established industries to finance risky, new ventures. The industrial groups are a specific Japanese invention dating from the nineteenth century, when Japan launched its drive to catch up with the advanced industrial nations that were threatening it. Their contemporary successors have been modernized: they have eliminated the old family holding companies in favor of guidance through banks and trading companies. Perhaps the most important feature of the *keiretsu* system in Japan is that there is more than one group: only one conglomerate would lead to monopoly, but five or more involved in every industry in fact generates cut-throat competition. . . .

Many significant implications flow from this form of industrial organization. Let us consider just one. The industrial groups are relatively impervious to the effects of the international business cycle because of their large concentrations of capital and conglomerate structure. This means that they can leverage their positions during the business cycle to gain advantages over their international competitors. Japanese firms in the *Keiretsu* can continue to invest in R & D and productive capacity right through a cyclical downturn, whereas their American competitors, without comparable backing, will be forced to lay off workers, reduce investment, and cut back on research. When the recession is over, the Japanese will be ready to meet renewed demand, often with better prices and higher quality products. In the semiconductor industry, for example, the Japanese have pulled this stunt at least twice (with 64K and 256K memory chips). They are able to do so because the industrial groups can free leading enterprises from short-term profitability considerations.

A third key institution in Japan is the postal savings system, through which the government invests the people's savings in projects that the industrial policy organs have designated as strategic. At the end of 1984, the deposits in the postal savings system amounted to some ¥86.3 trillion (c. $350 billion), or two-and-a-half times the assets of Citicorp. These deposits form the basis of the Fiscal Investment and Loan Program, a financial institution that is wholly in the hands of Japan's industrial policy bureaucrats. It is, in fact, the largest single financial organ in the world today.

Japanese citizens save at their post offices, because the system offers higher interest rates and better terms than the government allows commercial banks to offer, and because the Japanese cannot freely invest their money abroad, in, say, U.S. banks, where they might get still higher rates of interest. The Japanese government also induces its people to save by not providing the full range of welfare and retirement services found in most other democracies. During the 1950s, at the start of high-speed growth, postal savings contributed some 40 per cent of all investments in Japan's priority industries. That figure is much lower today, not because postal savings are smaller but because bank lending has grown phenomenally. The postal savings system, given its size and the bureaucrats' track record in managing it, still possesses almost irresistible powers of guidance for the economy as a whole.

The fourth set of institutions I would like to mention are the official forums through which bureaucrats, businessmen, experts, journalists, and representatives of the people consider and decide on virtually all public policies. These are the *shingikai*, or "deliberation councils," of which, during 1984, there were some 214. At present the Ministry of Finance operates fourteen of them, MITI twenty, the Ministry of Agriculture fourteen, the Ministry of Transportation eleven, the Economic Planning Agency three, and so forth. . . . The *shingikai* contribute to the smooth government-business relationships of Japan, which is a distinct comparative advantage when Japan is competing with systems that cannot produce widely supported or effectively implemented public policies. In the U.S., similar deliberations on laws go on in Congress and are subjected to the full range of lobbying pressures, including pressure from foreign lobbyists. In Japan, they are conducted in private, shielded from interest groups or the press and under the control of Japan's elitist state bureaucracy. . . .

The fifth institution on my list is actually one of the 214 deliberation councils. This is the Tax System Investigation Council (*Zeisei Chosakai*), which is the key Japanese organization for trying to depoliticize the national and local tax systems and to make them as economically rational as is possible in a democracy. No tax system is politically or economically neutral, certainly not Japan's. But Japan's system is more closely coordinated with industrial policy than in other countries, and its overall tax burden is the lowest of any OECD nation. One of the ways Japan achieves these things is through its very prestigious Tax System Investigation Council.

In its current form the Council came into being in April 1962. It is composed of some thirty tax experts, representatives of enterprises, bankers, and opinion leaders who are appointed for three-year terms by the Prime Minister on the recommendation of the tax bureau of the Ministries of Finance and Home Affairs (the latter representing local governments). The Council deliberates in secret and each year produces a long report of recommended revisions to the tax codes. Many of these changes are timely, narrowly focused tax breaks for industry . . . . The Council's recommendations are communicated directly to the Diet, where, with rare exceptions, they are automatically enacted into law.

The Council is influential because of the reputations of its members and because of the relative invulnerability of its sponsoring ministries to lobbying. There has been some increase over the years in the representation of politicians on the Council, but during the 1980s its head was the country's most distinguished former Vice-Minister of Agriculture, Ogura Takekazu. Members included [newspaper] editors . . . ; professors . . . ; and the governor of Kagoshima prefecture; and the chief executive officers of Toshiba Electric, Komatsu Tractors, Mitsui Bank, and Suntory Whisky. . . . The Council has more authority in the eyes of the public than any group of elected politicians, and this is the key to its success. The Diet has the legal power to overrule the Council, but it rarely does so because of the rationality and seriousness of the Council's recommendations.

A sixth set of very important institutions in Japan are those concerned with labor negotiations. Nowhere does Japan achieve a greater comparative advantage over its competitors than in its utterly flexible, strike-free ways of avoiding labor conflict. Many people. . .conclude that Japan's tranquil labor relations must be a reflection of cultural propensities. Nonetheless, the evidence is building daily that Japanese-run factories in the United States and elsewhere also achieve greater loyalty and commitment from their workers than do factories under ordinary American management. Culture thus has little or nothing to do with Japan's achievements in this area.

During the late 1940s and all of the 1950s Japan was torn apart by very violent labor strife. The result of this era, however, was a decision by management not to buy the unions off (as in the American steel and automotive industries) but to fight them to the bitter end. . . . Since then trade unions in Japan have been replaced with enterprise unions, which are supported by the workers because of a simultaneously enlarged career employment system for male heads of households. The result is a labor force that is sensitive to international competition in order to keep their enterprises healthy, that has no incentive to oppose technological innovation of even a labor-saving type (such as robotics) because of career job security, and that does not have or seek a major role in politics. This last achievement is critical to Japan's success with industrial policy. Japan does not exploit its labor, but it also does not give labor a veto power over its industrial policy initiatives—and that is a real competitive advantage.

The seventh set of institutions to consider are conspicuous by their absence. That is to say, Japan garners some advantages by *not* allowing certain American-type institutions to flourish. These are the institutions of anti-trust and anti-monopoly policy, which Americans claim are needed to promote competition. Japan actually achieves much more vigorous domestic competition for an advanced, oligopolized industrial economy than the United States does, but it manages to do so without the benefit of thousands of anti-trust lawyers. . . .

Japan in fact generated its vigorous domestic competition through industrial policy and its structure of industrial groups. When one of MITI's deliberation councils designates a particular industry as important for Japan's future growth, industrial groups vie with each other to enter it. This is because of the reduced risks that follow from investment in a designated industry and because of the longer time perspectives of Japanese managers. At the same time, given a less legalistic orientation than the United States, Japan is able to employ all manner of cartels—recession, export, import, rationalization, research, and so forth—to implement its policies. Each of these is authorized as an exception to the Anti-Monopoly Law, usually for fixed, relatively short periods of time. Japanese economic ministries also tailormake policies for particular industries of enterprises through discretionary and non-justiciable "administrative guidance." Above all, Japan is not burdened with the huge and wasteful diversion of human resources into the legal profession that is so conspicuous a part of the American economic system. . . .

An eighth set of Japanese institutions illustrates the country's creative use of cartels. These are the "research cartels" *(kenkyu kumiai)* that the Agency for Industrial Science and Technology, and integral part of MITI, authorizes and funds in order to promote Japan's research and development.

Such cartels allow competing firms to collaborate on specific research projects—projects that may advance Japan's overall technological level but that, in any case, save Japanese firms the costs of duplicating R&D. Research cartels are currently authorized for a range of microelectronics, biotechnology, telecommunications, new materials, and energy conservation projects. The government also sponsors a group of closely related R&D efforts, including the well-known attempt to build a "fifth generation" computer and one to give Japan its own capacity to produce and launch telecommunications satellites.

A ninth set of Japanese institutions are those that supply domestic information, intelligence, publicity, and propaganda concerning commercial trends and new economic challenges. Japan actually operates something similar to the National Security Council, the Central Intelligence Agency, and the Rand Corporation in the industrial and commercial spheres. In Japan, however, these kinds of operations are not secret; instead they are aimed at achieving the greatest possible publicity.

Among Japan's information organs there are: the Trade Council (known as the "Supreme Export Council" before 1980), which is led by the Prime Minister and the cabinet and is intended to give maximum authority and publicity to national economic initiatives; the Economic Planning Agency, which is an organization for economic monitoring and analysis, one that is indefinitely more effective than the American Council of Economic Advisors precisely because it is not authorized to give advice; JETRO, which is a worldwide commercial intelligence and support organization for Japanese importers and exporters; and MITI, the Ministry of Finance, the Bank of Japan, and the semi-official Bank of Tokyo, each of which produces innumerable "visions" of the future, indicative plans, and analyses of various industries and markets. All of this material is readily available in any Japanese bookstore. The Japanese businessman who does not know what his foreign competitors are doing, or who does not know where to turn if he wants more information, is probably illiterate. . . .

The tenth and final set of institutions to be discussed in this survey are those charged with making and implementing industrial location policy. These institutions are particularly relevant to the United States because of the very high social and political costs associated with the shift of American industries from the rust-belt to the sun-belt. In Japan, industrial location policy is as politically salient an issue as in the United States. . . . The Japanese answer to these problems has been a combination of local initiatives, massive government investments in infrastructure to assist relatively backward areas (for example, the bullet trains in the north-east, the bridges to Shikoku island,

and the world's longest tunnel connecting Honshu and Hokkaido), and the establishment of a number of public corporations to provide incentives for labor mobility, relocation of industry, and foreign investment.

In implementing its industrial location policies, Japan relies primarily on public corporations. This means that although politicians establish industrial location policy—something particularly true under the leadership of former Prime Minister Tanaka Kakuei—the actual implementation is fairly depoliticized and technocratic. . . .

In addition to the activities of these organizations, in 1983 the Diet passed a MITI-sponsored law to create and give tax breaks to some fifteen high-tech cities throughout the country, known as "technopolises." The technopolises are modelled on California's Silicon Valley and are based on the hopeful idea that high-technology industries located adjacent to each other will generate synergisms of innovation and new jobs. One of the Japanese technopolises, Miyazaki city in Kyushu, even claims that it lies in the same "isothermal zone" (in other words, has the same weather) as Silicon Valley, which is thought to be of possible advantage to it, or perhaps just a good omen. To celebrate this latest aspect of industrial policy location, MITI, during 1985, sponsored a high-tech world fair at Japan's first "science city," Tsukuba, where from the early 1970s MITI has located many of it most important laboratories and research cartels.

At least two lessons seem to emerge from the Japanese experience with industrial location and relocation activities. First, political initiative is necessary to get anything done. The leader in Japan was Tanaka Kakuei, who, as Prime Minister from 1972 to 1974, made industrial dispersal one of his main priorities. Second, local initiative is equally important; the central governments are responsive not just to depressed areas but also to those areas that are most active in terms of self-help. Japan's programs have not been perfect, but the most pervasive impression one gets of the country as a whole is of the relatively equitable distribution of income and amenities.

The ten sets of institutions outlined here of course do not add up to the totality of the Japanese industrial system. Aspects that have not been mentioned include measures for the relief of structurally recessed industries, Japan's trade policies, and its measures for administering economic diplomacy (unlike the United States, Japan never entrusts its foreign economic diplomacy to its Ministry of Foreign Affairs). Equally to the point, not everything the Japanese do in the name of industrial policy succeeds. . . .

In my opinion, what does emerge from the Japanese case is that the Japanese government takes its responsibilities in the economic sphere more seriously than do most other democratic governments: It staffs its government with the best minds in the country; it tries to depoliticize important economic decisions; it sticks to them long enough for households and enterprises to adjust; and its interventions in the privately managed economy are market-conforming rather than market-displacing. Firms or nations wanting to compete with the Japanese must become at least as serious.

The key to what makes Japan so different from the other advanced industrial democracies is its institutional innovations. Japan has outperformed the rest of the world in inventing new institutions through which the relationships of modern capitalism are realized, Japan has altered, experimented with, and reinvented both democracy and capitalism to such an extent that it has evolved a qualitatively different structure as a nation state from the norm in the West. . . .

Europe's New Game Plan

In modern society, research and technology play an increasingly important and central role. After steadily gathering momentum since the mid-14th century, scientific and technical progress ushered in some years ago in the western world a period of radical change dubbed variously 'the scientific and technical revolution,' 'the third industrial revolution,' 'the intelligence revolution,' etc. . . .

The second industrial revolution in the 19th century gave man the physical capacity to influence his environment on an unprecedented scale: the steam locomotive and internal combustion engine extended the physical potential of the human body. The fruits of the third industrial revolution are for the most part of a different sort: they allow man to transfer his intellectual capacities to external devices. At the same time, they extend his range of action to an extent unimaginable a hundred years ago by enabling him to influence the very heart of matter and of life . . . .

In the plethora of discoveries, developments and innovations generated by the third industrial revolution, what part does European R&TD [research and technological development] play? Europe is the cradle of science and technology in the forms in which we know them today: until recently it was the home of all major breakthroughs. Sadly, Europe can no longer claim the lead in most of the major areas of research and technological development. In some fields (such as research on controlled thermonuclear fusion or particles physics), European research still leads the world but on the whole it has clearly lost ground—a situation all the more disastrous in sectors of exceptional economic importance such as electronics, information technology, the life sciences and materials science.

A few figures and examples show the scale of the problem: of the 37 technological sectors of the future that have been identified, 31 are dominated by the United States of America, nine by Japan and only two by Europe:

Excerpted from Research and Technological Development Policy *(Luxembourg: Office for Official Publications of the European Communities, 1988).*

software and electronic switching (some sectors being dominated by two countries equally). In 1986, four out of five patent applications for new materials were filed by U.S. or Japanese companies. Of the 10 leading companies in the world in the computer industry, seven are American, two Japanese while the leading European company is back in 10th place. The picture for biotechnology and many other areas is similar. What are the reasons for this state of affairs? . . .

[I]nsufficient attention to the problems involved in the follow-through from scientific research to technological development and then on to the market place; poor marketing techniques: the persistence in companies of organization principles and training methods unsuited to the circumstances of the scientific and technical revolution; the lack of financial instruments to stimulate R&TD and the meager venture capital available for investment in this field. All these factors will continue to constitute a drag on European R&TD until there has been a radical revolution in attitudes, practices, behavior, culture and education in the Community.

Alongside these reasons, another group of factors can be identified; funds spread too thinly, research teams working in ivory towers, a lack of coordination, poor dissemination of information, inadequate mobility of research scientists, duplications in national programs, differing strategies, disparities in standards, the lack of a real single market, et. All these factors are obviously interrelated and at root they all stem from a single cause that is easy to identify: the division of Europe into many different countries.

Whatever might appear advisable in other fields, there is at least one idea that no one disputes today: European cooperation in research and technology is a vital necessity. . . . It is clear today that in research and technological development Europe's only salvation lies in systematic and purposeful cooperation. . . .

Information technology [IT] and telecommunications, now vital factors for industrial competitiveness, constitute the fastest growing sector in the world and one in which European technological dependence is high: the Community's trade deficit for electronics was approximately 15000 million ECU in 1986 and European manufacturers today hold no more than 25% of the world market in information technology and telecommunications. The European market represents 12% of world demand for integrated circuits and 26% of world demand for information processing and office systems and yet the share of the world market going to European firms in those two subsectors in only 9% and 24% respectively.

A look at the economies that have succeeded most spectacularly in this field shows that their success is due to a combination of factors that until recently were not found in the European economy. Two of these factors are particularly significant. The first is the existence of a strong scientific and technical base resulting from spontaneous or organized cooperation between universities, research centers and industry. The second is the existence of a vast internal market capable of absorbing a large production and offering economies of scale to its industries. These two factors tend to ease the severest constraint on industry in the information technology and telecommunications sector, the steadily increasing cost of R&TD investment. . . .

On the basis of these findings, the Community has defined a policy for IT and telecommunications incorporating several inseparable features which should help European industry to increase its competitiveness in IT and telecommunications and to acquire both on the world market and on its own European market a position more in keeping with its considerable, if poorly exploited, technological potential. The two most important components are the strengthening of the Community's technological capacity through R&TD programs carried out by cross-frontier cooperation between universities and industry and the establishment of a vast internal market for IT and telecommunications products and services with all that this involves in the way of a common standardization policy: encouraging the early definition of standards, protocols and technical specifications, in particular on the basis of the work done under the Community's R&TD programs. . . .

The first of the Community IT and telecommunication programs to be implemented (and the most ambitious in volume terms) is the Esprit program. Esprit (European strategic program for research and development in information technology) first saw the light in the early 1980s. It was devised by the Commission after extensive consultations with the academic world and the industries concerned, both large and small firms, and was designed for a 10-year period (1984-93). . . .

After a brief pilot phase, Esprit got off the ground in 1984. The first phase covered five major sectors: two basic technologies, advanced microelectronics (very large-scale integrated circuits) and software development; two application areas, office systems and computer-integrated manufacturing (robotics, computer-aided design, automatic assembly, computerized management networks, etc.) and finally advanced information processing to provide the link between the other two (highly parallel architectures, voice and image recognition and synthesis, etc.).

The first phase of Esprit had a budget of 1500 million ECU (750 million of which came from the Community) which financed 219 projects involving 450 different partners, more than half of whom were manufacturers; amongst these were some 170 companies with less than 500 employees. It is generally recognized that the first phase of Esprit, in which some 3,000 researchers were involved, was instrumental in sparking off genuine European cooperation in information technology. . . .

The first phase of Esprit rapidly yielded significant results: one example from the field of microelectronics is the design of a bipolar gate array circuit of 10 K gates with an access time of 200 picoseconds, for which a production line has just been set up. In advanced information processing several Esprit projects led to interesting developments concerning the logical programming language Prolog. . . . The budget for the second stage of Esprit was double that of the first. Three R&TD areas were selected for the second phase: microelectronics and peripheral technologies, information-processing systems and IT application technologies. In each of them the emphasis is on topics shown by a study of the current IT situation to merit priority: high-density integrated circuits, multifunction integrated circuits, peripheral technologies, systems architecture and knowledge engineering, etc. Generally speaking, special importance is given to application technologies (computer-integrated manufacturing, robotics and office systems) and to technology transfer.

Related as it is to information technology, telecommunications is a sector of an importance that cannot be exaggerated: the telecommunications infrastructure will have an extremely strategic role to play in the general economy in the years ahead since its influence on all aspects of economic life is growing at an exponential rate. In only a few years it has become the focus of both public and private investment. . . .

Consequently the Community has defined, and is now implementing, a coordinated development strategy for telecommunications as well. . . . Once again an R&TD program plays an important part in the Community strategy: this is the RACE program. The strategy is designed to ensure that the different telecommunications systems and services now being developed in Europe remain consistent. The specific aim of RACE is to enable the Community to move towards integrated broadband communications (IBC) based on integrated services digital networks (ISDN). This system would be able to handle a very wide range of new and conventional services, one-way or interactive including telephones, video-phones, cable and pay television, data transmission and electronic mail. . . .

The first phase of RACE covers the period 1987 to 1991 and has a budget of 1100 million ECU, 50% of which is provided by the Community. Following up the results of the definition phase, this first phase was divided into three parts. In the first the IBC reference model will be extended and functional specifications developed for systems, the second continues and amplifies the research on IBC technologies, hardware and software (opto-electronic equipment, audio and video signal processing, digital image recording techniques, etc.) while the third consists of the simulation and testing of IBC techniques to enhance their capability for integration in a standardized IBC system. . . .

One of the vital aspects of the development of both telecommunications and information technology in Europe is clearly standardization. This is obviously receiving special attention from the Community as otherwise the community IT and telecommunications policy would be virtually meaningless. Launched in 1985, the Community policy on IT and telecommunications standardization is designed to encourage the harmonized application of international standards in the European context. Developed in close cooperation with the industry and in collaboration with the European standards institutions, CEN and Cenelec, the main plank of this policy is the promotion of standards defined by reference to the OSI (Open System Interconnection) model of the international Organization for Standardization (ISO), so as to guarantee effective compatibility between different equipment and systems and their ability to communicate on networks. In the implementation of the standardization policy a specific role falls to R&TD programs such as Esprit and RACE, in which a large number of projects are relevant to standardization problems (28 Esprit projects have led to the development of IT and telecommunications standards).

The Community's R&TD activities in the field of information technology and telecommunications are not confined to the two flagship programs Esprit and RACE. There are also a number of more specific initiatives. In 1987 the Commission prepared three programs for the integrated application of IT and telecommunications in new services. These are the Delta program (Development of European learning through technological advance) in the field of computer-aided education (development of a reference model for a learning system, personal computer technologies, satellite transmission systems, etc.); the AIM program (Advanced informatics in medicine) in the two fields of biocomputing and medical computing (expert systems, data banks, biosensors, imaging techniques, patient monitoring and medical record systems, etc.) and the Drive program (Dedicated road infrastructure for vehicle safety in Europe) on computer aids for road traffic (route guidance, navigation systems, vehicle-to-vehicle communications, etc.).

Industrial technologies

The action line covering industrial technologies in the framework program identifies four separate sectors: Manufacturing industry, advanced materials, raw materials and technical standards and reference materials. The first is covered by the Brite program. Brite is typical of the second-generation Community programs. Its specific field is the application of new technologies in manufacturing industries: the motor industry, chemicals, textiles, aircraft, shipbuilding, machine tools, civil engineering, etc. These 'traditional' industrial sectors are of considerable economic importance. They account today for the greater part of the GDP generated by industry and provide jobs for more than 24 million people in the Community. In all these sectors a whole series of recent technical advances (lasers, computer-aided design, mathematical modeling, powder metallurgy, etc.) heralds radical innovations and far-reaching changes in both products and production processes.

Like Esprit, Brite was prepared by the Commission in close cooperation with industry. . . . Nine key sectors were identified: reliability, wear and deterioration; laser technology; joining techniques; new testing methods; computer-aided design and manufacture (CAD/CAM) and mathematical models; polymers, composites and powder metallurgy; membrane science and technology; catalysis and particle technology; new technologies for products made from flexible materials. Since it was launched in 1985 Brite has aided several hundred projects. . . .

The Community has devoted a complete program to materials technology, which has widespread applications and is essential to progress in many areas (microelectronics, the motor and aviation industries, biomedical techniques, etc.). This is the Eram program, designed to help Europe develop and produce for itself a whole range of sophisticated materials that it currently has to import or manufacture under American or Japanese license. It covers virtually the full range of advanced materials: metal materials (aluminium, magnesium and titanium alloys, superplastic forming techniques and powder metallurgy); engineering ceramics for gas turbines or high-temperature internal combustion engines; a whole range of composites: organic matrix, metal matrix (magnesium or aluminium alloys), vitreous matrix, etc. . . .

The framework program (1987-91) contains a number of closely linked activities on the intelligent exploitation of living resources (from the double viewpoint of scientific exploitation and respect for the constraints on human action imposed by living matter itself and its balances). . . .

The Community effort first took the form of a small research and training program in molecular biology (1982-86). This was the BEP (Biomolecular engineering program). . . . It covered research sectors relevant to biotechnological applications in agriculture and agro-industry. . . . [The] second Community program covered the same research areas as its predecessor and also tackled new fields, with projects in the following sectors: bioinformatics (data capture, data banks, modelling techniques); collections of biotic materials; enzyme engineering (development of advance bioreactors, protein design); genetic engineering (genetic engineering of micro-organisms of importance to industry, plants and associated microorganisms, breeding animals); assessment of risks (development of method for detecting and assessing risks associated with biotechnology and, in particular, risks associated with the release of engineered organisms); *in vitro* test methods (development of methods to evaluate the toxicological properties of molecules). During the second half of the framework program, the Community's biotechnology activities are to be further expanded and the industrial world will be more closely associated with them. . . .

Away from the immediate environment of the Community's R&TD acitivities, a more general look shows that they have numerous links with many of the major policies that have gradually been defined and implemented by the European Community.

This is particularly obvious in the case of industrial policy, as is clear from a review of the main action lines of the framework program (1987-91): almost two-thirds of the activities have a direct industrial purpose. The framework program concentrates much of its resources on diffusing technologies (information technologies, materials, biotechnology, etc.) that are rapidly spreading through the whole fabric of manufacturing industry. . . .

The link between R&TD and the Community telecommunications policy is just as obvious. Anxious to ensure that the many new telecommunications services now emerging are developed at European level, the Community has been making a great effort since 1984: it is promoting the establishment of an advanced European telecommunications infrastructure, together with the building of a single European market for terminals and equipment and the introduction of advanced services and networks in the least prosperous peripheral regions of the Community. . . .

VI

Coming Back: Domestic Obstacles

One of the principal arguments against America adopting an economic strategy holds that most of our economic problems are home-grown. If only our workers worked harder and our managers managed better, the argument continues, the U.S. economy would bounce back in no time. And government supposedly can't do anything about such problems; they reflect the failures of individuals. A domestic focus, however, is essential for a true economic strategy. In particular, it reveals the flaws in emphasizing individual shortcomings as the root of our problems. First, the assumption underlying this argument is simply unconvincing—that Americans do not work as hard as foreigners, and that American executives are less intelligent than their counterparts abroad. Second, a strategic perspective underscores the factors that do separate America from its leading competitors.

As indicated in the preceding chapter, countries succeed economically in a strategic world when they take such success seriously, and when this attitude is reflected in fiscal and monetary policy as well as regulation, science and technology promotion, education, financial practices, corporate structures, and other dimensions of public and private life.

The selections in Part Six reveal that the United States has a long way to go in all these respects. Some of the biggest self-made obstacles to better U.S. economic performance are intellectual. Robert Kuttner argues that the sociology and organization of the economics profession itself have been part of the problem. Tightly controlled by the Orthodoxy, most of our university economics departments determinedly churn out generations of students who value pristine theory over messy reality.

Another set of intellectual obstacles involves outdated thinking about government's proper role in promoting excellence. George C. Lodge traces many U.S. government failures to promote business effectively to a political tradition that immediately denigrates any departures from individualism as "suspect, illegitimate, and likely to fail." And when the eventually half-hearted measures taken do fail, the idea of government intervention itself gets another black eye. This individualistic ethic assumes that capitalism and economic planning are like oil and water. But Saburo Okita, another key shaper of Japan's postwar economic success, argues that this belief confuses a "planned economy with economic planning." The former is typified by the Soviet system; government monopolizes all economic activity. The latter "sets an economic framework" but "allows a free hand" to private citizens and firms.

Erich Bloch challenges the idea that government officials can and should draw a sharp distinction between promoting basic science and encouraging applied research. For years, Washington has enthusiastically funded such "pure" scientific endeavors as research in astronomy and nuclear physics. But promoting technological development has been equated with such taboo notions as "picking winners and losers." Bloch observes that basic and applied research are increasingly inseparable. Nowadays in particular, each drives the other forward.

Yet more concrete problems are afflicting the U.S. economy as well. David Alan Aschauer documents the link between anemic U.S. spending on transportation and communications networks—our infrastructure—and anemic U.S. productivity growth since the 1950s. The Council on Competitiveness describes the tangle of government regulations that often needlessly slow down the process of bringing new U.S. technologies to the market. The staff of Data Resources, Inc. focuses on the domestic financial and tax-policy factors behind American industry's productivity troubles. As a result, U.S. firms must borrow money at much higher rates than companies in many other countries, and face much more pressure to sacrifice long-term competitive position for short-term gain.

At the same time, according to Robert H. Hayes and William J. Abernathy, a seductive but dangerous new gospel has taken hold in the executive suite. The importance of offering superior products has been forgotten. Too many executives today seek financial short-cuts to success.

Finally, Edwin J. Coleman describes the problems created when governments and businesses lack the most basic economic information—on the size of the economy, its makeup, its rate of growth. In Coleman's view, short-sighted Reagan-era statistics policies have put U.S. producers at a major competitive disadvantage.

The Poverty of Economics

Robert Kuttner

. . .Since 1970 an outpouring of serious and ideologically diverse articles and books has pronounced that economics is in a state of severe, perhaps terminal, crisis. Some titles convey the sentiments: *The Crisis in Economic Theory, Economists at Bay, What's Wrong With Economics, the Irrelevance of Conventional Economics, Why Economics Is Not Yet A Science, Dangerous Currents: The State of Economics,* even a scholarly article titled, "Let's Take the Con Out of Econometrics . . . ."

...Yet despite the apparent soul-searching, the teaching of economics, the hiring of young economists and the granting of tenure, the financing of research, the pages of prestigious "refereed" journals all evidence deep resistance to change.

Neoclassical economics, the reigning school, marries the assumptions of the classical invisible hand—the principle of a self-regulating economy—to the Keynesian insight that macroeconomic stabilization by government is necessary to keep the clockwork operating smoothly. In method, standard economics is highly abstract, mathematical, and deductive, rather than curious about institutions. Neoclassical economic theory posits an economic system of "perfect competition." All transactions in the economy are likened to those that occur in simple marketplaces, like fish markets, in which prices rise or fall exactly enough to move the merchandise. As economists say, adjustment of price based on supply and demand serves to "clear the market . . . ."

...The model also assumes that markets are composed of many sellers and many buyers, who individually have too little market power to dictate prices or to manipulate choices, and can only offer or accept bids. As economists say, each seller is a price taker, not a price maker—for otherwise

Robert Kuttner, *an economics correspondent for* The New Republic *and a columnist for* BusinessWeek, *is co-editor of* The American Prospect *and the author of the forthcoming* The End of Laissez-Faire *and other books. Excerpted with the author's permission from "The Poverty of Economics,"* The Atlantic Monthly, *July 1985.*

there could not be perfect competition.

Perfect competition requires "perfect information." Consumers must know enough to compare products astutely; workers must be aware of alternative jobs, and capitalists of competing business opportunities. Otherwise, sellers could charge more than a competitive price and get away with it, and workers could demand more than their services were worth. Moreover, perfect competition requires "perfect mobility of factors." Workers must be free to seek the highest available wage, and capitalists to shift their capital to get the highest available return; otherwise, identical factors of production would command different prices, and the result would be a deviation from the model. Economists argue that monopoly prices or wages can't last very long, because some entrepreneur soon perceives an opportunity, enters the market and forces prices back into equilibrium.

The introduction of concrete social institutions like banks, corporations, currencies, and the modern state complicate only the details, not the fundamentals.   Likewise, deviations from perfect competition in actual economic life require embellishments of the model, not a revision of its promises. With Keynes, standard theory conceded that disequilibria might intrude upon the economy as a whole, but it held that these could be remedied by judicious stabilization of aggregate demand—that is, combined government and consumer purchasing power.

The neoclassical model assumes that economic behavior is based on the concept of "marginal utility": individual consumers express choices by continually calculating and refining their preferences "at the margin"—the point at which they have extra dollars of income or hours of time to spend—and firms likewise make adjustments at the margins to maximize profits. We know these things by assumption and inference: an individual who did not maximize his well-being would be behaving irrationally, and a firm failing to maximize profits would fall by the wayside. In most models the state of technology is assumed to be constant, and so are cultural and institutional environments. Technological, cultural, and institutional changes that do occur over time result from individuals constantly adjusting their preferences at the margin. If individuals have cultural attachments, and motivations other than utility maximization, these are not of theoretical significance.   Charles Schultze, a senior fellow at the Brookings Institution and recent president of the AEA [American Economics Association] says, "When you dig deep down, economists are scared to death of being sociologists. The one great thing we have going for us is the premise that individuals act rationally in trying to satisfy their preferences. That is an incredibly powerful tool, because you can model it."

When the standard model is presented in the classroom, an impertinent freshman invariably protests that is plainly unrealistic. The professor has heard the complaint before. He tells the student that we must walk before we can run, that we must oversimplify for the sake of analytic clarity, and that after the student is more accomplished in analytic technique, refinements will be added to adjust the model to the nuances of economic reality. The model indeed becomes more elaborate, yet the basic assumptions persist. By then the student either will have decided that the entire exercise is unrewarding and moved on to history or sociology, or will have mastered the difficult mathematical proofs and acquired a certain fondness for deductive logic, as well as a professional loyalty to the discipline.

Neoclassical economic analysis grows out of the Enlightenment mentality, which substituted a scientific natural order for a metaphysical one. An invisible hand that shaped individual egoism into general harmony reconciled the Enlightenment predilections for personal liberty and natural laws. Adam Smith's concept of equilibrium in market economics is also a variation on eighteenth-century Newtonian mechanics. Physics has served ever since as a model to which economics should aspire.

The difficulty is that economic phenomena are neither so universal nor so predictable as physical phenomena. If, for example, most actual markets do not automatically clear according to price, then standard economics is building elaborate models of a world that doesn't exist.

. . .Of several major theoretical problems the most basic is that economic theory reasons deductively, from axioms . . . .

. . .By reasoning deductively from axioms economics confuses the normative with the descriptive. Theory stipulates, *a priori,* that perfect competition is both a description of the optimal world and a useful approximation of the actual world. When it is pointed out that high unemployment, or segmented labor markets, or oligopolistic corporations, or national economic-development strategies, or big public sectors, or regulated banks, or protected agricultural markets—or the logic of social organizations in general—suggest a world very far from the textbook picture of perfect competition and self-correcting markets, the economist has essentially two choices. He can turn pamphleteer, as so many economists do, and insist that the world would be a better place if it did conform to the textbooks. (As the Cambridge University economist John Eatwell has said: "If the world is not like the model, so much the worse for the world.") Or he can scrap the formalism, get out of the office, and study the profane world of real institutions. There are some economists of this sort, but they are mostly of an older generation—men like Herbert Simon, of Carnegie-Mellon University, and Albert Hirschman, of the Institute for Advanced Study, who challenge the psychological assumptions of the orthodox model. However, you will find very few under age fifty in tenured chairs at major universities, or in the prestigious economics journals; and you will not find work of this kind in the body of theory taught to aspiring young economists.

The deductive method of practicing economic science creates a professional ethic of studied myopia. Apprentice economists are relieved of the need to learn much about the complexities of human motivation, the messy universe of economic institutions, or the real dynamics of technological change. In economics, deduction drives our empiricism. Those who have real empirical curiosity and insight about the workings of banks, corporations, production technologies, trade unions, economic history, or individual behavior are dismissed as casual empiricists, literary historians, or sociologists, and marginalized within the profession. In their places departments of economics are graduating a generation of idiots savants, brilliant at esoteric mathematics yet innocent of actual economic life.

In a spoof entitled "Life Among the Econ," published in 1973 in Western Economic Journal, the Swedish-born economist Axel Leijonhufvud proposed that the methods of the economics professions might best be understood anthropologically, as the rituals of a primitive tribe.

> Among the Econ. . .status is tied to the manufacture of certain types of implements, called "models". . .most of these "models" seem to be of little or no practical use, [which] probably accounts for the backwardness and abject cultural poverty of the tribe. . . . The priestly caste (the Math-Econ) [ranks higher] than either Micro or Macro . . . . The rise of the Math-Econ seems to be associated with the previously noted trend among all the Econ towards more ornate, ceremonial models . . . .

. . .It matters that economists are trained to view the world the way they do. Lately, almost all public policy questions have been defined as economic ones. The experts with the professional authority to pronounce on such questions are, of course, economists. Civic issues of public values, political power, the nature of democratic society, are mistaken for narrowly technical issues, with conclusions ordained and alternative solutions foreclosed.

An equally serious consequence of the professional obsession with model making is that the most pressing *economic* questions lie outside the frame of reference. The issues that standard economics can't explain and doesn't address are of far greater moment than the ones "solved" by the formal proofs. A non-economist reading the economics journals is struck mainly by what is left out. The literature of standard economics recalls Tom Stoppard's *Rosencrantz and Guildenstern Are Dead*. Minor subjects have usurped center stage, while the truly important ones remain tantalizingly out of view.

One could imagine a wholly different sort of economics, which empirically investigated when the assumptions of the standard model apply and when they don't. How do technological and institutional changes influence economic growth? What institutional circumstances merit public intervention? What are the links between economic performance and cultural and political value? When is the famous trade-off between equality and efficiency a genuine imperative, and when is it only a rationalization for privilege? Which markets behave like the textbook market? Under what cultural, technological, and institutional circumstances does interference with the market allocation of capital investment produce dynamic gains? What really accounts for the wide disparities in the degree of technological success achieved by different nations in different historical eras? What practical costs and what benefits to dynamic efficiency do different forms of redistribution incur? What really motivates human behavior, and under what circumstances are impulses cooperative and altruistic as well as self-interested?

Adam Smith wrote, in a famous passage celebrating economic egoism, "It is not from the benevolence of the butcher, the brewer, or the baker that we expect our dinner, but from their regard to their own interest." But are there any circumstances under which cooperation is more "efficient" than the pursuit of self interest? If so, what are they? Why are some labor unions in some nations friendly to productivity and technological progress and wage restraint, while others are obstructionist and self-seeking? Which sorts of deregulation lose in stability what they gain in innovation? Maybe it is appropriate to deregulate airline routes but not aircraft safety. Maybe trusting market discipline to deal with bank failures produces a loss to institutional stability that outweighs the gain to allocational efficiency. These subjects are seldom treated in the economics journals, except at impenetrable levels of abstraction and assumption . . . .

. . .A generation ago economics was far more committed to observation, disputation, and its own intellectual history. The lions of the mid-century had lived through depression and war, had watched real economic institutions totter, had worked in economic agencies, and had appreciated the power of wartime statecraft. Most of them are now gone. In the 1920s and 1930s and eclectic school of economics known as institutionalism flourished. Inspired by Veblen, institutionalists were committed to the empirical study of corpora- tions, banks, labor unions, an so on as concrete social organizations. Ironically, they were displaced partly by econometricians, who promised a more rigorous empiricism. Institutionalists still exist, they have their own professional guild, the Association for Evolutionary Economics (after a word favored by Veblen, who argued that economic institutions evolve). They still have strongholds in economics departments at state universities in the South and Midwest. But few institutionalists are to be found at the fifteen or twenty elite graduate schools that turn out tenured faculty for one another. The very term has become a pejorative.

The other two main schools that today compete with neoclassicism— neo-Marxism and post-Keynesianism—are intellectually lively but effectively isolated from mainstream economics . . . .

. . .The third dissenting school, the post-Keynesian, is the weakest and apparently the most despised of them all. The post Keynesians want to rescue Keynes from the neoclassical synthesis—which Keynes disciple Joan Robinson has called "bastard Keynesianism." They, along with the institutionalists, insist that large corporations and labor unions are major facts of economic life and that economic intercourse cannot be modeled as mechanical transactions in equilibrium. But neoclassical economists are mostly contemptuous of the post-Keynesians . . . .

. . .In the interstices between the schools are a handful of brilliant eclectics—an older generation, including Galbraith, Leontief, Albert Hirschman, and Herbert Simon, and a few people in their thirties and forties like Lester Thurow, James Medoff, Richard Freeman, George Akerlof, of Berkeley, and Michael Piore, of MIT. Piore's recent book, *The Second Industrial Divide*, which he wrote with the political economist Charles Sabel, painstakingly re-examines technological innovation throughout history and concludes that the present macroeconomic woes are due in part to unsettling changes in the organization of corporations, financial systems, technologies, and consumer markets. This sort of insight depends on the concrete study of institutions.

The difficulty is that eclecticism, no matter how brilliant, doesn't add up to a contending school. The great idiosyncratic economists of the last generation, like Galbraith and Simon, disseminated their work to a broad audience, but left few spores within the profession. In recent years the fields of inquiry that deal with applied economics have been driven from the standard curriculum. Thirty years ago an economics student took courses in money and banking, labor economics, economic history, and perhaps industrial organization, economic development, and international trade. All of these courses grounded the grand theory in a sense of how actual economic institutions operate. Today these are considered remnants of an older, not quite scientific tradition. A student looking for the fast track to a tenure position at a prestigious university tends to avoid them . . . .

. . .The economic historian Robert Heilbroner titled his book on the history of economic thought *The Worldly Philosophers*. As a description of the moral philosophers of the Enlightenment who abandoned metaphysics for the investigation of commercial life, the phrase fits perfectly. As a description of today's economists, however, Heilbroner's title would be a misnomer. Economists have become the least worldly of all scientists . . . .

. . .Virtually all of the heretics I have talked to agree that if they were young assistant professors attempting to practice their brand of economics today, they would not get tenure . . . . [N]o dissenting paradigm seems able to gain a foothold within economics. Thus the economic orthodoxy is reinforced by ideology, by the sociology of the profession, by the politics of who gets published or promoted and whose research gets funded. In the economics profession the free marketplace of ideas is one more market that doesn't work like the model.

Our Paralyzing Individualism

George C. Lodge

The polar paradigms of individualism and communitarianism. . .provide a way to consider the structures of government: where power lies, how it is used, and who uses it. The communitarian state, with its planning and vision-setting functions, tends to be relatively powerful, coherent, and centralized. The executive bureaucracy is more important than the legislature and attracts to its ranks society's best and brightest. It therefore commands the respect of business and the general public.

Communitarian systems are often characterized by strong political parties, with one party or a coalition of parties retaining control over a long period of time. Some examples are the various party coalitions that have governed Germany since World War II, the Liberal Democratic Party in Japan, and the Social Democratic Party in Sweden. More authoritarian variations of one-party rule have prevailed in South Korea, Taiwan, and Singapore. Communitarian government's structure is thus consistent with its overriding role: to establish a consensus behind a coherent strategy for the nation's development. . . .

In contrast, the individualistic state sees government's role as essentially limited. In the United States, for example, power is widely dispersed, checked and balanced. . . . Federalist Paper No. 51 spoke in the 1780s, for example, of the need to design controls over the power of government so "that the private interests of every individual may be a sentinel over the public rights." Samuel Huntington echoed that idea when he wrote,

---

George C. Lodge, *Professor of Business Administration at the Harvard Business School, is the author of* The American Disease *(1984) and co-editor of* Ideology and National Competitiveness *(1987). He is a member of the Advisory Board of the Economic Strategy Institute. Reprinted by permission of Harvard Business School Press, Boston from George C. Lodge,* Perestroika for America: Restructuring Business-Government Relations for World Competitiveness. *Copyright* © *1990 by the President and Fellows of Harvard College; all rights reserved.*

"Because of the inherently anti-government character of the American Creed, government that is strong is illegitimate, government that is legitimate is weak. . . ."

Communitarian governmental structures evolved from those of feudalism, in which the stratification of the "estates" and the obligations of both rulers and ruled were clear and accepted. The governmental structures associated with individualism either emerged from the feudal forms and were affected by them, or grew fresh in soil virtually uncontaminated by old forms. Since the United States stands alone in the world in its degree of independence from feudal traditions, individualism and its governmental structures exist in their purest form. That is not to say that U.S. practice never departs from its ideal; indeed, it does so frequently, especially in times of crisis. During the Great Depression, for example, the National Recovery Administration sought to convert the structures of government into something capable of industrial planning in cooperation with big business. But the quick and ignominious death of the NRA at the hands of the Supreme Court serves for many as a reminder that such ventures are not for America.

American departures from the individualistic mode are regarded as suspect, illegitimate, and likely to fail. These departures create a "legitimacy gap" between ideology and practice. . . . As a result, authority falters and the community faces two choices: pull the wayward institutions back into line and practice what you preach, or install a new ideology and preach what you practice. However it is resolved, a legitimacy gap causes ambivalence on the part of decision makers in government and business, as exemplified by the uncertain efforts of the U.S. government in 1987 and 1988 to encourage national competitiveness in certain key industries, especially semiconductors, superconductivity, and biotechnology.

Harvard professor Steven Kelman in his study of government regulation in Sweden and the United States elaborates on the distinction between these governmental structures:

Out of the Swedish tradition grew dominant values encouraging individuals to defer to the wishes of government and encouraging leaders to be self-confident in charting a course of how people should behave. Out of the American tradition grew values encouraging self-assertion and refusal to bow before the desires of rulers.

It was this difference that made agreement between government and business about such issues as health and safety regulation much more difficult in the

United States than in Sweden. Kelman explains further:

> Contemporary Swedish society, like many European societies, emerged
> from a history of brutally sharp distinction between ruler and ruled.
> The Swedish word *overhet* is a generic term for those on top of society,
> seen as an undifferentiated presence by those at the bottom . . . . It
> translates literally as "those over us" and consisted of those—kings,
> aristocrats, bishops—born to rule over others.

Even with Sweden's contemporary democratic structures, elements of
overhet can still be seen in the deference that citizens show to government.
This is not unlike the respect the Japanese have for the young "summa cum
laudes" who run the Ministry of Finance or the Ministry of International
Trade and Industry. In Japan and Sweden, the words of the Swedish poet that
mark the entrance to Uppsala University ring a responsive chord: "To think
freely is great, to think correctly is greater." Such expressions are not found
in America, where the supremacy of individual rights over the rights of the
state is woven deep into the fabric of national thinking.

In such places as Japan and Sweden, a strong government is associated
with virtue. In the United States, as Huntington points out, it is at least a
cause for suspicion if not an outright sign of evil. Other countries are arrayed
between these extremes. It cannot simply be said that communitarian governments are strong and individualistic ones weak, for such is clearly not the
case. For example, no one would attribute strength to Lebanon's communitarian government. . . .

We might say that a government is strong if it can (1) create a
consensus in society sufficient to allow government to design and implement
goals for the community as a whole; (2) change the behavior of important
groups, such as business, to further its policies; and (3) change the structure
of society—the nature of ownership, the degree of industrial concentration, and
the importance of particular sectors—in pursuit of its goals.

Planning impediments for the United States government start with a
fundamental principle: The responsibility for linking domestic economic
management with the international economy is not an appropriate role for
government. When such linking does occur, it does so with little, if any,
coordination among a disparate group of departments and agencies, including,
for example, the Departments of Commerce, State, Defense, Treasury, and
Agriculture; the White House Office of the United States Trade Representative, Office of Management and Budget, and Council of Economic Advisers;

and a welter of congressional committees and subcommittees. The link is considered to evolve automatically from the interplay of market forces in a world of free trade and free enterprise; that is to say, it is taken for granted. It is significant that in the three years during which the 1986 tax bill was being framed, the inner circles of government never discussed its effect on national competitiveness in the world.

During the 1980s, inaction and budgetary pressures in Washington forced increased planning activity at the state level. For example, in Michigan, which was hard hit by foreign competition, state government, working with business and labor, developed strategies for competitiveness. Interest groups also went to the states seeking action on a variety of fronts, including boycotts of companies doing business in South Africa, plant closings and antilayoff res-trictions, pay based on "comparable worth," and safety and health regulations.

In government, as in business, strategy often dictates structure. But the reverse may also occur. The structure—personified, for example, by the young men of Japan's MOF [Ministry of Finance] or by the traditional economists of the President's Council of Economic Advisers—conditions and constrains strategy. Furthermore, in both business and government, different structures may serve the same strategy, some more efficiently than others. The governments of the United States and Japan promote exports, but they employ quite different structures and tools to do so.

Finally, there is the question of what happens when old structures meet new challenges. Japan's emphasis on employment security, respect for elders, and consensualism through bottom-up decision making may have worked in periods of rapid growth. But will it serve as well the needs of contraction, conversion, and restructuring that the nation faces now? "There is no harmonious way to move 3,000 jobs offshore," wrote Bernard Wysocki, Jr., Tokyo bureau chief of *The Wall Street Journal*. Furthermore, Wysocki notes, pushing decision-making control down to the level of assistant section chiefs may have given government offices an atmosphere of collegiality, "but it also has produced ministries that are highly turf-conscious, inbred, and inflexible . . . ." When a nation confronts tough choices about which there is no consensus—taxes, land prices, and so forth—does it not need strong, tough, quick leadership? In this regard, Wysocki likens Japan's prime minister to the king in a game of chess. "He is surely important, but his own power is limited. He can only move one space at a time. To succeed, he has to persuade other, more powerful and agile players to move on his behalf."

What Is the Use of Economic Planning?

Saburo Okita

Postwar Japan has thus far formulated three formal, long-term economic plans; first was the Five-Year Plan for Economic Independence worked out at the end of 1955, second the New Long-Term Economic Plan formulated at the end of 1957, and third the National Income-Doubling Plan mapped out at the end of 1960. At issue now is the so-called "after-care" of the income-doubling plan, and the Economic Deliberation Council is studying the problematical points by comparing the achievements with the plan.

Economic planning now constitutes one of the Government functions, but the general public does not appear to understand well the purpose of economic planning and its use in actual work. For instance, an argument is made now and then that economic planning is unnatural for Japan where a free economy is adopted. Also often heard is the criticism that the Government, while formulating an economic plan, does not take a firm attitude concerning its implementation.

In answer to such criticisms I must first point out the meaning of economic planning under a free economy and say that those criticisms confuse a planned economy with economic planning. A planned economy, as opposed to a free economy, is typified by the Soviet Union's socialist planned economy and is the structure under which the national economy and every social phase is run along Government plans. The free economy, or the so-called market economy, on the other hand, is the structure under which individual enterprisers determine their production and sales activities in consultation with prices and the market situation. In prewar years economic planning was considered a monopoly of a planned economy, but after the War many countries have come to conduct economic planning, while adopting the free economy system. It is

---

Saburo Okita, *former Foreign Minister of Japan, is Chairman of the Institute for Domestic and International Policy Studies. He is a member of the Advisory Board of the Economic Strategy Institute. Excerpted from* Jitsugyo No Nippon, *June 15, 1963.*

because the need for economic planning in a broad sense has come to be felt in view of various evils of laissez faire economy.

Postwar economic planning sets a large economic framework on the one hand but on the other it allows a free hand, unlike a planned economy, to individual enterprises, individual industries and individual economic activities from the standpoint of withholding the Government's bureaucratic control and intervention as much as possible. In short, how to combine the merits of free economy and the need for planning is the problem of contemporary countries.

Many estimates

By way of answering the second criticism that the Government does not take a firm attitude concerning the implementation of an economic plan, I must make it clear that economic planning under a free economy is largely estimation in character. Inasmuch as economic activities are mostly left to individual enterprises, only a limited range of individual, economic phenomena is left to Government management.

This problem must be considered by dividing the economy into the civilian and governmental-public fields. In the civilian field, where economic functions are automatically adjusted, as a rule, by the mechanism of prices and the market, Government plans are mostly outlooks or estimates for the future. Planning in this field, if any, is done by individual businessmen who possess the means of implementing plans. The Government may influence the framework of civilian economic activities and guide them as to the direction of their future development, but it does not possess the means of implementing individual plans in this field.

The mechanism of prices and markets wields no power on road construction, city planning and other governmental and public projects. It is the central and local governments that formulate plans in this field. Public projects have hitherto been liable to be planned, as the occasion demands, in the framework of each fiscal year's budget, but such a practice is haphazard and must be held responsible for the inconsistency and confusion seen in Tokyo. . . . The basic stand taken in working out the income-doubling program was that economic planning should give estimates and guidance to the civilian economic field and consistency to governmental and public projects.

Planning gives a concrete direction to policies

If economic planning is largely estimation in character as mentioned before, figures given for future economic activities are largely estimates. Yet, they are not pure estimation but show targets at the same time especially in governmental and public projects. Figures given by an economic plan on the gross national product, living standards and iron and steel production ten years hence are apt to be taken as showing the extent of the governmental guarantee for their materialization. Nevertheless, they are an estimation of one possibility. Their important meaning is that they offer a clue to the measures to be taken now for the estimation and to passing a long-range judgment on the decision to be made now.

Economic planning under free economy is rather aimed at formulating estimation for the economy five or ten years hence and clarifying beforehand the problems which may arise in the future so as to take timely measures than at fixing a target for five or ten years hence and urging efforts or its realization.

Separation of long-range plans from annual plans

There has been a view, as was advanced by Mr. Tatsunosuke Takasaki some years ago when he was the EPA [Economic Planning Agency] Director General, that a five-year plan must be made and projected one year ahead every year. The All-America Planning Association also recommended, in its publication commemorating the tenth anniversary of the Employment Act, that the Government should annually formulate an economic estimate for six years hence and use it as a clue to budget compilation and economic measures. The British Government, too, compiles an economic estimate for the coming four years, prior to budget compilation, although it is withheld from publication, to use it as an intra-governmental datum and for formulating a budget and economic measures. It has hitherto been considered that an economic plan is fundamentally worked out for every five years as illustrated by the Soviet Union's first, second and third five-year plans.

Science and Technology: The False Dichotomy

Erich Bloch

One of the most important changes in recent years has been the rise of the global economy. Increasingly, national markets are being supplanted by new international markets, made possible by advanced transportation, communications, and information technologies.

This global economy is a knowledge-based, skill-based economy. A nation's competitiveness today is determined less by natural resources, access to low-cost labor, and other classical comparative advantages of the past, than by the generation, access, and rapid deployment of new knowledge, as well as by technical insights and their conversion into quality processes and products. Thus comparative advantage today must be measured in terms of new knowledge generation, the access to new knowledge, and the availability of a technically trained workforce to use this knowledge.

This new environment has brought with it increased economic competition. Technological capability has spread rapidly around the globe, and the size of the world's technically trained workforce has grown dramatically. One result is that the United States, enjoying a dominant position in nearly all technologies at the end of World War II, is now challenged on many fronts.

In this new environment, basic scientific research, technology development, and education have become critical sources of economic competitiveness and prosperity. Their funding is no longer simply another public expenditure; it is an investment in the future of the nation.

Coping successfully with virtually every major public issue—defense, health, education, the environment, energy, urban development, international

Erich Bloch, *a Fellow of the Economic Strategy Institute, was Director of the National Science Foundation from 1984 to 1990. Previously he held several senior positions at IBM Corporation and played a key role in developing IBM's revolutionary 360 line of computers.*

relationships, the space program, and economic competitiveness—depends on generating new knowledge and, just as important, on expeditiously exploiting that knowledge.

In recent years, however, serious U.S. weaknesses in the latter field have become apparent. America continues to excel at generating new knowledge—a national comparative advantage whose preservation is imperative. But the nation is lagging at quickly turning that new knowledge into new commercially viable products, and in particular in developing the detailed insights, understandings, and processes that are prerequisite to product design and product manufacturing.

The gap between America's performance in knowledge generation (basic science) and knowledge exploitation (applied science) has been widely noted and exhaustively analyzed. One important contributing factor, however, has been overlooked in the current debate—the assumption too often made by the makers of U.S. science and technology policy that a sharp distinction can and should be drawn between basic research and technology. The conclusion drawn is that a prominent government role is proper in the former but improper in the latter. The public sector, in other words, should promote "pure science," but the private sector should be responsible for picking and creating technology winners from these findings.

Increasingly, however, the dichotomy perceived between basic and applied research is a false one. In many fields, the boundary lines between basic research and technology are shrinking, if not overlapping completely. In these areas, generic technologies at their formative stages are the base for entire industries and industrial sectors. U.S. science and technology policy must begin to take this development into account.

The origins of this dichotomy go back at least to the close of World War II. On July 5, 1945, Dr. Vannevar Bush, then director of the U.S. Office of Scientific Research and Development submitted to President Harry S. Truman his report "Science—The Endless Frontier." The report, commissioned by President Franklin D. Roosevelt, outlined this country's first federal science policy and science machinery. [*See Part IV*]

Bush stated clearly, "Progress in the war against disease depends on the flow of new scientific information. New products, new industries and more jobs require continuous addition to knowledge of the laws of nature, and the application of that knowledge to practical purposes . . . . This essential new knowledge can be obtained only through basic scientific research."

The report stated further that "the impetus can come promptly only from the Government . . . [since] basic research is essentially non-commercial in nature. It will not receive the required attention, if left to industry." Five years later, this report led to the establishment of the National Science Foundation, which for 40 years, together with other research and development (R&D) agencies of the federal government, has kept the United States at the leading edge of basic scientific research.

But what about technology?

In advocating the new role for government, Bush made short shrift of technology support and declared that "Industry will fully rise to the challenge of applying new knowledge to new products. The commercial incentive can be relied upon for that."

His confidence no doubt stemmed in part from instances in which the government for its own reasons—like the war effort and subsequent defense effort—set the course and supported the development of basic technologies. For example, Washington made the initial investments in research technology development and product design, as well as in plant and facilities for semiconductors and computers, sectors that after the war developed into new and important industries for the country and the world. Even television gained immensely from the radar and electronics research undertaken initially for military and defense reasons.

Yet over the postwar decades, the federal government too often treated science and technology as if they were neatly separable worlds of activities. In fact, they are a continuum: "Applied science" or "applied research" (or, as it is often called, "generic technology" or "strategic technology" or "pre-competitive technology") is an important part of this continuum. In much the same way, generic technology development resembles basic science research: It is expensive, diffuses fast to one's competitors, requires a constant two-way interplay with basic science, and in many cases not only serves one company or one industry, but underlies several different industry sectors. In addition, the gestation period for generic technology development is long.

Still if the development of the generic technology base was once a matter for the private sector, why all of a sudden does it need the support of the public sector?

In the first place, as already pointed out, the public sector has been heavily involved in such activity in the past. Support for generic technology by the Defense Department and the National Aeronautics and Space Administration (NASA) gave America world leadership in integrated circuits, advanced computers, aerospace, lasers, nuclear energy, many new materials, and other fields. But two recent developments in particular have undermined this strategy of supporting generic technology.

First, the strategic technologies of the future will be increasingly developed in civilian contexts rather than in military or space programs. Biotechnology, semiconductor manufacturing, robotics, artificial intelligence, advanced imaging technologies, and materials technology are all being developed for and finding earlier applications today in the civilian sector than in the military sector. This is the reverse of the situation that existed prior to about 1980.

Second, the fundamental shift away from U.S.-Soviet military confrontation is likely to reduce R&D budgets available to the military and hamper efforts by military agencies to develop important dual-use technologies.

Further, American industry is facing international competitors that are supported by their governments in fashioning private/public sector partnerships for the development of generic technologies, both in the Pacific Rim countries and lately and increasingly in the European Community. These countries have targeted successfully key sectors of developing industries.

Counting on the private sector alone for prompting new technologies is also complicated today by their increasing cost. In the 1970s, developing a new generation of semiconductor manufacturing technology, at a feature size of about 10 microns, cost approximately $3-5 million. In the 1980s the feature size was down to 1-2 microns, but the cost of developing a new generation of technology had shot up to about $30-50 million. In the 1990s, the feature size reduction will have decreased by another order of magnitude, to about .1-.2 microns. But the cost will rise by another factor of ten, to about $300-500 million.

Investments of this magnitude are beyond the capability of any American semiconductor company. Without government support, they may well be beyond the capability of the entire American semiconductor industry. And the same is true of other important industries.

This cost escalation is aggravated by U.S. companies' continuing loss of market share in these sectors not only abroad but at home. Consequently, the ability of these firms to invest in new and risky technology efforts is further reduced.

Strategic technologies are "pre-competitive" and underlie entire industries. It should always remain the responsibility of individual companies to turn them into products for the competitive marketplace. Strategic technologies are also inherently high risk technologies, and require sustained investment over a long period before they are ready to produce returns. In the past, when the costs were lower, some companies were willing and able to make these investments as a bet on the future. But in most cases this is no longer possible. Today, an industry decision to stay competitive in these technologies depends on partial support by government.

President Bush has acknowledged his administration's determination to support strategic-technology development. He stated in a March 1990 speech to the American Electronics Association that, in addition to other crucial investments in the future, "the administration is committed to working with [industry] in the critical pre-competitive development stage, where basic discoveries are converted into generic technologies."

This commitment is welcome. Action needs to be taken now if we want to stop further slippage in our technology base. Coalitions involving industry, government, and academia should be created to foster a small number of strategically important generic technologies to maintain America's economic strength as well as to assure its leadership in critical technologies into the 21st century.

New funds are not necessary. Federal support for R&D is large enough already. But the funds must be redirected. In particular, at least some government laboratories must be encouraged to support industrial coalitions directed towards creating leadership positions in strategic technologies. As military budgets decline, many government laboratories must find new missions or go out of business. Today, many have no well-defined mission.

Industry must get in on the ground floor and contribute skills and resources to this cooperative effort. In fact, industry should set the strategy and direct day-to-day activities. SEMATECH, the U.S. Semiconductor Manufacturing Technology Consortium set up with public and private funds, provides an example of an imperfect but nonetheless valuable guide to organizing such an effort.

Over the last decade, the United States has lost much of its strategic technology base. If we do not reverse this trend, we will sustain irreversible damage.

The end of World War II was a critical time for the country to establish the science base, strategy, and organizational mechanisms to remain at the leading edge of scientific research. Today, the end of the Cold War should spur the long overdue effort to put in place the technology strategy and implementing mechanisms needed to return America to that leading edge.

Required is a multi-sector effort, involving industry, academia, and the federal and state governments. Required as well is an understanding of the close and mutually supportive relationship between progress in science and progress in technology, plus a clear understanding of where and how U.S. policy must change.

Infrastructure Roadblocks

David Alan Aschauer

A six-car collision on Tampa's two-lane Howard Frankland Bridge—the locals call it the "Frankenstein"—causes a three-hour traffic jam during rush hour. A dam bursts near Toccoa, Georgia, killing thirty-nine residents—mostly children—of a tiny Bible college. A bridge collapses on Interstate 95 in Connecticut, hurling six people into the river some 75 feet below, killing three and injuring several others.

Such accidents and disasters happen almost daily in the United States. They are outward signs of a growing affliction—the decay of our national infrastructure. But not only safety and convenience are affected. There are deeper implications of this national neglect for the health of the U.S. economy. Indeed, as Bill Clinton, Governor of Arkansas, recently wrote, "America is falling apart, literally. Federal budget pressures and changes in the Federal tax law in the 1980s have steepened a decline in public works spending that dates to the 1950s."

This *Letter* looks at recent trends in public works expenditures and relates the fall-off in such spending with the productivity slowdown that became evident in the United States around 1970. The decline in public capital spending—on dams, highways, sewers, mass transit, etc.—relative to employment and private investment in plant and machinery forces private business to absorb higher costs, and thereby lowers productivity. And lower productivity, sooner or later, means a lower standard of living.

A stronger commitment to America's infrastructure by the public sector is necessary for at least two reasons. First, a well-maintained public works system contributes to an expanding, robust economy. Second, directly and indirectly, it contributes to an improved standard of living.

David Alan Aschauer, *a former senior economist at the Federal Reserve Bank in Chicago, is currently Elmer W. Campbell Professor of Economics at Bates College. Excerpted from "Rx for productivity: Build infrastructure,"* Chicago Fed Letter, *September 1988.*

A check-up

On the basis of most external appearances, the economy's health is robust. We are experiencing an expansion of output that is progressing into its sixth year; economists are raising their forecasts for this year's growth rate of gross national product (GNP); we see surging employment and a declining unemployment rate. To be sure, we see some threats of inflation, but not the inflation fever of other periods.

A complete physical examination, however, produces evidence of economic atrophy. The growth of output that is not explained by increases in labor and private capital inputs—generally called "total factor productivity"—has slumped during the last decade and a half. Indeed, the annual growth rate of total factor productivity in the private business economy has plummeted from 1.5% from 1951 to 1960 and 1.8% from 1961 to 1970 to 0.8% in the 1970s and a dismal 0.7% in the first half of the 1980s.

Previous diagnoses

Prior studies of the fall-off in productivity have centered on a relatively small number of potential causes. A surge in aggregate productivity can be expected whenever resources are shifted from less to more productive sectors of the economy. The migration of labor from farm to nonfarm occupations had such an effect, but mostly came to a halt by the mid 1960s. Certain economists, most notably Zvi Griliches of Harvard University, have emphasized a general slowing of expenditures on research and development and a related slowing of technological change.

But the combination of these factors does not go far enough in explaining the productivity decline. The Bureau of Labor Statistics, for example, estimates that these factors probably account for only one-fourth or so of the slower productivity growth in the private economy. Lower rates of capacity utilization also may explain some of the reduction in total factor productivity; after averaging 84.1% during 1951 to 1970, the rate of capacity utilization fell to 79.5% in the period 1971 to 1985. But changes in capacity utilization rates, largely driven by erratic fluctuations in aggregate demand for goods and services and transitory technological shocks, are more likely to explain short-term, rather than long-term movements in productivity.

A new diagnosis

One place to search for a plausible reason for the productivity decline is in the government accounts—how the government gets and spends its money. Many have insisted that the financial status of the public sector—the budget deficit and consequent creation of government bonds—may play an important role in influencing the economy's performance. Specifically, it is argued that high public sector bond issuance forces up real interest rates and drives down the new private investment spending that is essential for fostering economic growth and technological improvement.

I suggest, however, that it is more reasonable to look at the physical aspects of the government budget, at the distribution of government spending across various broad categories.

As it happens, there is a remarkable correlation between the level of total factor productivity and the level of the nonmilitary public capital stock over the last thirty-five years. My empirical results suggest that movements in public capital are capable of explaining a large portion of the longer term movements in productivity in the private sector over the period 1949 to 1985.

Roughly, a one percentage point increase in the level of the net stock of public capital relative to the level of private sector inputs of labor and capital brings forth a one-third of one percentage point (.33) rise in productivity. . . . While productivity growth fell from 2% to 0.8% per year [between 1950 and 1985]—a fall-off of 1.2 percentage points—the growth rate of the net stock of nonmilitary public capital shriveled from 4.1% to a mere 1.6% per annum. Even more strikingly, the growth rate of the public capital stock *relative to* a "combined" unit of private labor and capital went from a strongly positive 2.4% [between 1950 and 1970] to a *negative* 0.6% in the slowdown period [1971-85] .

Multiplying the slump in the growth in public capital by the sensitivity of productivity to public capital growth—the previously mentioned 0.33—shows that fully (3.0) x (.33) = 1.0 percentage point of the total decline in productivity of 1.2 percentage points can be attributed to the neglect of infrastructure. . . .

[T]he tight relationship between public nonmilitary capital and total factor productivity [can be illustrated] by comparing levels of total factor productivity and the stock of public structures and equipment after removing time trends. . . . [T]his relationship holds for the period of rising productivity growth during the 1950s and 1960s as well as for that of falling productivity growth during the last decade and a half. And, as low productivity growth leads a low standard of living by the hand, insufficient investment in the economy's infrastructure will soon force individuals to trim their style of living; Senator Quentin Burdick of North Dakota warns, "We have produced a high standard of living, but we are beginning to see cracks in that high standard, and a less than adequate infrastructure has been identified as the cause."

We would also expect that countries that sustain a high level of public investment relative to output would experience higher productivity growth than countries that do not invest in infrastructure. . . . [From 1973-85] Japan ...invested about 5.1% of output in public facilities and achieved productivity growth of 3.3%; at the other end of the spectrum we find the United States with a low public investment of 0.3% per year and low productivity growth of 0.6% per annum. At the same time, productivity growth in [the industrialized] countries was negatively related to government consumption spending.

While total government outlays relative to GNP have risen from 26% in the late 1950s to 35% in the middle of the 1980s, public nonmilitary capital expenditures have slid precipitously. Dana Huestis, President of Associated General Contractors of America, has stated in Congressional testimony, that "the infrastructure crisis is real. As a nation, we have not been investing enough in our public facilities to either keep up with new growth, or to rebuild and protect what is falling into disrepair."

Thus, a root cause of the decline in the competitiveness of the United States in the international economy may be found in the low rate at which our country has chosen to add to its stock of highways, port facilities, airports, and other facilities which aid in the production and distribution of goods and services. Just as thoughtful athletes would not think of neglecting their health for fear of failing to compete well on the playing field, we as a country should be vitally concerned with the viability of our economic lifelines that enable us to meet the challenge of an increasingly competitive world marketplace.

In the words of Nancy Rutledge, Executive Director of the National Council on Public Works Improvement:

"If we spend too little on public works. . .society loses more than the direct public cost. In the long run, our ability to compete in the international economy will be weakened, and our standard of living will suffer."

Nearly echoing her remarks, Peter Butkus, a public works manager for the State of Washington, has said that "good public works becomes the single most important thing that local governments can provide in the nation's effort to maintain and expand foreign trade and competitiveness."

Prognosis

The chance for a recovery from a physical condition such as a minor hardening of human arteries is usually quite good if it is identified early enough, and the patient adopts a proper counting of calories, a good diet, and a certain amount of exercise. Similarly, given the stability of the relationship between the economy's infrastructure and the productivity of private factors of production, we may be confident that a more balanced distribution of public sector resources, shifting some from consumption and into capital accumulation, will rejuvenate the economy's lifelines.

Raising the level of public investment spending from its current abysmal level of less than one half a percent of GNP to a modest two percent—some 80 to 90 billion dollars per year—would work wonders, quite likely wonders comparable to those of modern medicine in dealing with the human disease.

Regulatory Gridlock

If new technologies are to be commercialized successfully, they must overcome a set of economic, legal and regulatory barriers. These barriers arise from private agreements (such as contracts, licenses and corporate structures); from common law (tort and property concepts enforceable in court); and from public law and regulation. Just as the competitive context for American technology has changed enormously over the past decade, so, too, has the legal environment.

The effect of law and regulation on technological innovation cannot be characterized simply. They affect industries differently and often require amendment in the face of new technology and new markets. Some regulations are intended to encourage new technology—intellectual property rights being the prime example. Other regulations—pharmaceutical, pesticide and chemical registrations, for example—create deliberate barriers to ensure that new products are safe and environmentally sound. Yet even in this context, the government imprimatur can aid market acceptance.

Laws and regulations like these that directly affect technological innovation are only part of the problem. In fact, most laws and regulations are enacted to address a particular social issue that has little to do with technology. Although, in the aggregate, the impact of these laws and regulations on technology is enormous, it is almost entirely unmanaged—typically unforeseen by lawmakers, ill-considered by enforcement officials and often unpredictable.

Clearly, the legal and regulatory environment could be better planned and controlled. With foresight, laws and regulations could be designed to encourage technological innovation—or at least minimize negative impacts. This is not done, however, for several reasons: legislative ignorance of the issue; inadequate analytical resources to study the issue; an adversarial legal process that impedes informal discussion; and the absence of a forum where industrial concerns can be aired. All of these deficiencies must be addressed

Excerpted with permission from Picking Up the Pace: The Commercial Challenge to American Innovation *(Washington, D.C.: The Council on Competitiveness, 1990).*

in reformulating national technology policy.

The growth of government regulation

Federal regulation of industry today extends throughout the economy. The American penchant for making rules to guide the market, coupled with a reluctance to intervene in other ways, has caused the United States to be characterized as a "regulatory state." Other countries, notably Japan, take a different approach in which the state has taken on a "development" role, intervening more frequently to promote, rather than regulate, economic development.

Indeed, a different approach was taken in America in earlier eras. Throughout the pre-Revolutionary period, for instance, the colonies saw themselves as promoters of economic growth. During the first hundred years of nationhood, the federal government dedicated itself largely to infrastructure development. During this era, the nation emerged as an exporter. The first regulatory agency, the Interstate Commerce Commission, was not established until 1887. Since then, laws and regulations have accumulated in waves: antitrust and trade laws at the turn of the century; labor and securities regulations in the 1930s; environmental and consumer-protection regulations throughout the 1970s. In recent years, the nation has imported massive amounts of goods and services and run up large trade deficits. It is important to shift the focus of national policy back toward facilitating exports.

The wave of consumer-protection legislation in the 1970s is perhaps the most problematic from the point of view of technological innovation. New and radically reformulated regulatory mandates arose: air pollution, water pollution, chemical registration, strengthened pesticide and pharmaceutical controls, equal employment opportunity, consumer financial protection, export controls, advertising limitations, and occupational safety and health. Ironically, this new wave of regulation was being enacted just as established regulatory regimes—such as trucking, natural gas and airlines—were being dismantled. The new regulations differed from the old not only in terms of their focus—consumer and environmental protection—but also in that their mandates typically were applied irrespective of industry boundaries. As a result, there was no way for regulators to consider the cumulative impact or to coordinate across regulatory regimes.

Developments in private legal practice intensified the regulatory changes ushered in during the 1970s. In some instances—environmental impact statements and civil rights, for example—legislative mandates opened the door to private civil actions that supplemented government enforcement. Elsewhere, the courts created major doctrines that enlarged consumers' and workers' rights and their ability to bring suit. An explosion of litigation, which has continued largely unabated through the 1980s, is most visible in the area of product liability. A doctrinal movement away from fault-based torts to compensation in the absence of fault was accompanied by procedural innovations that allowed consumers to join in large-scale tort actions. Although product-liability reform has generated extensive discussion at the national level, by and large it has remained within the ambit of state law, and, thus, is highly variable across jurisdictions.

The regulatory process

Dramatic changes in administrative law and in the structure of private-public relationships also arose during the 1960s and 1970s. As a result, the American regulatory process has become more adversarial, political, legalistic and highly pluralistic. In part, these developments were fashioned by the courts, which transformed the Administrative Procedure Act into a powerful tool for challenging government action and ensuring public debate of regulatory decisions. Congress also chose to open government to the public through actions such as the Freedom of Information Act. This pluralism, while desirable, often has also caused uncertainty in the direction of public policy and has hampered the implementation of new policies and programs.

Along the way, the regulatory decision process itself has become a subject of controversy. Since the Nixon Administration, each President has attempted changes, but only in the first four years of the Reagan Administration did "regulatory reform" become well-institutionalized. By and large, reform has not altered legislative mandates, nor has it eliminated many existing regulations. Instead, it has focused on how regulatory decisions are made, as expressed through four principal actions: paperwork reduction, as mandated by the 1980 Paperwork Reduction Act; economic impact analysis of major regulations, as mandated by Executive Order 12291; the establishment of a regulatory planning process, as mandated by Executive Order 12498; and executive oversight of the regulatory process through the Office of Management and Budget. These initiatives in regulatory reform have primarily addressed economic regulations, with very little attention being given to social regulations in areas such as health, safety and the environment.

While valuable, these policies and procedures generally do not address issues pertaining to commercial technology. In a few specific instances, notably antitrust reform through the National Cooperative and Research Act of 1984, the promotion of new technology in industry was moved to center stage, but for the most part regulatory reform only considers technology within the generalized rubric of "economic impact." The indirect impacts of social regulations on technology development are significant in many industrial sectors and these regulations need review and streamlining. Nor does the reform process effectively attack institutional and organizational difficulties. For example, there is currently no neutral forum where industry can have its concerns about regulation and technology aired and discussed. Similarly, the ability to consider and coordinate the impact of regulatory requirements across different agencies and statutory mandates is inadequate. And few alternatives to adversarial regulatory procedures have been explored seriously.

Impacts on commercial technology

Laws and regulations have a pervasive impact on the process by which technology is introduced to the commercial marketplace. On the most micro-level, their impact is felt as products and the processes are "engineered" to cope with applicable legal specifications. In the aggregate, they strongly shape the overall climate for technological innovation. The sheer breadth and variety of legal requirements make a full discussion here impractical, nor can simple conclusions be drawn. Nevertheless, a number of areas, discussed below, stand out as particularly important to the business community today.

Intellectual property rights are widely recognized as essential to technological innovation. Appreciation of this relationship has led to recent decisions strengthening these rights: the Supreme Court and Patent Office have upheld the patentability of life forms, patent-term restoration for pharmaceuticals and the right of government contractors to claim title to inventions.

At the same time, however, some industries face uncertainty about the extent of legal rights (for example, in the area of computer software). In the context of government regulation, it is not clear that officials adequately protect trade secrets from disclosure to the public or competitors under the Freedom of Information Act. Perhaps the most pressing problems are in international markets where intellectual property "piracy" is common. The ability of foreign companies to legally "infringe" on U.S. process patents abroad has been a subject of legislative concern, and provisions to address this problem are included in the recently passed omnibus trade bill.

Direct restrictions on research are occasionally imposed by funding and regulatory agencies. Notably, genetic engineering experiments are subject to guidelines from the National Institutes of Health as a condition of funding, as well as regulations from the Environmental Protection Agency, the Department Agriculture and other agencies. Similarly, new drug testing is subject to Food and Drug Administration controls on experimentation.

Pre-market and pre-manufacturing approval for new products moves government regulation beyond research into direct control of innovation. This occurs for pharmaceuticals, pesticides, food additives and industrial chemicals. The government's power to halt the marketing of a new technology, in turn, increased testing costs and delays. Although the need for these regulator regimes is hard to question, there is also a need to strike a better balance between legitimate public health goals and the competitive position of the firms that produce new technology. Few legislative mandates have followed the lead of the Toxic Substances Control Act in this regard, which causes regulators to avoid "undue" adverse effects on innovation. Even the best legislative intent, however, can be frustrated by staff shortages in the regulatory agencies, an area of special concern today.

Restrictions on commercial transfers of technology occur mostly in the context of international sales, where concern for national security has led to a comprehensive system of export licenses under the Export Administration Act. Controversy here centers on the need for regulation, but on the details of implementation. This issue was addressed most recently in the omnibus trade bill when Congress attempted to better define strategic technologies subject to strict control and to streamline the administrative process.

Government standards also establish performance criteria for products and processes in commercial use—air pollution, water pollution, waste disposal, product safety and occupational safety and health are the main examples. These standards influence technology in diverse ways. For example, because new sources typically are treated more strictly than old ones, some bias against modernization may arise. On the other hand, the regulations that mandate use of "best available technology" encourage diffusion of new techniques to lagging firms. Because environmental and safety standards have such significant economic impact, their costs and benefits are carefully weighed in rulemaking. Nevertheless, the analysis typically pays insufficient attention to the affect on commercial technology. In addition, because the rulemaking process is so lengthy, subsequent changes to adapt to new technical developments are made with difficulty. Greater use of informal consultation or negotiating strategies between industry and regulators may be useful in remedying these problems.

State product-liability laws also significantly influence the development of technology. Here, the laws are problematic because they cut two ways. On the one hand, high insurance and liability risks now associated with untried products deter the introduction of new technology. On the other hand, court awards made against old, unsafe products make it imperative to introduce improvements or substitutes. Because liability is imposed *ex post facto*, and is based on ever-evolving precedents, the law is also highly uncertain. Reform efforts therefore have focused on means of creating a more predictable legal environment. For the most part, these actions have occurred at the state level; Congress has been reluctant to enter this traditional area of state jurisdiction.

Evaluating the impact of regulation

The precise impact that the legal and regulatory environment has on technology is extremely difficult to assess. Analysis is hampered by methodological problems, lack of appropriate data and disagreement about evaluation. Perhaps the most troublesome issue is that the analysis can only be done in the particular: each regulation is different; each industry's technology is different; and each company will have different responses.

While the impact of regulation is specific to industries and companies, regulatory decisionmaking is oriented toward broad problems that span industries. Discontinuity and controversies emerge as regulatory and legal mandates are applied without a unified perspective. Nowhere has this been more evident than in the biotechnology industry.

Biotechnology research has long been supported by the National Institutes of Health and the Department of Agriculture, both of which have been thrust into a regulatory role. In addition, the Environmental Protection Agency (under both pesticide and toxic substances authority), the Food and Drug Administration and the Occupational Safety and Health Administration all exercise regulatory control over certain aspects of biotechnology. Environmental impact litigation has cast the judiciary as a major player as well.

At least two fundamental problems have arisen in this regulatory scenario. First, the overlap among the regulatory agencies, their many scientific advisory committees, Congress and the courts has created a highly inefficient, often confusing and conflicting system. These difficulties have not been addressed adequately by attempts at coordination at higher levels (for example, the Biotechnology Science Coordinating Committee). Second, the current institutional structure lacks a forum for overall consideration of the balance that needs to be struck among the competitive position of this industry, the development of its technology, and public health and safety.

Reforming the legal and regulatory system

The regulatory and legal apparatus represents the accumulation of many years of federal activity. Throughout it s history, America was responding to diverse sets of pressing social issues, as has been discussed earlier. By and large, however, today's laws and regulations were enacted during a period when the United States was more insulated from the international economy, and the competitiveness of American industry was a matter of little concern. The changed competitive circumstances now demand reforms in the regulations and laws to harmonize their legitimate objectives with a new national economic agenda.

Regulatory and legal reform should be directed toward four broad goals. First, changes need to be made in obsolete legal structures. Inadequate protection against international intellectual property piracy and tax provisions that discriminate against domestic R&D investments are priority issues. Second, more consideration needs to be given to the potential negative impact of certain regulatory measures. Restrictions on international transfers of technology and slow or overly strict new product-approval procedures (for example, in pharmaceuticals) may present the most pressing problems of this nature. Third, the promotion of technology must become an integral element in regulatory strategies. Regulators must consider explicitly the impacts of their actions on the development of new technology, and, to the extent possible, craft regulations that encourage technological innovation. All legal and regulatory regimes need to reflect this orientation. Fourth, better mechanisms of coordination, analysis of industry impacts and consideration of the technological dimension of law and regulation must be developed.

These goals can be accomplished through various legislative, administrative and private sector initiatives. Specific amendments to the legal and regulatory systems need to be considered along with enabling statutes on a general "technology mission." The novel decision-making criterion in the Toxic Substances Control Act—to minimize undue impacts on innovation—may provide a model.

Inside Executive Branch agencies, analyses of the impacts of regulation on technology must become more important. Regulatory strategies that promote innovation in industry must be considered. These objectives could be added to the existing analytical requirements contained in Executive Order 12291 or they could become a separate, complementary analytical effort.

New institutional mechanisms may be necessary to build a technology focus into law and regulation. It also may be desirable to change the skill mix and orientation within the federal regulatory apparatus, which is currently dominated by lawyers and economists. More technically trained individuals are needed, perhaps drawn from industry on a temporary basis. Last, coordination of regulation needs to be made a high-level, high-priority concern.

During the 1980s, the federal government has initiated a number of promising pro-technology initiatives. All too often, however, these policies were piecemeal, *ad hoc* and inconsistent. In some cases, promising new laws were enacted, but never funded. In other cases, a benefit bestowed by one Congress—the R&D tax credit, for instance—was denied by the next.

The Tax and Finance Connection

The causes of the inability of American manufacturing industry to respond to the challenge of Japan and other new competitors can be traced to numerous factors. But high on the list was an exceptionally high cost of capital. . . .

A manufacturing company finances the larger part of its investment by means of internal and external equity sources. On the debt side, bank loans and commercial paper are routinely used to finance inventories and other working capital needs; and bonds can be sold in limited quantities. But access to debt is relatively limited, as the financial community insists on preservation of strong balance sheets which are largely defined in terms of relatively low debt-to-equity ratios. Thus, even though debt-equity rations rose in recent decades, debt represented only about one-third of the balance sheet of the typical large capital-intensive manufacturing company at the end of the period.

Other sectors of the economy are able to make greater use of debt. Residential and commercial construction are largely financed by mortgages, with equity representing a relatively small percentage. The electric utility industry, which uses immense amounts of capital, shows debt representing nearly 60% of its balance sheet.

Equity capital is expensive. The return that has to be paid on it is not deductible in calculating corporate income taxes, doubling the effective cost compared to debt financing. Further, equity financing, particularly the issue of new stock, dilutes existing ownership by surrendering to the new providers of capital a share of the permanent ownership of the business. Thus, the typical cost of equity capital is more than twice as high as the cost of debt capital.

Why is manufacturing so limited in its use of debt? There are two

Excerpted with permission from The DRI Report on U.S. Manufacturing Industries, *prepared by Otto Eckstein, Christopher Caton, Roger Brinner and Peter Duprey, in Collaboration With the Staff of the U.S. Economic Service of Data Resources, Inc. (Lexington, Mass.: McGraw Hill, 1984).*

primary reasons. First, because of the continued prevalence of the business cycle and the vulnerability of the demand for manufactured good, earnings of manufacturers are relatively unstable. Consequently, if debt financing were the principal source of capital, many companies would be making large losses in recession times because of their leveraged balance sheets, and some of them would be forced into bankruptcy. Thus, because of the lender's risk on debt capital in an unstable economy, it is necessary to hold down the share of debt in total financing.

Second, the tax laws are less favorable to debt financing in manufacturing. Many provisions of the tax code push in that direction. Despite tax provisions that lower average effective rates, many manufacturing companies pay corporate income tax at the margin in the general range of the statutory tax rates. Financial institutions, on the other hand, are able to reduce their corporate taxes to very low figures, giving them an advantage in attracting capital. Further, tax shelters provide cheap equity capital for the financing of commercial and residential construction, and put a premium on leveraging that equity capital with the heavy use of debt to make large tax loss writeoffs possible. These differences in the cost of capital help create differences in profitability.

Utilities are also able to use more debt capital than manufacturing. Their earnings are less volatile and their prices are set on a cost-plus basis by regulation. Because they provide services that are relatively essential in the short run, their volume is less variable over the business cycle. . . . As a result, utilities are able to obtain 50% to 60% of their capital from debt sources.

The Japanese economy suffers less from these disparities. One of the elements of her strategy of industrialization has been the use of cheap debt capital to finance large-scale manufacturing investment. The close relationships between the Bank of Japan, the commercial banks and the large industrial corporations operating under the friendly eye of the government make possible a preponderant use of debt, even in manufacturing. While high historical growth may have reduced the risk of such debt financing, Japan' industries also suffer from the business cycle and from earnings swings. It is the close relationships among the public and private and financial and nonfinancial sectors which allow Japanese manufacturing to make much heavier use of debt than is done in the U.S. Indeed, in recent years, Japanese financing has moved toward the American pattern. But in the period of particularly high manufacturing investment, heavy use of debt financing was a key supporting element.

The Japanese government has understood the important role of a low cost of capital to a successful industrialization process. In the last four years, the cost of capital in the United States was boosted by a monetary policy designed to bring an end to double-digit inflation. Japan also pursued a vigorous policy of disinflation but avoided the use of high interest rates, limiting the use of credit by more quantitative guidance, whereas the United States relied almost entirely on the price mechanism of record interest rates. A recent study by Hatsopoulos[1] analyzes the cost of industrial capital in the United States and in Japan. The study calculates the typical composite rental price of capital, using the actual cost of debt and equity capital as the two financing sources. . . . [T]he after-tax cost of industrial capital for fixed investment in Japan was 7.8% in 1980 whereas in the United States it was 20.8%.

One of the most common observations of critics of U.S. business decisions is their myopic character. . . . Japanese business, on the other hand, is credited with greater farsightedness, including willingness to build new basic capacity and create worldwide marketing and distribution systems. The typical American corporation must use high "hurdle" rates in judging investment proposals, given the high composite cost of capital that it pays. While internally generated funds may appear to be very cheap to management, they become, in effect, very expensive when their supply falls far short of the investment opportunities open to the firm. In the typical capital budgeting process, projects compete for the scarce funds, and the high hurdle rate is one mechanical rule which reflects the high opportunity costs. If the firm has to raise external capital, it faces the constraints on long-term debt financing or must pay the very high effective returns on new stock issues. In summary, the difference in the cost of industrial capital between Japan and the United States can explain much of the difference in the levels of industrial investment. It also affects the degree of farsightedness or myopia which governs investment strategies in the two countries.

Comparisons with European countries produce intermediate results. The use of debt is greater in Germany and France than in the U.S., though not as high as in Japan. One reason for their greater willingness to use debt is the lesser role of stockholders and of stock markets. Lenders of debt, particularly banks, play a larger role than in the United States, and so there is less emphasis on steady earnings-per-share growth on common stocks.

The special problem of underdepreciation

The high cost of capital in U.S. manufacturing industry is also partly attributable to the depreciation provisions of postwar tax laws. While there were liberalizations of depreciation allowances, in 1954, 1962, and 1971, these changes were insufficient to keep pace with the accelerating consumption of capital and the increasing inflation. Economic lives were shortened and the depreciation paths were made more generous, but the basic principle of depreciation remained the writing down of historical cost. As inflation worsened, the gap between the funds needed to replace capital and the depreciation allowances generated by historical cost writeoffs widened. Only with the adoption of the Accelerated Cost Recovery System in the Economic Recovery Tax Act of 1981 was the average depreciation allowance raised to an economic level, but differences among industries remain great, with high-tech industries gaining little benefit.

The Bureau of Economic Analysis of the Department of Commerce publishes estimates of the under—or over—depreciation, which is, of course, on a replacement basis. . . . [T]here was underdepreciation until the reforms of 1981, except for some years in the mid-1960s following the depreciation reforms of 1962.

Total taxation of capital income

While depreciation is a particularly important aspect of the tax system, federal and state tax rates and local property taxes also affect the total burden of taxation of capital. A recent study by King and Fullerton[2] analyzes the total burden on taxation of capital income. Their study calculates marginal rates on a typical investment yielding a 10% pretax return. . . .[T]he marginal tax rate on capital income in manufacturing is about four times as great as the marginal tax rate in nonmanufacturing industry. The commercial sector pays intermediate marginal tax rates. Their study also shows that the burden of taxation of capital rises substantially with the inflation rate, ranging from a marginal rate of 38.4% in the absence of inflation to 49.0% at 10% inflation in the case of manufacturing.

King and Fullerton also analyze the effective marginal tax rates on capital financed by different methods. These results are even more extraordinary and cast light on the disparities in the cost of capital between the United States and Japan. Debt-financed capital actually faces a negative marginal tax rate, i.e., a disguised subsidy, and as the rate of inflation rises, this subsidy grows. This negative tax rate is produced by the reduction in the real burden of debt under inflation, a reduction which is not recognized by the tax law which allows all interest to be deductible.

On the other hand, the marginal tax rate on capital derived from new stock issues is extremely high and at high rates of inflation exceeds 100%. A 10% return in a period of 10% inflation is actually no return at all, yet whatever nominal profit is earned is subject to taxation, making the effective tax rate over 100%. . . .

A low saving rate

While institutional and tax factors played a critical role creating the high cost of capital for U.S. industry, the relatively low level of national saving was also of importance. The United States has operated with a substantially lower personal saving rate than the other principal industrial countries. The personal saving rate has varied from 6% to 8% over the last 20 years, and has been even lower in 1982-83. In Japan, the personal saving rate has been close to 20%, and in Germany over 14%. Even the United Kingdom saves more than the U.S. . . .

There are numerous institutional and historical factors which explain these differences in savings rates. The use of consumer credit is more highly developed here. Until recently, government deficits represented a larger form of dissaving in the other countries and required correspondingly higher personal savings rates. Differences in private and public pension arrangements also account for some of the differences. . . .

Nonetheless, the low volume of personal saving is a fundamental characteristic of the U.S. economy. With personal saving providing very little industrial capital, companies are dependent on cyclically vulnerable retained corporate earnings and on open capital markets that show large price fluctuations caused by variations in foreign and domestic flows-of-funds and in monetary policies.

Notes

[1] George N. Hatsopoulos, *High Cost of Capital, Hardship of American Industry*, American Business Conference, Inc., Thermo Electron Corporation, April 26, 1983, p. 118.

[2] Mervyn King and Don Fullerton, eds., "The United States," *The Taxation of Income From Capital*, Discussion Paper No. 37 (Princeton University, Woodrow Wilson School of International and Public Affairs, December 1982).

Managing Our Way to Economic Decline

Robert H. Hayes and William J. Abernathy

During the past several years American business has experienced a marked deterioration of competitive vigor and a growing unease about its overall economic well-being. This decline in both health and confidence has been attributed by economists and business leaders to such factors as the rapacity of OPEC, deficiencies in government tax and monetary policies, and the proliferation of regulation. We find these explanations inadequate . . . .

Our experience suggests that, to an unprecedented degree, success in most industries today requires an organizational commitment to compete in the marketplace on technological grounds—that is, to compete over the long run by offering superior products. Yet, guided by what they took to be the newest and best principles of management, American managers have increasingly directed their attention elsewhere. These new principles, despite their sophistication and widespread usefulness, encourage a preference for (1) analytic detachment rather than the insight that comes from "hands on" experience and (2) short-term cost reduction rather than long-term development of technological competitiveness. It is this new managerial gospel, we feel, that has played a major role in undermining the vigor of American industry . . . .

The new management orthodoxy

We refuse to believe that this managerial failure is the result of a sudden psychological shift among American managers toward a "super-safe,

Robert H. Hayes *is William Barclay Harding Professor of Management of Technology at the Harvard Business School. The late* William J. Abernathy *was Professor of Business Administration at the Harvard Business School and the author of* The Productivity Dilemma: Roadblock to Innovation in the Automobile Industry *(1978).*

no risk" mind set. No profound sea change in the character of thousands of individuals could have occurred in so organized a fashion or have produced so consistent a pattern of behavior. Instead we believe that during the past two decades American managers have increasingly relied on principles which prize analytical detachment and methodological elegance over insight, based on experience, into the subtleties and complexities of strategic decisions. As a result, maximum short-term financial returns have become the overriding criteria for many companies.

For purposes of discussion, we may divide this new management orthodoxy into three general categories: financial control, corporate portfolio management, and market-driven behavior.

Financial control

As more companies decentralize their organizational structures, they tend to fix on profit centers as the primary unit of managerial responsibility. This development necessitates, in turn, greater dependence on short-term financial measurements like return on investment (ROI) for evaluating the performance of individual managers and management groups. Increasing the structural distance between those entrusted with exploiting actual competitive opportunities and those who must judge the quality of their work virtually guarantees reliance on objectively quantifiable short-term criteria.

Although innovation, the lifeblood of any vital enterprise, is best encouraged by an environment that does not unduly penalize failure, the predictable result of relying too heavily on short-term financial measures—a sort of managerial remote control—is an environment in which no one feels he or she can afford a failure or even a momentary dip in the bottom line.

Corporate portfolio management

This preoccupation with control draws support from modern theories of financial portfolio management. Originally developed to help balance the overall risk and return of stock and bond portfolios, these principles have been applied increasingly to the creation and management of corporate portfolios—that is, a cluster of companies and product lines assembled through various modes of diversification under a single corporate umbrella. When applied by a remote group of dispassionate experts primarily concerned with finance and control and lacking hands-on experience, the analytic formulas of portfolio theory push managers even further toward an extreme of caution in allocating resources . . . .

Market-driven behavior

In the past 20 years, American companies have perhaps learned too well a lesson they had long been inclined to ignore: businesses should be customer oriented rather than product oriented. Henry Ford's famous dictum that the public could have any color automobile it wished as long as the color was black has since given way to its philosophical opposite: "We have got to stop marketing makeable products and learn to make marketable products."

At last, however, the dangers of too much reliance on this philosophy are becoming apparent . . . .

The argument that no new product ought to be introduced without managers undertaking a market analysis is common sense. But the argument that consumer analyses and formal market surveys should dominate other considerations when allocating resources to product development is untenable. It may be useful to remember that the initial market estimate for computers in 1945 projected total worldwide sales of only ten units. Similarly, even the most carefully researched analysis of consumer preferences for gas-guzzling cars in an era of gasoline abundance offers little useful guidance to today's automobile manufacturers in making wise product investment decisions. Customers may know what their needs are, but they often define those needs in terms of existing products, processes, markets, and prices.

Deferring to a market-driven strategy without paying attention to its limitations is, quite possibly, opting for customer satisfaction and lower risk in the short run at the expense of superior products in the future. Satisfied customers are critically important, of course, but not if the strategy for creating them is responsible as well for unnecessary product proliferation, inflated costs, unfocused diversification, and a lagging commitment to new technology and new capital equipment . . . .

Two very important questions remain to be asked: (1) Why should so many American managers have shifted so strongly to this new managerial orthodoxy? and (2) Why are they not more deeply bothered by the ill effects of those principles on the long-term technological competitiveness of their companies? . . . .

The road to the top

During the past 25 years the American manager's road to the top has changed significantly. No longer does the typical career, threading sinuously up and through a corporation with stops in several functional areas, provide future top executives with intimate hands-on knowledge of the company's technologies, customers, and suppliers . . . .

. . .Since the mid-1950s there has been a rather substantial increase in the percentage of new company presidents whose primary interests and expertise lie in the financial and legal areas and not in production . . . .

Far more important, however, than any absolute change in numbers is the shift in the general sense of what an aspiring manager has to be "smart about" to make it to the top. More important still is the broad change in attitude such trends both encourage and express. What has developed, in the business community as in academia, is a preoccupation with a false and shallow concept of the professional manager, a "pseudo-professional" really—an individual having no special expertise in any particular industry or technology who nevertheless can step into an unfamiliar company and run it successfully through strict application of financial controls, portfolio concepts, and a market-driven strategy . . . .

Complex modern technology has its own inner logic and developmental imperatives. To treat it as if it were something else—no matter how comfortable one is with that other kind of data—is to base a competitive business on a two-legged stool, which must, no matter how excellent the balancing act, inevitably fall to the ground . . . .

. . .At the strategic level there are no such things as pure production problems, pure financial problems, or pure marketing problems . . . .

The Statistical Vacuum

Edwin J. Coleman

Item: In 1965, the preliminary estimates of the GNP (gross national product) gave no indication that a sharp upturn in the economy had begun, and that a shift to more restrictive economic policies was needed.

Item: In late 1973 and early 1974 the inventory component of the GNP was seriously underestimated, disguising the unwanted inventory build-up at the outset of the 1974-75 recession. As a result the necessary policy response was needlessly and damagingly delayed.

Item: During the late 1970s when the need for more investment was vigorously debated, the business fixed-investment component of GNP—the data on which the discussion was based—seriously understated the actual rate of investment growth by as much as 20 percent.

These economic policy-making horror stories all point to a serious obstacle to American economic revitalization: the rapidly deteriorating U.S. economic record-keeping system.

By the beginning of the 1970s the United States was a world leader in keeping economic statistics. Yet developing and maintaining reliable economic statistics requires continuous support from a nation's business community and from its government. This support was dramatically cut in the United States during the late 1970s and 1980s. As a result, the statistical system began to lose its capacity to reflect economic reality accurately. Thanks to more than a decade and a half of public and private sector neglect, by the beginning of the 1990s the U.S. record-keeping system had sunk into a state of general disrepair. An economic strategy requires not only a clear vision of the future but an accurate picture of the present. Consequently, the

Edwin J. Coleman *is head of Coleman Consultants in Annapolis, Md. He was formerly a Senior Economist at the Bureau of Economic Analysis, U.S. Department of Commerce.*

importance of good economic statistics to political and business leaders cannot be overestimated.

The GNP, for example, is an indicator of the general economic condition of the economy, and obviously has an enormous impact on monetary and fiscal policy. The consumer price index (CPI), which measures the increase or decrease in the total price of a set of goods and services, shapes the lives of nearly every citizen in the United States. Wage negotiations are tied to the CPI along with the cost of living adjustments for 45 million Social Security beneficiaries and military and civil service retirees, and for the 24 million children in the National School Lunch program. The CPI is also used to prevent inflation-induced tax rate increases. Billions of dollars are allocated to state and local governments according to formulas based on state and county estimates of total and per capita personal income, population, and tax burden.

Yet the determination of the Federal statistics effort can only be reversed if the Bush administration overturns its predecessor's shortsighted policy of underfunding and undermanaging the system.

The price of fragmentation

The United States is the only major industrialized country with a highly decentralized record-keeping system. The data is collected, processed, estimated, and disseminated by a loose system of 70 statistical agencies. Directing the effort is the Statistical Policy Office, a bureau of the Office of Information and Regulatory Affairs (OIRA) in the Office of Management and Budget (OMB).

This highly interdependent system also depends on considerable coordination among federal producers and federal users. For example, the Department of Commerce's Bureau of Economic Analysis (BEA) draws on information from more than 400 reports, surveys and tabulations prepared by 42 other federal agencies to produce the National Income and Product Accounts.

The economic factors behind the U.S. government's record-keeping crisis are pervasive and include the ongoing alteration of the domestic economy due to structural changes; and the increased complexity of the global economy due to the rapid changes in the patterns of international transactions.

As will be discussed below, because economic activity around the world is growing ever more complex, producing accurate statistics has become a greater challenge as well. But Washington's record-keeping crisis can be traced to a recent, momentous shift in the federal government's view of its proper role in providing information to the public. During the Reagan administration policymakers questioned Washington's basic responsibility to gather and disseminate statistics, and encouraged a shift of important statistical activities to the private sector.

In 1985, OMB issued new guidelines for managing federal information resources. The document, circular no. A-130, attempts to lay the groundwork for privatizing the statistical system, and prescribes a relatively restricted and passive federal role. It calls inter alia for Executive Branch agencies to:

> collect only that information necessary for the proper performance of agency functions and having "practical utility";

> satisfy new information needs through legally authorized interagency or intergovernmental sharing of information, or through commercial sources, where appropriate;

> to distribute only those products and services specifically required by law; and

> to cut costs by shifting as much of the dissemination of information products and services to the private sector as possible and by assessing user fees.

As Douglas Ginsburg, the administrator of OIRA, said in a 1984 speech:

Each of these information collections requires the expenditure of public and private resources that might be more profitably spent on something else. The more money we spend to collect, process and disseminate information, the less there is available for government services. The more industry spends, the less money is available for production.[1]

Thus, as the need for better information grew, federal funding for statistical programs shrank. The operating budgets of the nine agencies that produce economic statistics declined (in constant 1988 dollars) from $570 million in 1980 to $498 million in 1988, a decrease of more than 12 percent.

In addition, the Reagan administration dismantled the system's only credible central planning mechanism for coordinating and directing the system's statistical output. In the spring of 1982, OMB abolished its separate statistical unit, the Office of Federal Statistical Policy and Standards, and merged the statistical policy functions mandated by the Paperwork Reduction Act of 1980 with other functions within OIRA. At present, a bare handful of professionals is struggling with the mounting work load.

The coordination and management of federal statistical policy is still in the hands of OIRA, where it is not only subject to neglect but where, as Courteney Slater, former chief economist for the Commerce Department observes, it easily becomes confused in the public's perception with collection of information for regulatory purposes.[2]

The administration acknowledges that "the integrity and accuracy of Federal statistics are paramount to effective government."[3] But deeds, not words, count, and President Bush has done almost nothing to halt the deterioration of U.S. economic statistics set in motion by the Reagan administration's policy of malign neglect.

Currently, the recordkeeping crisis shows up in a number of specific ways. Information needed to measure accurately the current patterns of economic activity is often not available, or increasingly often is late due to delays in the availability of source data. Resources are not available to develop alternative sources to replace the data lost as a result of deregulation. Estimates are becoming less reliable due to a lack of staff to edit and refine source data. Statistics formerly included in surveys are being discontinued, postponed, or released in truncated form, and unedited administrative records are being provided to other federal users due to reduced funding.

Complicating matters is the growing government and business demand (frequently legitimate) for more current information. This demand is forcing statistical agencies to divert resources from producing "current" estimates, which are based on comprehensive data, to producing "preliminary" estimates, which are based on fragmentary data well as on economic forecasts of doubtful value.

Priority measurement problems

As pointed out earlier, two of the most critical measurement problems facing the statistical agencies stem from the increased complexity of the domestic economy due to structural changes, and the increased complexity of the global economy due to the rapid changes in the patterns of international transactions.

For example, is the U.S. domestic economy indeed deindustrializing? Is productivity growth low and dropping, particularly in the service industries? Has job creation in recent years been concentrated in low-wage industries? The only certainty is that no one knows. The available data is insufficient to answer these questions. And the statistical agencies today lack the resources to remedy such problems.

The biggest problem is that structural change has blurred the very distinction between goods and services. Newspapers, for example, are goods, but information obtained through radio or television is generally classified as services. Measurement is also complicated because manufacturing firms are increasingly contracting out services that used to be produced internally and classified as goods output.

The data gaps in the service sector stem from a statistical system centered on the goods producing sector economy rather than on the rapidly growing service producing sector, and from Reagan-era deregulation. The latter crippled the statistical activities of the regulatory agencies that had been the primary source of data for the communications, finance, and transportation sectors of the economy. Data gaps also resulted from the emergence of new industries along with changes in foreign trade patterns and in business and consumer behavior.

The conceptual problems in the service sector are equally formidable. Consider the task of valuing the intellectual content of goods and services. The problem is how, conceptually and statistically, to separate changes in the value of goods and services resulting from increased intellectual content (quality changes) from price changes that do not reflect real changes in value. Without such a separation, price increases tend to be overstated and real GNP, along with productivity, is understated. Definitional problems are equally difficult and complicate measures of output—especially defining the output of service sector firms (e.g., banks and hospitals).

Just as restrictive Reagan-era policy has thwarted the statistical agencies' efforts to cope with problems of structural change, it has hampered attempts to upgrade international trade and financial statistics. Thus, the current widespread concern that today's global statistics and analyses cannot adequately guide business and governments is well-founded.

To be sure, information on international trade and financial flows has long lagged behind the rapid evolution of international transactions. The statistical system created in the 1930s was designed to measure America's domestic activities, particularly those involving manufacturing, mining, and agriculture. Some adjustments have been made to expand the coverage of foreign trade and investment but not nearly enough. Statistics on international trade and financial flows still reflect the former relative isolation of the American economy.

Moreover, however intrinsically complex the data collection and analysis problems associated with international activities, support for improvements in this area continues to be inadequate because the importance of foreign trade and investment transactions is still inadequately recognized in the public and private sectors. A partial list of the problems with international trade and financial statistics would include:

>   The lack of monthly trade flows on a seasonally adjusted basis

>   Huge gaps in the information on international capital flows—both purchases of assets denominated in foreign currencies and purchases of dollar-dominated assets by foreigners;

>   Significant underreporting of exports;

>   Failure to seasonally adjust quarterly price figures on exports and imports;

>   A lack of detailed breakdowns of exports;

>   Inadequate data on transactions in services; and

>   Significant understatement of total trade in services and failure to cover many individual service sectors at all.

Some progress is being made in making import data collected by different countries comparable. A 1987 OMB Report of the Working Group on the Quality of Economic Statistics points out that a potential source for improvement in the import and export trade statistics is the Harmonized Commodity Description and Coding System, developed by the Customs Cooperation Council (CCC). This international system standardizes the customs nomenclature of participating countries and permits import data collected by different countries to be compared more accurately. Since import data are the principal information used in trade negotiations, the Harmonized System will provide a common basis for negotiations if fully implemented. (The United States is also planning to implement the new international commodity classification now used by most of its trading partners.)

Priority statistical problems

Before Washington can adequately resolve the conceptual and definitional problems of measuring the prices and qualities of products and services, and before it can close the data gaps in the measures of domestic and international economic activity, the government's programs for locating and classifying businesses will have to be revised and upgraded. A more comprehensive list of service businesses will have to be developed as well.

The government's statistical programs for locating and classifying businesses are its standard industrial classification system (SIC) and its business directory lists. The validity of virtually all industrial analysis depends on the quality of these two statistical programs.

Most government surveys of nonfarm businesses rely entirely or partly on large lists of firms or establishments to assure adequate coverage. The problem is that rather than sharing a common sampling frame that would improve the quality of the data, the three statistical agencies that collect the largest share of basic economic data through surveys (the Bureau of Labor Statistics [BLS], the Census Bureau, and the National Agricultural Statistics Service [NASS]) use different business lists to conduct their surveys. The BLS and NASS business list is based on the administrative records maintained by the Departments of Agriculture and Labor and affiliated state agencies, as well as by the agencies' own surveys. The business list used by the Census Bureau is based on income and payroll tax records and on the Bureau's censuses and surveys. The result is redundancy and a lack of comparability among statistical programs.

Equally important, if an industry cannot be defined, it cannot be measured. Currently, there is a lack of service industry detail below the 4-digit SIC level on outputs, inputs, and productivity, which in turn significantly affects the measurement of structural changes in the economy. This system for defining and classifying business is out of date. Most seriously, the fastest growing industries are not being identified and tracked. And apparently they are not being tracked because they are not identified by the SIC system. Without a complete SIC overhaul, the industrial detail needed to measure service outputs, inputs, and productivity will continue to fall short.

Although the importance of both of these basic statistical housekeeping chores—locating and classifying businesses—has been belatedly recognized by the Bush administration, there is no concrete indication that these programs will receive priority or the resources they need. Until this happens, many basic questions concerning the changing industrial structure of the U.S. domestic economy will go unanswered.

Losing the international competition for economic statistics

How well do the U.S. government's record-keeping efforts compare with the efforts of our major economic competitors—especially Japan? Although few comprehensive comparative studies exist, there are clear indications that the United States is falling behind. Other countries, notably Japan, are outspending the United States in the development of their statistical output.

Japan's current work on its International Input/Output Model Project is in striking contrast to the U.S. government's efforts in this area. At the cost of one million dollars a year over 6 years, this Ministry of International Trade and Industry (MITI)-directed project will construct a series of input/output tables connecting Japan and its major economic partners. Not only is this effort impressive on its own terms. But because U.S. statistics were deemed inadequate by Tokyo, data for the United States had to be estimated by a private contractor. Equally serious from an American standpoint, since the United States lacks data on the use of imports by industry—an important characteristic of I/O models—the Japanese had to estimate these figures by surveying Japanese firms about which U.S. industries buy which types of goods from them.[4]

Japan is also engaged in constructing an international input/output table in an effort to build capability for analyzing "bilateral and multilateral economic issues and conflicts," "analyzing the economic impact of international economic activities," and "clarifying the magnitude of international interdependence."[5]

The Japanese are spending $1 million a year over 6 years on a *supplement* to their main domestic Input/Output work, compared with America's expenditures of $1.4 million in fiscal year 1989 for its total input/output budget. Admittedly other countries may emphasize I/O analysis because it plays a more fundamental role in their policy making. Yet input/output statistics are extremely important to the United States as well. Because the U.S. I/O tables continue to be many years behind schedule, other

Federal agencies and private analytical firms are forced to update them using a mix of methods that result in conflicting analyses.

The National Trade Data Bank (NTDB)

The U.S. government has, however, made some encouraging progress in the area of data access. In 1988, Washington established a National Trade Data Bank (NTDB), designed to be a central source for a large body of economic statistics.

The NTDB is the product of the Omnibus Trade and Competitiveness Act of 1988 and is located in the Department of Commerce. It will be divided into two components: an international economic data system and an export promotion data system. Areas covered will include imports and exports, international service transactions, international capital markets, foreign direct investments in the U.S. economy, international labor markets, foreign government policies affecting trade, and U.S. import and export data on a state-by-state basis aggregated at the product level.

The export promotion data system will include information on the industrial sectors and markets of foreign countries determined to be of greatest interest to U.S. exporters as well as to economic policy analysts. Areas covered will include specific business opportunities in foreign countries; specific industrial sectors with high export potential; foreign economic conditions, business practices, and trade policies affecting imports, licensing, and the protection of intellectual property; export financing information; and transactions involving barter and countertrade.

The trade data will be disseminated through optical disks, an electronic bulletin board, and magnetic tapes. The disks will be the primary medium. NTDB disks containing the entire data bank, including all updated information, will be produced every month. Yet this ambitious program has a long way to go before it is fully implemented.

Although worldwide economic change is at the root of the U.S. government record-keeping crisis, the erosion in the quality of the U.S. inventory of economic statistics can be traced to more than a decade and a half of declining budgets and a lack of support and interest on the part of both business and government. Unless the current administration reverses the Reagan policy of neglecting the development of economic statistics, the quality of U.S. statistics will surely continue to decline.

Notes

[1] Douglas H. Ginsburg, "Federal Information Resources Management: The Challenge of Change," Information Industry Association Conference, September 20, 1984, p. 4.

[2] Courtenay Slater, Chair of the Council of Professional Associations on Federal Statistics. From testimony given to the House Committee on Government Operations, Subcommittee on Legislation and National Security, Hearing on the reauthorization of the Paperwork Reduction Act, August 1989.

[3] *The Statistical Programs of the United States Government, Fiscal year 1989*, U.S. Office of Management and Budget, p. 1.

[4] "Statistical Needs for a Changing U.S. Economy," Background Paper, OTA-BP-E-58 U.S. Congress, Office of Technology Assessment, (Washington, D.C.: U.S. Government Printing Office), September 1989, p. 1.

[5] M. Sato, Japan's Minister of International Trade and Industry, "Compilation of an International Input/Output Table," paper presented at the OECD Workshop on International I-O Tables and Performance Analysis of Structural Adjustment, December 14, 1988, Paris, France, p. 23.

VII

Coming Back: Foreign Policy Obstacles

Part Seven indicates that, for all the importance of domestic obstacles to better U.S. economic performance, the way that American foreign policy have been pursued has also continually undermined efforts at economic revitalization. The biggest foreign policy obstacle has been the Orthodoxy's view of the economic world as being non-strategic. Whatever international competition the Orthodoxy recognizes in the military and political realms is thought to be completely unaffected by economics, and vice versa. As a result, one of the major instruments that states have used to secure important foreign policy objectives has been greatly devalued by the United States, and, in fact, all but assumed away.

Throughout the post-World War II era, Washington confidently assumed that as long as the free world community's overall GNP growth continued, dangerous economic tensions and conflicts would never break out, and none of its members would even seek advantages at the expense of others, for all realized their vital interest in the prosperity of the whole. And in the unlikely event that important economic tensions did emerge, America would farsightedly make the sacrifices or incur the costs needed to calm the waters—for example, buying other countries' exports even if they refused to buy ours, or periodically slowing down domestic economic growth to keep the world monetary order stable. And, of course, the United States would indefinitely shoulder the lion's share of the costs and risks of defending the free world militarily.

The comfortable foreign policy establishment that developed this strategy called these practices "exercising leadership." What this inspiring phrase concealed, however, was the reality that the free world was being held together by squandering critical building blocks of national economic strength. Yet one of the key reasons for holding the coalition together, American leaders believed, was to preserve and increase U.S. economic strength. In other words, U.S. leaders have viewed America's resources and technology as little more than a collection of trinkets to be doled out periodically in the form of political favors, not as integral parts of America's national arsenal. Yet while it was relatively easy to sacrifice economic strength 30 or even 20 years ago, when America had so much of it, it is much more difficult and costlier today.

Alan Tonelson and Ronald Morse contend that the U.S. strategy of maintaining alliance cohesion by sacrificing U.S. economic strength was not only unwise, but unsustainable. For America's determination to smother international political and economic conflict by assuming costly international leadership responsibilities could not survive the inevitable fading of overwhelming U.S. military and economic superiority after 1945.

Walter Russell Mead observes that when this postwar Pax Americana ran into its first crisis, U.S. leaders responded not by developing new, more strategic economic and military policies, but by abandoning the only truly strategic dimension of the postwar structure—monetary policy. Even the Cold War utopians who set up the postwar order realized that the value of various national currencies could not simply be left to the market without inviting 1930s-style economic chaos. But when this order collapsed in 1971, this insight fell by the wayside. As Mead concludes, the run-up of inflation and unemployment, the slowdown in growth, and the monetary volatility that followed show that this experiment failed. Ironically, in the 1980s, U.S. leaders convinced themselves that solving these problems required one more innovation: an abdication of most government responsibilities for domestic economic affairs.

Reviewing the voluminous literature on the relationship of defense spending and economic performance, Steve Chan sheds important light on the recent debate over whether high U.S. military spending has damaged American economic competitiveness. The key to understanding the relationship, Chan observes, is not to compare the defense spending burdens of the United States and its chief economic competitors at specific moments in time, but to identify the long-term effects of defense spending on the productive use of resources. Chan also describes the various means by which high defense budgets can sap a national economy's long-term strength.

Outdated Alliance Strategies

Alan Tonelson and Ronald A. Morse

Despite the waning of the Cold War, Americans are finding themselves once again in the fight of their lives: the struggle to retain international economic preeminence. This struggle is not as dramatic as the was the Cold War but the stakes are just as high—maintaining national independence, and preserving the American way of life. For economic power is the base on our national power, values, and dreams, ultimately rests. Yet the United States is not equipped to wage this struggle materially or organizationally. Most important, America is not equipped for it intellectually—indeed, few U.S. leaders, in particular, even want to acknowledge that a struggle is underway.

Some of the domestic requirements of this struggle are slowly dawning on Americans—principally the need to foster technological innovation and cultivate our human resources. But some of the biggest obstacles to many of these reforms are found in America's antiquated concept of foreign policy, and particularly in policy towards America's most important international relationships, its alliances with Western Europe and Japan.

Created at the height of the Cold War 40 years ago, the existing alliances understandably were geared toward fending off military and ideological threats.

Yet as structured today, they are of little or no help to America in confronting the new economic threats. In fact, the alliances and the strategy behind them have been a big part of the problem. The security imperative at their core has in effect defined these new challenges out of existence. It has held—inconsistently, to be sure—both that the current economic struggle

---

Alan Tonelson *is Research Director of the Economic Strategy Institute. He is an Adjunct Scholar of the Cato Institute and author of a forthcoming Twentieth Century Fund study of U.S. foreign policy.* Ronald A. Morse *is Executive Vice President of the Economic Strategy Institute. A former State Department and Energy Department official, he directed the East Asia Program at the Woodrow Wilson Center and served as private-sector liaison officer and special assistant to the Librarian of Congress.*

cannot break out, and that it must not be allowed to break out. And to the limited extent that it has tried to cope with economic problems, the traditional alliance strategy has strapped the United States with a second-best approach—an addiction to arm-twisting its allies to solve its economic problems that has encouraged American leaders to mortgage long-term economic strength for short-term geopolitical benefit.

The goals originally set by U.S. alliance strategy remain essential—peace and security for the world's other great centers of economic power, and profitable U.S. relations with them. But fundamentally new means of achieving these goals are equally essential. The United States needs an entirely new vision of its relations with Western Europe and Japan. This new vision would fully recognize the need for economic as well as military preparedness. And to safeguard the American economic future, it would rely first and foremost not on increasingly vain efforts to manipulate alliance relationships, but on actively nurturing and rebuilding real national economic power. In this way, the United States could enable itself to deal with whatever problems may be caused by Western Europe and Japan (or anyone else) in the most dependable way possible—from a position of genuine strength.

In recent years, Americans and American leaders have tacitly admitted that the military and even the economic strains of U.S. alliances have been getting out of hand. Thus even before Mikhail Gorbachev's revolutionary changes in Soviet foreign policy, Washington was pressing its allies to pick up more of the costs of free-world defense and open their markets wider to American goods. During the last year, President Bush has proposed negotiating with the Soviets significant troop cuts in Europe, as well as formulating new economic and political missions for NATO in an era when the map of Europe is being redrawn. Meanwhile, talk of fundamentally new approaches for U.S.-Japan relations, has been prompted not only by U.S. impatience with Tokyo's unfair trading practices and defense free-riding, but by America's fears of losing international economic and technological preeminence to Japan, and by Japan's own growing resentment of such American complaints. The administration even agreed to impose trade sanctions on Japan in 1989.

But however welcome, such individual steps are unlikely to accomplish much because they have been taken within the old framework of military and ideological priorities, and are designed to carry out its underlying mission. To resume serving American interests, U.S. alliances must be relieved of this mission—one that may have been realistic in the days of early post-World War

II U.S. global supremacy, but that has since moved completely beyond our reach. U.S. alliance strategy must give up the goal of removing any incentive for the West Europeans or the Japanese to conduct independent foreign policies of their own.

Since 1945, U.S. alliance strategy has aimed not only to protect Western Europe and Japan against Soviet military aggression and political intimidation—that has been made clear by the insistence that sizeable U.S. conventional and nuclear forces stay in these regions even after Soviet forces leave. Nor can U.S. alliance strategy be accurately portrayed simply by adding the task of preventing German and Japanese revanchism to its agenda. Instead, both aims flow from a larger strategy, one of filling all of the major needs that would have led the Western European countries and Japan to conduct their own foreign policies in the first place—principally, security and prosperity. This is why Washington has been as determined to provide an enormous, guaranteed market for these now prosperous, heavily trade-dependent, and highly protected countries (often at considerable cost to its own fortunes) as it has been to cover them with a nuclear shield (often at considerable risk). In other words, since 1945, the United States has been struggling to contain not only the Soviets, but all the great nations of the world—to do nothing less than to prevent them from acting like great nations in the first place.

The most obvious problems with this strategy of smothering West European and Japanese foreign policy independence are imposing enough. America has been paying the lion's share of free-world defense costs and incurring most of the nuclear risk—even though the allies would clearly suffer the most from Soviet aggression. The short-sighted economic dimension of this approach, meanwhile, forces America to make most of the near-term sacrifices needed to keep the world economy on an even keel.

But there has been an equally troubling long-range cost to America's current alliance strategy. As the allies caught up with America economically and Moscow caught up militarily, the risks and particularly the economic costs of this strategy became too large for the United States to shrug off. Yet rather than generate the new resources needed by rebuilding its own economic strength, Washington has become hooked on the habit of using its political and military clout to attempt to wring various forms of compensation from the allies—sometimes in the form of specific trade concessions, but more often by leaning on Western Europe and Japan to finance its balance of payments deficits. This strategy not only contains a fatal internal flaw—for ultimately the military clout upon which it is based cannot be wielded without the real economic strength that it neglects. But its ultimate goal is not worth the risks and costs, and is something that in fact a country like the United States does not need.

Why did America choose this ambitious, intricate, risky, and costly smothering strategy to begin with? And once its costs became apparent, why did the United States settle for simply trying to slow the hemorrhage of its economic strength? In other words, what other goals did the United States consider to be even more important? Simply put, U.S. leaders believed that smothering was the strategy likeliest to prevent World War III in a nuclear age.

As planning for the postwar world began, American foreign policy-makers felt themselves to be in a deep and complex quandary concerning Western Europe and Japan at the end of World War II. Both regions were of course viewed as great strategic prizes. Economically, Western Europe and Japan were seen not only as centers of military-industrial potential, but as vital trading partners. If their markets were denied to America by Soviet overlords, American exports would shrivel and living standards would sink like a stone. And though rarely stated in public, U.S. leaders also believed that alliance relationships gave them much of the clout they needed to fight restrictive trade practices in Western Europe and Japan when they got out of hand.

Nevertheless, encouraging the recoveries of Western Europe and Japan raised the possibility of restoring the pre-World War II global balance of power. And this balance had proven highly unstable; in less than half a century it had collapsed into two terrible international conflicts. And plainly the problem went far beyond the defeated Axis powers. Centuries of bloody history indicated that, when it came to foreign policy, all the major European states were completely irresponsible. Enabling them to return to their old warring ways was a horrifying prospect in the nuclear age. Today, some view a world of multiple, independent power centers as a welcome development. State Department policy planner Francis Fukuyama has even written that we are nearing the "end of history"—at least in terms of big-power conflict. But at the end of the late-1940s, a truly multipolar world was exactly what American foreign policy-makers were striving to prevent.

Not everyone at that time shared these fears. In the late 1940s, two of the leading voices arguing that America would benefit from restoring Western Europe, in particular, as an independent world power were George F. Kennan and Walter Lippmann. And initially, Washington leaned toward promoting West European unity as the way to encourage both self-reliance and responsible foreign policy behavior. American leaders knew that a united Western Europe could become too independent in foreign policy. Thus the early interest in Washington in deindustrializing Germany and the heavy pressure on Britain and France to dismantle their colonial empires—precisely the assets that helped make the latter two global powers before 1939, and in theory could do so again. But as indicated by the Marshall Plan (a crash program of economic recovery) and NATO-as-originally-advertised (a stopgap measure to give Western Europe a breathing spell), American foreign policy-makers eventually came to consider the problem manageable.

Others in the bureaucracy, however, were convinced that rising East-West tensions demanded a strong U.S.-Western Europe alliance, whatever the long-term impact on European self-reliance. When the Cold War further intensified, U.S. calculations underwent a subtle but significant change in favor of the NATO enthusiasts. The militarized, global version of containment toward which America shifted—especially after Korea—required creating a maintaining a solid, cohesive anti-communist front. Significant Western European independence was no longer tolerable. Most U.S. policy-makers realized that the North Atlantic Treaty would jeopardize their aspirations for Western Europe's political and economic unification. But the new consensus came to accept this possible setback as a necessary tradeoff of protecting the region from Soviet encroachment.

Still, how could America encourage the emergence of a Western Europe vigorous enough to relieve it of major defense burdens and to strengthen NATO, but unlikely to challenge U.S. leadership? Could America have it both ways? Washington believed that it could. Its solution to the Europe quandary—which emerged gradually over the next decade—was the smothering strategy. The United States would guarantee Western Europe's security by maintaining its massive troop presence and its nuclear umbrella. It would guarantee Western Europe's prosperity by opening its markets wide to allied exports, by tolerating and even encouraging their own protectionism—steps that became doubly necessary as the West Europeans grudgingly gave up their profitable third world possessions—and by upholding a stable international monetary order.

What gave American leaders hope that Western Europe would remain content as a junior partner was the U.S. nuclear arsenal (for which the West Europeans knew they could develop no adequate substitute for many years) and America's own economic strength (which not only enabled the United States literally to buy Western Europe's continued cooperation whenever the

West Europeans began grumbling about the terms of their alliance-protectorate, but to do so without requiring visible sacrifices by the American people).

America's postwar policy toward Japan followed a similar, although not identical, course. During the war, the Japanese were seen both by the American government and by the American people as a brutal, barbarian enemy. Indeed, this image was carefully cultivated by the U.S. government's wartime propaganda apparatus and by the news media. As a result, the occupation forces under General MacArthur set out completely to revamp not only Japan's foreign policy and economy, but its politics and government, schools, and land tenure system. Americans rewrote the Japanese constitution to include the famous Article 1, which renounces war and prohibits Japan from maintaining any military forces beyond those needed for self-defense.

Yet coexisting with this profound distrust of Japan and its history of racial imperialism was fear of Soviet geopolitical expansion into Asia. Thus even as it encouraged Japan to become a military and political midget, America was consciously turning the country into an economic titan. Japan's evolution into a highly bureaucratized, monomaniacal, mercantilistic export powerhouse followed a detailed American blueprint. In addition, however, the United States encouraged Japan to rely on America, not its Asian neighbors, for most of its export market—in large part to prevent fears of Japanese economic predominance from feeding regional tensions, and creating opportunities for Moscow and Beijing to expand their influence.

As the postwar era wore on, however, America's ability to maintain its smothering strategy at low cost and risk decayed. In fact, the terms of the security and economic bargains inherent in America's major alliances began to turn decidedly against the United States. Today, because it possesses thousands of intercontinental-range nuclear weapons, America no longer needs nuclear bases on the Soviet periphery. These same weapons have also made the United State invulnerable to the threat of invasion from a united, hostile Old World. Nuclear weapons have long been accurate enough to vaporize any invasion force seconds after it left port—if not while troops were massing to board ships—without attacking the enemy's homeland and thus risking a retaliatory strike. Indeed, as early as the mid-1950s, President Eisenhower realized that nuclear weapons were bringing to a close the days of fighting great-power wars by shipping vast armies around the world. Consequently, forward defense has lost most if its value as well for the United States; we can prevent invaders from coming "over here" without fighting them "over there."

By greatly reducing the likelihood of protracted conventional wars between the great powers, nuclear weapons have also loosened the link between America's core security and the capacity to mobilize huge amounts of resources for massive military operations. As a result, even though economic recovery in Western Europe and Japan have made them vastly more important centers of economic might, this power is much less important to America's security—either in terms of adding power to the Western camp, or denying it to the Soviets.

Worse, today, the greatest security risks to America itself still come from the nuclear guarantees at the heart of its major alliances. When the United States enjoyed a nuclear monopoly or overwhelming superiority, these guarantees arguably promoted important U.S. goals at negligible risk. But once the Soviets built significant intercontinental nuclear forces of their own—much less achieved parity—their ability to launch a fearsome retaliatory strike on the United States became apparent in Moscow, Washington, and the allied capitals.

Despite the new situation of nuclear parity, NATO in particular has largely been able to suppress these nuclear conflicts since the mid-1960s. Still-formidable U.S. nuclear forces seem to have provided a strong measure of what strategists have called residual or existential deterrence—raising too many nuclear questions in the minds of Soviet planners to make attacking the West a rational decision. And periods of East-West detente helped as well. But as shown by the INF and Lance missile crises of the 1980s, transatlantic nuclear tensions have never been very far below the surface.

Nor can it be argued convincingly today that U.S. alliances with Western Europe and Japan significantly enhance America's ability to project power into the third world. Of course, the bases that make this possible still exist. But despite impressive initial Western unity during the 1990 Iraq crisis, America's access to them is anything but assured. Recall the refusal of most of the NATO allies to help America resupply Israel in the 1973 Middle East War, and of France to grant overflight rights to U.S. bombers en route to attacking Libya in 1986. In fact, in 1988, U.S. access to West European bases in the event of a Persian Gulf crisis was characterized as "uncertain" by President Reagan's Commission on Integrated Long-Term Strategy. The panel included former Secretary of State Henry Kissinger, former national security advisor Zbigniew Brzezinski, former Chairman of the Joint Chiefs of Staff Gen. John W. Vessey, and former NATO commander Gen. Andrew Goodpaster—some of the prototypes of the American mental paradigm for a past era.

In strictly economic terms, the alliances may be draining the U.S. of more strength than they are contributing. When the alliances were formed in the late 1940s, they could be self-financing in a sound manner, for all practical purposes. The U.S. economy was so much larger than any other that it could easily absorb any short-term costs were needed to aid economic recovery in Western Europe and Japan, and maintaining Western solidarity by extending favors whenever complaints arose. Moreover, because only the United States could provide the goods and services needed for allied recovery, America's trade surpluses with both regions could cover the long-term costs of military protection and foreign aid. In fact, through the early 1960s, U.S. surpluses with Western Europe could also significantly offset deficits with other parts of the world and other elements of the balance of payments—the foreign exchange costs of maintaining large military forces abroad, foreign aid, and private foreign investment.

Yet as early as the late-1950s, the first signs of trouble emerged for the smothering strategy. The first U.S. balance of payments deficits signalled that American economic largesse had limits after all. By the early 1970s, dollar outflows in the rest of the balance-of-payments categories had come to dwarf the U.S. trade surplus with Western Europe. Moreover, the European Community's extensive trade protectionism suggested to Treasury Secretary John Connally that without these trade barriers, the surplus with Europe would be even higher, and the trade account could make a greater contribution towards narrowing the overall international deficit. In other words, as early as 1971, senior American officials were complaining that the allies were not allowing America's costly military commitment to pay for itself. But few made the connection between the economic burden of U.S. foreign policy and the growing ills of the domestic economy.

In the 1980s, the situation dramatically worsened. Not only did the U.S. trade balance with the rest of the world plunge deeply into the red, so did its trade balance with Western Europe. From 1985 to 1988, these deficits averaged nearly $22 billion annually. Simultaneously, America's deficit with Japan bottomed out at roughly $50 billion annually.

Of course, during the 1980s, the United States ran up huge deficits virtually everywhere. Thus the perversities of Reaganomics, not U.S. alliance relationships, are usually blamed for America's trade woes. This analysis begs the question of why Reaganomics was adopted in the first place. In particular, its tax reductions, budget deficits, and massive foreign borrowing are best understood as an attempt to finance costly alliance commitments and other elements of America's ambitious, universalistic foreign policy without imposing heavy, visible, and immediate sacrifices on the American people or sparking ruinous inflation. And although the trade gap narrowed considerably in 1989 and early 1990, the larger problem remains: U.S. alliances are still a long way from being self-financing in a sound manner—through encouraging the creation of real economic strength.

Not surprisingly, as the credibility of America's nuclear guarantee faded, as Western European and Japan regained self-confidence, and as American complaints about the costs of alliances multiplied, the most important pillar of the smothering strategy has weakened—the allies' willingness to accept subordinate status and entrust their fate to U.S. leadership. Ironically, however, the first great crisis of the smothering strategy began just when it achieved its fullest expression—during the Kennedy years. Kennedy's Grand Design promoted West European unity but the purpose was to construct a transatlantic community or partnership, with America as the senior member of the firm. Japan's economic takeoff, meanwhile, was simply contrasted with China's ruinous Great Cultural Revolution and welcomed as proof of the superiority of capitalism over communism. Nonetheless, throughout the 1960s, the relative power required for this version of the smothering strategy waned at an accelerating rate.

The allies' economic recovery and their growing trade power helped to worsen America's persistent balance of payments deficits. Moreover, Lyndon Johnson's determination to buy guns (primarily for Vietnam) and butter without raising taxes triggered an inflation that would soon help drag down American productivity growth, and undermine the international monetary system.

Vietnam also triggered a major political dispute between the United States and its major allies. Most allied leaders supported the American military effort in public—albeit unenthusiastically. But Washington's willingness to incur such phenomenal costs for so marginal an objective undermined allied confidence in American judgement and leadership. Finally, in mid-1966, came the first major failure of the smothering strategy—de Gaulle's decision to leave NATO's integrated military command, and his challenge to U.S. nuclear, diplomatic, and economic preeminence in transatlantic relations.

Plainly, the passive version of the smothering strategy was not working. As the 1960s wore on, worsening inflation, declining trade performance, and a series of ever more acute monetary crises raised the consequences of failure to dangerous levels. In response, American leaders gradually introduced a more active version of the smothering strategy—an openly hegemonic version. The strategy, brilliantly described by political scientist David P. Calleo of The Johns Hopkins University, has consisted of America using the clout generated by its military role to wring various kinds of compensation from the allies for the domestic economic problems created by its disproportionate, alliance-fueled, military spending.

After all, Americans would never have tolerated the various combinations of high taxes, domestic austerity, huge trade deficits, or high inflation made inevitable by massive defense budgets, foreign military deployments, and foreign aid disbursements. Therefore, U.S. leaders reasoned, maintaining these policies required passing the costs on to others. Washington pressed Japan and the NATO allies—chiefly West Germany—to make major purchases of U.S.-made weapons and to help pay for the American troops on their soil. It tolerated allied protectionism in exchange for their agreement not to exchange for gold the growing quantities of dollars flooding international markets. And it stepped up the policy of exploiting the dollar's international reserve currency role. Specifically, Washington greatly increased the world dollar glut by continuing to run large budget and international payments deficits without paying the penalties imposed on less privileged members of the Bretton-Woods monetary system. As de Gaulle so bitterly complained, America thus exported its inflation to the rest of the noncommunist world.

Over the short- and medium-term, this strategy worked to America's advantage. America could balance its international books better. More important it could continue playing a superpower role without requiring major sacrifices from the American people. In other words, a hegemonic policy allowed the United States to live beyond its means, and to exert more influence than its real economic strength would have permitted. Not surprisingly, it was continued for decades by Democratic and Republican presidents alike; Richard Nixon's unilateral decision to yank the United States off the gold standard, bring down the Bretton-Woods system, impose tariffs on imports, and devalue the dollar was only the most spectacular example of this policy. Ronald Reagan's policy of bolstering alliance defenses by launching the biggest peacetime military buildup in American history and financing it by borrowing may have been the cleverest.

But the hegemonic strategy never linked security and real economic strength in any meaningful way. The United States enjoyed hegemonic privileges and influence but never asked what good such benefits were if the real strength underlying them was continually eroding. More disturbing, the economic troubles responsible for the hegemonic strategy to begin with kept growing worse. The country's productivity growth continued to lag behind that many of most allied countries, its savings rate plummeted, its rate of investment stagnated, and its trade deficit soared.

Yet largely because the strategy worked so well to mask these troubles, American leaders felt free to neglect their root causes. Confidence that such profligacy would carry no real risks peaked during the Reagan years. For unlike the America of the Vietnam era—and unlike the Soviet Union of the Gorbachev era—the United States found foreign creditors willing to bankroll its self-indulgence. But viewed from the perspective of the Bush years, the Reagan version of the new imperialism—featuring unheard of peacetime indebtedness and reliance on foreign capital to finance consumption rather than productive investment—only created an entirely new set of economic problems and vulnerabilities. In other words, the long-term economic costs of U.S. alliance strategy are only now beginning to become apparent.

Nor did the West Europeans and the Japanese become notably more willing to follow American leads. Rather, their new economic and political clout enabled them to place limits on traditional American unilateralism—a quality that the Founding Fathers gave the less pejorative and more accurate name "freedom of action." Still reeling in the early 1980s from the second oil shock, the allies generally acquiesced in Reaganomics. But fiscally conservative West Germany in particular continued to resist U.S. calls to promote faster economic growth. And the strengthening of the Deutschemark-based European Monetary System attested to the Europeans' continuing interest alternatives to the dollar. Japan, meanwhile, hedged its own bets on the dollar.

Further, the allies generally stonewalled on U.S. trade demands, ultimately prompting Congress to pass the toughest trade legislation of the postwar period. The Super 301 provision of the Omnibus Trade Act of 1988 mandates sanctions on "unfair" trading powers that do not negotiate improved access to American goods within one year. Moreover, the European Community adamantly opposed a U.S. plan to negotiate an end to the subsidies that distort agricultural trade. And by financing U.S. deficits, these more independent-minded countries gained broad new influence over America's economic future. Both Reagan and Bush, however, stubbornly refused to view this influence as a problem at all, especially with regard to Japan. Indeed, they were confident that they held a critical "America card" that they could play any time because of Japan's desperate need for a special political relationship with its protector, and for U.S. markets.

Signs of growing allied—and especially West European—foreign policy independence mushroomed as well. Just as the allies resisted President Carter's call for sanctions to protest the Soviet invasion of Afghanistan and the Iranian seizure of American hostages, they opposed President Reagan's bid to retaliate economically for the Moscow-backed crackdown on Poland's Solidarity movement and initially pressed ahead with the Soviet gas pipeline deal over his protests. Japan quietly took the same positions.

Allied opposition to America's preferred security and nuclear strategies were apparent in the controversy over deploying intermediate-range nuclear forces (INFs) on the continent, the row between Washington and Bonn row over modernizing short-range nuclear missiles based primarily in West Germany, allied unhappiness over Reagan's Strategic Defense Initiative, and over Reagan's proposal at Reykjavik to ban all ballistic missiles by 1996. The Europeans became convinced that Reagan the superhawk was bent on decoupling America's nuclear forces from the continent's defense. In the meantime, the West Europeans generally opposed America's new determination to resist Soviet thrusts in the third world, fearful that third world conflict could endanger detente in their own neighborhood.

Throughout the decade, the members of the EC also continued to make progress—however incremental—towards developing a unified foreign policy. The Community, as well as Japan, was especially interested in staking out positions independent from America's on Middle East diplomacy, repeatedly calling for recognition of Palestinian rights and peace talks under UN auspices. And giving powerful new momentum to Europe's resolve to gain more foreign policy independence has been the Community's decision to achieve economic integration by 1992. This momentous process has also stimulated notable progress toward the still-distant goal of European political integration.

Finally, the smothering strategy did nothing to reduce the risks to American security; if anything, it was increasing them. Despite the onrushing Soviet nuclear and conventional military buildups of the 1960s and 1970s, America maintained sizeable forces in Europe. Too small and weak to beat back a Soviet conventional attack unaided—largely because the West European allies refused to field adequate conventional forces of their own—they were nonetheless large enough and deployed close enough to the front lines to serve as a tripwire. That is to say, they would almost automatically ensure America's involvement in any East-West conflict in Europe. As Senator Sam Nunn (D.-Ga.) and many other critics noted, American strategy had to count on the early use of nuclear weapons because the allies would not defend themselves. The result, as military analyst Col. Harry G. Summers has written, is a "Mel Brooks strategy: Attack me and I'll commit suicide."

Indeed, although the crumbling of the Soviet's European empire has all but eliminated the prospect of Soviet military aggression against Western Europe for many years, it has also raised a new danger to American security. Both halves of Europe are now much less stable than they have been for 40 years. In Eastern Europe, myriad national, ethnic, and religious rivalries have resurfaced. And the German question is back on to the world agenda. Thus, despite America's Herculean efforts, balance-of-power politics, preemptive alliance formation, and the wars they produced may well make a comeback in Europe. Smothering in Europe, in other words, had a dirty secret: It required Germany's division. Today, if Europe does turn into a powderkeg again, the presence of thousands of American troops and nuclear weapons in the heart of the continent raises the odds of U.S. involvement in future European wars whether we like it or not.

But despite its willingness to scale back the American military presences in Western Europe and the Far East, the Bush administration is sticking with smothering. No doubt sheer inertia accounts to some extent for this decision. But public statements by the president and his top advisors reveal the belief that genuinely independent European and Japanese foreign policies would simply be to dangerous to permit, and that smothering these regions continues to be worth practically every risk and cost. And most of the foreign policy community generally agrees.

Thus Bush's repeated insistence that American troops are needed in both regions to "maintain stability," and in particular to calm fears—held by local countries, of course, not by the United States—of a resurgent Germany and Japan.

The administration has been most explicit about its determination to contain any impulses toward independent foreign policies in the Far East. As Bush argued in a March 1989 interview, "I don't want to see us push Japan into a position that revives in the minds of some of the ASEAN countries this specter of Japanese imperialism." Nor is the smothering strategy a peculiarly Republican or conservative idea. Rep. Stephen Solarz (D.-N.Y.) has warned that if Japan's defense spending approached U.S.-level percentages of GNP, the country would become "not simply a regional military power, but a superpower. And that, in turn, would have enormously destabilizing consequences, both in Asia and around the globe."

One of the more extensive discussions of the importance of the strategy in the Far East was provided by Defense Secretary Cheney during his February 1990 trip to the Far East: "If continuing Soviet expansion was all that we cared about, we might be tempted to withdraw. But that is not what we intend to do." Without a U.S. presence, he added, "a power vacuum would quickly develop. There almost surely would be a series of destabilizing regional arms races, an increase in regional tensions, and possibly conflict." Cheney also acknowledged that in the past, "[W]e have not devoted enough energy to explaining the other dimensions of our security policy," beyond fighting communism.

In addition, the president seems determined to continue the hegemonic version of the smothering strategy in Europe. In his "New Atlanticism" speech of December 12, 1989, Secretary of State James Baker not only recommended that NATO busy itself with a series of new missions to replace its military raison d'être. He also proposed that the United States and the Community forge a set of new institutional links and intensify cooperation and warned that the new intra-European cooperation should not replace traditional transatlantic cooperation.

At the same time, Baker's approach underscored current U.S. weakness. For the 1992 program and its associated goals of greater European political integration and an all-European foreign policy have been conceived precisely to bring Europe out from under America's shadow. Before the Gorbachev era, the United States might have been able to win a seat at the EC table if it pressed hard enough. But today the military protection that gave America clout obviously is valued much less by Western Europe. Nor is it obvious what economic clout America can wield to achieve this goal. America has been reduced to the New Atlanticism, which is nothing more than a fancy way to say "Please." Even if the American economy could continue to support it, it is highly uncertain how much longer the allies will accept even the pretense of a smothering strategy.

The evolution of U.S. alliance policy highlights a huge and troubling irony: Although the expensive defense commitments extended to Western Europe and the Far East originally were conceived largely as a means of strengthening the U.S. economy over the long-haul (by preserving its opportunities to trade and invest in these potentially wealthy and powerful regions), by the mid-1960s, the United States had settled on a policy of sacrificing real economic strength in order to preserve defense commitments.

Yet without real economic strength behind it, neither military adventurism nor alliance arm-twisting can succeed. And the weaker America has become economically, the more its demands for compensation have grated on the increasingly powerful allies—even before the Gorbachev era—and the less cooperative they have become.

The United States, therefore, faces a fundamental choice in its alliance strategy. It can try to stay on the hegemonic course. Or it can dramatically cut its foreign policy expenditures by dismantling its major alliances, and therefore free up the resources needed for economic revitalization at home. Revitalization would permit the United States to depend on much more reliable methods than manipulating alliance relationships to achieve its principal foreign policy goals. Chiefly, it would use responsible fiscal policies to help assure international monetary stability, it would win adequate shares of world markets by manufacturing world-class products—not exerting pressure on its allies—and it would maintain the national military strength to handle whatever security threats it faces. True, the United States would lose much of its ability to defuse alliance tensions and mobilize allied consensuses behind its various international positions, and to maintain geopolitical stability around the world. In particular, Washington would lose much of its ability to contain the power of Japan and the new Germany.

But these capabilities are eroding quickly anyway. The Japanese, the Germans, and the Europeans are going to conduct more independent foreign policies no matter what the United States does. The question facing Americans is whether we will continue to try to stop the inevitable, or focus on the much more realistic goal of coping successfully with the consequences of a much less stable world. Revitalization can put America in a much better position to deal with Europe and Japan from a position of strength and to secure vital security through its own power. Indeed, revitalization is the only way to achieve what must become America's preeminent foreign policy goal in a multipolar world—expanding national strategic self-reliance wherever possible. In such a world, with all of its dangers and its intensifying economic competition, countries should want all the self-reliance they can get.

The very capabilities that make the United States a superpower—great military might, a favorable location, vast natural wealth, considerable economic self-reliance, and technological dynamism—make this revitalization strategy preferable to smothering for two principal reasons. First, as has been discussed, military strength that smothering exploits depends on the economic strength that it fritters away. Second, revitalization has the virtue of greater controllability. Obviously, America has much more influence over its own economy than it has over the economies of other countries. Therefore, all else being even only roughly equal, the revitalization strategy needs to take into account fewer wildcards and thus is more likely to succeed than a strategy of extorting prosperity from other countries.

The transition underway today from a Cold War era to an Age of Economics does not mean that power is shrinking in importance in world affairs. It simply signals that a new form of power is becoming decisive. Moreover, even if the United States continues to rely mainly on international cooperation to achieve its foreign policy goals, it will still need as much power as it can amass. For cooperative arrangements will entail continuous politicking and horse-trading. And the countries that bring the most chips to the bargaining table will see their positions prevail most often.

Precisely because Western Europe and Japan are too powerful and wealthy for America to keep trying to smother, America's security, political, and economic relationships with them will always be extensive. Further, even though the economic competition is likely to continue intensifying, it need not become dangerous and destructive.

But the days when the United States could rely on ordering these relationships to its liking are long gone. And the day when it can depend on good will and sentimentality to perform the same task is at best still distant. For the foreseeable future, Western Europe and Japan are going to act like fully independent powers no matter what America does, cultivating their own strength, pursuing their own goals, and placing their own interests above everyone else's.

The United States can afford to do no less. It must stop viewing its major allies variously as irresponsible children, paroled criminals, or even as protectorates and clients. Instead, the United States must abandon the illusion of perfect control over these countries, and perfect global stability. It must acknowledge the inevitability of friction and possibly conflict even among democratic countries, and concentrate more on dealing with the consequences. America must begin to view its allies as sovereign equals—both to build the foundations for healthy partnerships when their interests genuinely coincide, and to protect its own when they do not.

The Triumph of Neoclassicism

Walter Russell Mead

The breakdown of the Bretton Woods currency accords placed the world at a crossroads. Various pieces of the old system remained, but the keystone of the arch, the monetary accords, had fallen out of place. The international economy was left with an inadequate regulatory structure, a shoe that pinched but failed to support.

A stable framework for currency values is helpful in and of itself, but a working international system for stabilizing currencies has a significance that transcends its convenience in international trade. Stable currency values do not spring out of nowhere; they emerge from systematic and far-reaching agreements about economic objectives and policies. They do not cause stability so much as express it. Conversely, the failure to stabilize currency values after 1971 expressed a chaos that it reinforced but did not cause. In the absence of a broader consensus on economic objectives, the managers of the world economy could neither reform the Bretton Woods currency system not replace it with an adequate substitute.

Trilateralism, the first attempt at a new framework for U.S. policy, dominated the scene for most of the 1970s. This new consensus can perhaps more precisely be described as trilateral global neoclassicism. It was trilateral because it held that the burdens, and to some extent the direction, of the world economy should be shared among three powers—the United States, Japan, and Europe—principally West Germany. It was global because, as in the case of the Bretton Woods consensus, the trilateralists saw the world economy as essentially indivisible. Finally, it was neoclassical in its elevation of the free market, distrust of intervention, and diminished attention to demand-side problems. Where the Keynesians considered underconsumption and deflation to be the chief dangers of the modern economy, the

Walter Russell Mead, *author of* Mortal Splendor: The American Empire In Transition (1987) *is a Fellow at the World Policy Institute. Excerpted with permission from "The United States and the World Economy" by* Walter Russell Mead *in* World Policy Journal *Winter 1988-1989.*

neoclassicists worried about inflation and overconsumption. Where the Keynesians believed that intergovernmental cooperation ought to be expressed in enduring institutional forms, the trilateralists had lower expectations of international economic coordination. Bretton Woods had broken down; it could not, perhaps even should not, be replaced. The trilateral cooperation which, in the 1970s, would attempt to substitute for the unilateral American leadership of the 1940s, 1950s, and 1960s, would be ad hoc, expressed as a series of responses to specific problems rather than through institutions and binding commitments.

Most fundamentally, the neoclassicists disagreed with the Keynesians over the proper relationship between markets and governments. The Keynesians believed that the proper function of both intervention and the market was to stimulate investment by encouraging demand, and that, in tandem, regulation and the market produced stable growth in a liberal order. The neoclassicists believed that regulation was the enemy of free markets, and that free markets, so far as they were practicable, produced as if by the workings of an invisible hand the liberal order to which the Keynesians aspired. The dispute, like the historic dispute that split the Orthodox and Catholic wings of Christendom, boiled down to the *filioque*. For the orthodox neoclassicists, growth, the third member of the economic Trinity, proceeded only from the Father, the market; the catholic Keynesians added, *"filioque"*— "and the Son."

The triumph of neoclassicism created a policy gap—a principled refusal by policymakers to intervene in economic activity for the sake of maintaining a liberal order. In the Bretton Woods system, intervention and markets had, at least ostensibly, worked together. For the trilateralists, the two things worked at cross purposes. The trilateralists lacked the burning intensity of the free-market zealots who would attempt in the Reagan years to wage a *jihad* on all forms of state intervention, but they thought of regulation much as Abraham Lincoln originally thought of slavery: they would not seek to abolish it where it existed, but would steadfastly oppose its extension into new territories.

This meant that economic change would not be met with innovation in the economic structure. The 1970s saw the rapid expansion of manufacturing in the developing world, an explosion in international financial flows, steep declines in the value of the dollar against almost all major currencies, and even steeper drops in the value of all paper monies against gold. Where a Keynesian perspective would lead governments to deal systematically and strategically with these transformations, trilateralists—some from conviction, some from despair—were content to meet these challenges without a policy. Somehow, the trilateralists seemed to believe, a liberal order would emerge from this chaos if they could just stand aside long enough, intervening only when a crisis threatened to topple the system.

The market, a means under Bretton Woods, rose to the status of an end during the trilateralist era. The unshackling of markets from their fetters was believed to be the sole and necessary prerequisite for growth. The free market would cure the balance-of-payments problem, and floating exchange rates would yield the best currency values. And it was not only the web of currency regulations that the trilateralists disliked. They grew increasingly suspicious of all the forms of intervention by which the Keynesians had tried to protect mass purchasing power. Unions, in the neoclassical view, prevented manufacturers from realizing gains in productivity and also kept the labor markets inflexible by ensuring that nominal wages were slow to fall in response to rising unemployment. (To the Keynesians, this would be a sign of advanced degenerative social disease.) The trilateralists also turned on the monopolies and oligopolies inherited from the postwar era of regulation and nationalization. The high wages in these industries were deemed economically inefficient. Programs to stimulate employment were thought to impose unnecessary costs on employers. Countercyclical economic spending might still be necessary from time to time, but the trilateralists viewed even this with suspicion. Just as Lincoln eventually concluded that slavery must be abolished entirely, so the trilateralists came to believe that to stop the insidious spread of regulation was not enough.

Even with hindsight, one should not dismiss the trilateralists' position out of hand. Their view reflected the realities of the post-Bretton Woods world. The global economy had changed since 1950, but its basic institutional arrangements had not kept pace. In international finance, for example, restrictions on banking dating from the Bretton Woods era of controlled capital flows and stable currencies had begun to chafe. Banks needed more freedom to cope with the new risks and to exploit new opportunities. Domestically, interest-rate regulations that once were viewed by the banks themselves as safeguards against irresponsible competition came to feel stifling; banks needed greater flexibility to cope with the volatile interest rates that characterized the brave new world of international finance.

With the breakdown of the system, intervention tended to lose its constructive function and to degenerate into protectionism—internationally, into protectionist trade policies, and domestically, into efforts to protect the privileged positions of various industries and political constituencies. Small banks sought shelter from large ones; monopolies, state-owned or otherwise, sought protection from competitors; domestic producers called for help against imports. Losers sought protection from winners; the dinosaurs lobbied for state-subsidized nest patrols to keep the mammals away from their eggs.

Under the new global economic conditions, neither the free-market strategies of the neoclassicists nor the interventionist strategies of the Keynesians were effective; both tended to reduce the mass purchasing power on which Keynesian prosperity once depended. Market-opening policies achieved this directly by ending the high-wage monopolies, accelerating the transfer of production to low-wage labor markets in the developing world, reducing social benefits for the unemployed and unemployable, and cutting spending on programs designed to create jobs. Intervention produced the same results, but in a more roundabout way; rather than bolstering mass purchasing power, regulation had the opposite effect in the new protectionist context, since protection reduces the incomes of all those who do not benefit directly from its programs. Subsidies to farmers mean higher food prices for consumers; protected industries are able to raise their prices; the majority must suffer to benefit the few.

The trilateralists' diligent efforts to unshackle markets did not go unrewarded. From 1972 to 1980, real wages in the United States fell 15 percent; unemployment doubled in Europe. But did this brilliant success lead to faster rates of growth, more stable exchange rates, or even lower rates of inflation? In all cases, the answer is no. The 1970s were a signally less successful era of policy than the previous decades, so much so that the trilateralist consensus was abandoned by every participant by the end of the decade. Germany, burned by the inflationary consequences of its effort to take a turn as the locomotive of world growth (the larger locomotive could not pull the train, so the railroad had called on a smaller one to take its place), was not prepared to step forward again. Japan remained unwilling either to slow its drive for export-led growth or to allow the yen to be used as a reserve currency. In the U.S. presidential campaign of 1980, "trilateral" was a term of abuse that Ronald Reagan's supporters hurled at his foes. The stage was set for the final dissolution of the postwar consensus amid the disastrous deficits and the chaotic policies of the Reagan years . . . .

The Military Budget

Steve Chan

. . . . [T]he theoretical possibility of an impact of military expenditures on economic performance is not generally contested. Rather, the debate revolves around when, how, for whom, and in what direction and magnitude this impact is likely to be actually felt, and whether it can be mitigated or compounded by government policies and socioeconomic conditions. . . .

Whether we use the "impact," "consequence," or "effect," the analytic challenge is to arrive at valid causal inference: Whether and how a change in defense spending causes a change in economic performance. . . . [M]any studies have employed a cross-sectional design that is not very effective for establishing cause and effect relationships. To illustrate, if one finds that military spending is positively correlated with economic growth, in itself this result cannot tell us whether economic prosperity produces increased defense outlays or vice versa. One also cannot be sure whether and how much of the observed change in economic growth should be attributed to the current level of defense outlays, as opposed to the lagged influence of past levels or changes in these outlays. . . .

. . .[F]or the developed countries, the results suggest substantial cross-national and over-time variations in the relationship between defense spending and economic performance. In general, they do not support the view that defense spending encourages or facilitates sustained economic growth, but there are exceptions, such as when the pent-up demand and the expansion of production capacity during wartime result in a postwar economic boom. Also, in the short run military expenditures can stimulate demand and boost employment. In the long run, however, these expenditures are more apt to have a negative than a positive impact on investment, inflation,

---

Steve Chan *is Professor of Political Science at the University of Colorado at Boulder.* *Excerpted with permission from "The Impact of Defense Spending on Economic Performance: A Survey of Evidence and Problems." Taken from the Summer 1985 issue of* ORBIS: A Journal of World Affairs, *published by the Foreign Policy Research Institute.*

employment, balance of payments, industrial productivity, and economic growth. The evidence on the United States, the country that has attracted the most research attention, indicates especially significant costs.[1]. . . For this as well as the other developed Western countries, heavy defense spending seems to have a particularly important impact in dampening capital formation and investment, which in turn reduces economic growth in the long run.[2]

The distinction between the short-run and the long-run impact of defense spending points to a major deficiency in the current literature. . . . [M]uch of the impact of defense spending on the economy tends to be indirect and is apt to involve substantial time lags. The more important long-run negative effects of this spending can be concealed. . . . if we use relatively short temporal units of observation.

Indeed, given the customary preference of officials to finance defense and war by running budget deficits rather than by cutting other programs or raising taxes,[3] much of the cost of this spending is shifted to future generations. Mounting public debts and future governmental obligations (e.g., pension and other financial support for war veterans and their dependents) are only the most visible part of these postponed costs. The displacement of civilian research and development by military needs imposes another kind of cost on future productivity. It would be naive to expect this displacement to have an immediate negative impact on a country's industrial efficiency and trade competitiveness in the world market. Rather, it would require a chronic underemphasis of civilian research and development. . . . Moreover, this impact need not be constant over time, and is instead likely to involve cumulative and rising economic costs. In other words, there may very well be a threshold beyond which insufficient resource allocation to advance civilian technologies begins to exact an economic toll, and this will accelerate over time. And, just as it takes time for this to be manifest. . . . it will take time to decelerate and reverse it. . . .

How does this impact occur?

. . .[W]e need to distinguish between the first-order and second-order effects of military spending. As noted, the immediate direct impact of a rise in this spending is likely to be higher demand, production, and employment. These favorable effects, however, tend to be offset significantly by the indirect effects of military expenditures in reducing private saving and investment, which will hurt productivity and growth in the long run. Therefore, both the direct and indirect effects of these expenditures must be considered in a net assessment of their economic impact.

At the risk of some oversimplification, there are four main perspectives on this assessment. The first, the "modernization" model, is most closely associated with [the late sociologist Emile] Benoit's research [on developing countries] . . . . The second perspective, the "capital formation" model, stresses the importance of private investment as the primary determinant of future economic growth. To the extent that increased defense spending entails higher taxes or government borrowing in the capital markets, it absorbs funds that would otherwise have gone at least partly to investment. The cost-push inflation that this spending abets also encourages a mass psychology in favor of immediate consumption and against saving. . . .

[Ron] Smith's studies on the developed Western economies led him to suggest that there was roughly a one-to-one trade-off between a country's military expenditures and its total investment.[4] A recent study by [Karen A.] Rasler and [William R.] Thompson, however, shows that this trade-off tends to vary substantially for different countries and time periods.[5] A statistically significant trade-off had not existed for the United Kingdom, Japan, France, and West Germany in the post-World War II era, whereas such a trade-off was present for the United Kingdom during the period before 1945 and for the United States for periods both before and after that year. More research is needed to investigate the reasons for these cross-national and over-time variations. We also need to learn more about the temporal lags between increased defense spending and reduced investment, and between reduced investment and economic slowdown. In explaining the discrepancies between their cross-sectional and time series analyses, [Ron] Smith and [George] Georgiou properly observed that "the effect of military expenditure on growth through investment and capital formation is likely to be a long run one and so not picked up by the short lags used in [their] time series analysis."[6]

A third perspective on the chain of causality leading from defense spending to economic stagnation is offered by the "balance of payment" model, or the export-led model of growth. It points to the negative economic effects of a chronic and serious displacement of capital and talent from the most dynamic sectors of civilian production. Among OECD countries, those most adept in taking advantage of the rapidly expanding export opportunities have had the fastest economic growth.[7] Furthermore, as capital spending for defense tends to be concentrated precisely in the more important export sectors such as machinery and transport (and, more recently, electronics), it is not surprising that it reduces the available goods for export. Slower export growth in turn causes slower economic growth, further reducing a country's trade competitiveness. It appears that even after considering the large quantities of arms exports sold by the heavy defense spenders, the overall balance of payments position of these countries (including their significant military outlays abroad) still remains quite unfavorable.[8] Rising imports and falling exports in part explain the historical weakening of the U.S. dollar and the British pound, and the phenomenon of persistently high unemployment levels in these countries even in face of relatively robust consumer demand.[9] . . . [A] study of seventeen OECD countries has reported that these expenditures have a large positive effect on manufacturing output, although they also have a large negative effect on the investment rate.[10] Their resulting net impact on economic growth is negative (except for the Mediterranean members of the OECD).

The fourth perspective, "technological displacement," stresses the significant amounts of material and human resources consumed by the modern weapons industries for research and development. The diversion of these resources from civilian to military purposes can have a detrimental long-run effect on a country's productivity and technological position. This effect is offset somewhat when knowledge and technologies derived originally from military research are adapted for civilian uses. Although many analysts have commented on the effects of technological displacement and of technological spillover due to military spending,[11] there has been, thus far, very little systematic research on these subjects.[12] . . . . It is also difficult to estimate the impact of a specific new technical application in terms of its social and commercial values, and the role of military research and development in contributing to its discovery. . . .

The impact of what on what

So far, the discussion has proceeded as if the meanings of the terms "defense spending" and "economic impact" were self-evident and shared by all analysts. However, considerable ambiguity and doubt pervade both the conceptualization and measurement of the dependent and the independent variables. . . .

. . .[D]efense spending must be disaggregated according to different purposes. The economic impact of the military's personnel costs is similar to that of the government's civilian programs of income transfer. These costs should be separated from other types of defense spending, to see exactly how military expenditures differ from other kinds of government expenditures. Much of the theoretical literature has centered on the effects of military procurement on the economy. If this is the main concern, we should focus on military procurement rather than on gross expenditures in all defense-related activities. As the research to date has not generally tried to distinguish among types of military spending, there is the possibility of distortion in our analytic results and interpretations. In the case of the United States, total personnel costs for the Pentagon had climbed rapidly over the past decade to the point of consuming about half its budget. Some of the consequences attributed to military spending (e.g., cost-push inflation, production shortages in the capital goods industries) are accounted for by the nonpersonnel part of the defense budget and not by the entire budget. . . .

Current research has most commonly employed the annual or average levels of military spending and economic performance. This practice seems to be unsatisfactory, as the theoretical discussions usually imply a concern with the economic effects of persistently high defense expenditures. Accordingly, some weighted form of moving averages or the sum total of defense expenditures over a certain number of years are preferable to annual or average levels. If it is the cumulative costs of military spending—in terms of structural inflation, structural unemployment, the loss of comparative trade advantages, and the accustomed dependence of defense industries on government contracts—that ultimately concern us, then we should employ measures that can capture the cumulative size of this spending and of its effects.

On the other hand, if we are interested in the volatility of defense spending and especially in the economic effects of periodic swings in this spending, then measures such as first differences and deltas should be used. From the budgetary theories of incremental adjustment, there is sound reason to focus on the relative or absolute changes in the amount of defense expenditures rather than on the levels of these expenditures.[13] . . .

When is this impact most likely to be felt?

Recent longitudinal research has suggested. . .that the relationship between military expenditures and economic performance is hardly stable over time. . . . What can account for such over-time changes? Surely, time in itself is not the answer, or at least not the full answer. Instead, time is likely to be a proxy for such other variables as an economy's capacity to absorb defense spending, its government's fiscal and monetary policies, its technological and currency advantages over trade competitors, its vulnerability to foreign threats, and the effects of developments such as global wars and recessions.[14] It would especially be useful for future research to determine how a country's economic and military status in the international system might influence the relationship between its defense spending and its economic performance. . ..

There are substantial cross-national variations among the developed countries. Two recent studies on the OECD economies suggest that defense burden (especially measured in terms of its rate of change) tends to be positively correlated with economic growth for the Mediterranean countries (e.g., Greece, Turkey, Portugal, Spain, Italy).[15] Conversely, these variables tend to be negatively correlated for the more mature OECD economies. . . .

Causal explanation requires us to give attention to at least four terms: "there is first of all that which intervenes, secondly that state of affairs which is interfered with by the intervention, thirdly the actual effect of the intervention and fourthly the outcome that would have prevailed but for the intervention"[16]. . . .

However previous research on the defense-growth relationship tends to attend only to two of the four items: the "intervention" of military spending and its actual effect. The state of affairs that is interfered with and the state of affairs that would otherwise have obtained in the absence of military spending are usually not addressed. . . .

A sensitivity to "what if" questions in turn would lead us to stress more the idea of opportunity costs. . . . [T]here have been few experimental attempts to show how a given increase or decrease in defense spending would produce specific changes in private saving and investment, unemployment, inflation, and economic growth.[17] . . . It appears that for the United States at least, additional defense spending is more likely to be financed at the expense of consumption than investment, and that the savings from defense spending cuts are also more likely to go to consumption than investment.[18] The investment loss entailed by increasing defense spending may be small in absolute dollar amounts but significant in terms of its multiplier effects on demand, employment, output, and additional production capacity.   In cumulative terms, the opportunity costs are even greater because the lost production capacity is foregone for ever. In order to show these costs and the possible benefits of defense spending, we need realistic, explicit, and dynamic simulation models for asking "what if" questions.   Moreover, sound policy assessment requires us to contrast the current or recommended levels of military expenditures with the most probable (as opposed to the optimal) alternative use of these expenditures.

Notes

[1] See Robert W. deGrasse, Jr., *Military Expansion and Economic Decline: The Impact of Military Spending on U.S. Economic Performance* (Armonk, N.Y.: M.E. Sharpe).

[2] Karen A. Rasler and William R. Thompson, "Longitudinal Change in Defense Burdens, Capital Formation and Economic Growth," paper presented at the annual meeting of the International Studies Association, Atlanta, March 1984; and Ron P. Smith, "Military Expenditure Investment in OECD Countries, 1954-1973," *Journal of Comparative Economics* 4, March 1980.

[3] Earl J. Hamilton, "The Role of War in Modern Inflation," *Journal of Economic History* 37, March 1977, pp. 13-19. For an estimate of the total monetary cost of the Vietnam War to the U.S. taxpayers, see Tom Riddell, "The $676 Billion Quagmire," *The Progressive* 37, October 1973, pp. 33-37.

[4] Smith, "Military Expenditure and Investment in OECD Countries, 1954-1973"; "Military Expenditure and Capitalism," *Cambridge Journal of Economics* 2, 1977; and id., "Military Expenditure and Capitalism: A Reply," *Cambridge Journal of Economics,* 1978.

[5] Rasler and Thompson, "Longitudinal Change in Defense Burdens, Capital Formation and Economic Growth."

[6] Ron Smith and George Georgiou, "Assessing the Effect of Military Expenditure on OECD Economies," *Arms Control* 4, May 1983, p. 13.

[7] Kurt W. Rothschild, "Military Expenditure, Exports and Growth," *Kyklos* 26, 1973.

[8] Smith, "Military Expenditure and Capitalism: A Reply"; Eric Chester, "Military Spending and Capitalist Stability," *Cambridge Journal of Economics,* 1978; and Lloyd J. Dumas, "Economic Conversion, Productive Efficiency and Social Welfare," *Peace Research Review* 7, 1977.

[9] Dumas, "Economic Conversion, Productive Efficiency and Social Welfare."

[10] Adne Cappelen, Nils Petter Gleditsch, and Olav Bjerkholt, "Military Spending and Economic Growth in the OECD Countries," *Journal of Peace Research* 21, 1984.

[11] See, for example, Dumas, "Economic Conversion, Productive Efficiency and Social Welfare"; and Murray L . Weidenbaum, *The Economics of Peacetime Defense* (New York: Praeger, 1974).

[12] One recent effort in this area is by Goran Lindgren, "Military and Civilian Research and Development," paper presented at the annual meeting of the International Studies Association, Atlanta, March 1984. See also his assessment of the literature, "Armaments and Economic Performance," in "Industrialized Market Economies," *Journal of Peace Research* 21 (1984), pp. 375-87.

[13] See the argument in Richard C. Eichenberg, "The Expenditure and Revenue Effects of Defense Spending in the Federal Republic of Germany," *Policy Sciences* 16, June, 1984. For two other examples of research focusing on the changes in rather than the levels of military expenditures, see Riccardo Faini, Patricia Arnez, and Lance Taylor, "Defense Spending, Economic Structure and Growth,"*Economic Development and Cultural Change* 32, April 1984; and Rasler and Thompson, "Longitudinal Change in Defense Burdens, Capital Formation and Economic Growth: Evidence Among Countries and Over Time."

[14] Karen Rasler and William R. Thompson found that global wars tended to offer occasions for raising taxes and government spending (even more so for civilian programs than for military programs). See their "War Making and State Making: Governmental Expenditures, Tax Revenues, and Global Wars," *American Political Science Review* 79, June 1985, pp. 491-507.

[15] Cappelen, Gleditsch, and Bjerkholt, "Military Spending and Economic Growth in the OECD Countries"; and Steve Chan, "Defense Spending and Economic Performance: Correlates Among the OECD Countries," paper presented at the annual meeting of the International Studies Association, Atlanta, March 1984.

[16] Alasdair Mcintyre, "Causality and History," in Juha Manninen and Raimo Tuomela, eds., *Essays on Explanation and Understanding* (Dordrecht, Holland: Reidel, 1976), p. 148.

[17] For some examples of attempts to move in this direction, see Dumas, "Economic Conversion, Productive Efficiency and Social Welfare"; and W. Leontief and F. Durchin, *Worldwide Economic Implications of a Limitation on Military Spending* (New York: United Nations, 1980). Two other U.N. publications have examined the relationship between miliary expenditures and development; see *Economic and Social Consequences of Arms Race and of Military Expenditures* (New York: United Nations, 1978); and *Disarmament and Development* (New York: United Nations, 1973).

[18] Bruce M. Russett, *What Price Vigilance? The Burdens of National Defense* (New Haven, Conn.: Yale University Press, 1970), chapter 5.

VIII

Dimensions of a New Economic Strategy

Understanding the need for a comprehensive economic strategy is the first step toward developing one. Understanding the obstacles to better economic performance is the second step. The final step is identifying the components of a strategy. At this stage, there is still ample room for debate over specifics. Part Eight presents some of the most compelling proposals that have appeared in recent years for reviving American economic dynamism.

Although the particular recommendations and points of emphasis vary, these proposals all share several key assumptions about the basic requirements of a sound strategy. First, the strategy must be comprehensive. America's biggest economic problems are all closely related. They cannot be effectively attacked in isolation. Second, the conventional tools of post-1945 U.S. economic policymaking alone cannot solve these problems. It is especially important for an economic strategy to focus on micro-economics—the forces affecting the performance of individual American companies. Third, and perhaps most important, a sound strategy will not simply emerge from the natural workings of market forces. Individuals and businesses must be brought into the planning process, but only government can provide the overarching vision, the leadership, and the systematic coordination needed to produce a coherent program.

The section also looks at the domestic politics of competitiveness in America. Polls consistently show voters to be deeply troubled by the country's economic problems and, in particular, by the dramatic erosion in America's international economic superiority. But translating these concerns into a politically viable program is another matter. What are the ideological hurdles to galvanizing public support for an economic strategy? What new opportunities can politicians grasp? What messages will and will not work?

According to Clyde V. Prestowitz, Jr., an economic strategy must rest on four key elements: a macro-economic policy designed to raise U.S. investment rates to world-class levels; coordinated government policies to help boost productivity; measures to maintain across-the-board strength in key industries and technologies and to create corporate structures capable of winning in the global marketplace; and a "results-oriented" trade policy.

To speed up America's sluggish utilization of advanced manufacturing systems, William C. Norris advocates setting up a national network of computerized centers that would perform specific design and manufacturing tasks for U.S. companies on a contract basis.

Kevin L. Kearns and James P. Lucier write that U.S. competitiveness in the 21st century requires an entirely new kind of high tech national infrastructure—one utilizing fibre-optic networks, digital libraries, "smart" highways and cars, supercomputer networks, and other projects to move and manage enormous quantities of people, materials, and, above all, information. They emphasize that unless the federal government takes the lead in coordinating this effort and setting standards, the 21st century infrastructure will not materialize.

Competitiveness has become a major buzzword on Capitol Hill, but David Heenan notes that U.S. legislators are still unwilling to change American economic fundamentals. In particular, most members of Congress reject abandoning America's current adversarial economic and political system in favor of European or Japanese-style collaborative structures—both because they believe in the superiority of America's current free enterprise system, and because they doubt that our fiercely individualistic culture would stand for it.

Kevin Phillips takes American conservatives to task for dismissing the very idea of useful government-business collaboration to improve national economic performance, and thereby ceding the field to the Left—and its allegedly protectionist, hyper-regulatory impulses. In addition, Phillips criticizes as "absurd" the entire national debate over government's proper role in the economy. Both Left and Right, he argues, miss the central truth that the most successful economies today have found ways to exploit the strengths of both the public and private sectors.

Finally, Bruce Stokes reports on how Democratic and Republican party campaign strategists are planning to use the competitiveness issue in forthcoming elections. Democrats in particular face a delicate task: how to stoke the fires of economic nationalism without sparking a surge of racism and other forms of anti-foreign hysteria. But none of Washington's political insiders doubts that economic nationalism—and the much broader issues of economic strategy—will shape electoral politics in America for years to come.

Renewal From Within

Clyde V. Prestowitz, Jr.

The greatest challenges to American strength come from within, not from abroad. The world economic stage has changed and we have not changed with it. We continue to read from a script that no longer makes such sense to the rest of the world. We have seen our political ideals prevail, but our own economy has faltered.

Americans have time and again demonstrated their ability to unite and work together to meet major challenges. They can do so once more. But to rescue the present situation will require recognition of the sweeping changes that have transformed the world economy in the past forty years, and a concerted national effort to adjust to a new situation.

Specifically, America needs an integrated, multi-dimensional strategy to realize the full potential of America's rich material and human resources. Such a strategy must be based on four key elements: a macro-economic policy designed to raise U.S. investment rates to the levels of major competing nations; coordination of government policies with reference to overall productivity guidelines and objectives; an effort to assure the maintenance of a full range of industrial and technological capabilities in the United States and to create U.S. corporate structures able to compete in the international arena; and a result-oriented international trade policy.

We can no longer afford to look at the world as though it were still 1950. The United States must develop macro-economic policy that looks to the year 2000 and beyond. The United States needs and must have a production-oriented policy designed to avoid overconsumption by stimulating investment.

Clyde V. Prestowitz, Jr. *is founder and President of the Economic Strategy Institute. The author of* Trading Places: How We Are Giving Our Future to Japan and How To Reclaim It *(1988), he previously served as Counselor for Japan Affairs to the Secretary of Commerce from 1983 to 1986.*

Overconsumption adds $300 million to the U.S. debt burden each day. This is unsustainable in the long run, dangerous to ourselves, and dangerous to the many countries whose economies rely heavily on sales in the U.S. market. We can reduce our dangerous overconsumption level in one of two ways: by cutting back, or producing more. Sharp cutbacks would be undesirable. Producing more would preclude any need to even consider restricting foreign access to U.S. markets, and this could be achieved if macro-economic policy emphasized U.S. industrial production needs.

At the present time, American companies cannot compete effectively with producers in countries where the cost and risk of investment is far less than that of the United States. Correcting this imbalance is a prerequisite for American success. Left as it is, the investment rate in the United States will continue to lag behind that of its major national competitors and its industrial position will continue to erode. A macro-economic policy to redress the high cost of capital in this country would stimulate investment, stimulate production, and put American industry on a more equal footing with its foreign competitors. Future analysis should focus on ways to double the national savings and investment rate, and bring them into alignment with the rates of our principal foreign competitors; to adopt complementary budgeting and tax policies designed to reverse our international debt position; and to reduce U.S. investment risk to more acceptable levels.

Needed: Complementary micro-economic policies

All too often, the U.S. government's randomly set, microeconomic policies have a negative effect on the competitive health of American business. This has occurred in telecommunications, automobiles, aircraft, and dozens of other industries.

The entire U.S. telecommunications industry was restructured under a Federal court order. As an unintended consequence, the U.S. trade deficit in telecommunications equipment and services rose sharply. This occurred because the restructuring effectively opened the U.S. market to imports, but the United States did not ask its trading partners for similar openings abroad. This unintentional addition to the trade deficit could easily have been avoided had the court been required to review its restructuring plan with the United States Trade Representative.

U.S. auto industry regulations aimed at increasing fleet fuel efficiency have also produced adverse side effects. Though unintended, current regulations actually encourage U.S. automakers to move some production offshore, and they discourage foreign automakers in the United States from raising the U.S. content of their products beyond the 75 percent level. Reviewing such regulations in the context of broader productivity and investment considerations would preclude such anomalies.

Military co-production agreements struck in the interests of national security should not be exempt from economic review. Such unintended micro-economic consequences can be rolled back if the government takes steps to integrate and coordinate the way in which its thousands of presently random interventions affect both business decision and market forces. When that day comes, when economic leadership has become a formal national goal, the government must also begin to actively consider the composition and structure of the country's entire industrial base. The micro-economic criteria for determining how to focus this attention are not complicated. Industries and technologies that are critical to national defense are the obvious starting point. Beyond that it is obvious that industries characterized by rapid growth, high elasticity of demand, falling costs, knowledge intensiveness, and multiple linkages with other industries, will contribute more to economic growth, disinflation, productivity increases and wealth than industries without these characteristics. U.S. policies must be formulated to assure that such industries are encouraged to grow and prosper in the United States.

At present time, because such policies do not exist, a number of American industries have been decimated by aggressive foreign industrial policies. This unpleasant fact of life in the new world economic order will eventually require that government turn its full attention to such pressing questions as: How much of America's remaining industrial base should be manufacturing? How much in services? Does our economic well-being require an optical fiber industry, an automobile industry? Traditionally, most Americans think these are questions best left to free market forces. All things being equal, they are right. But all things are not equal. If the United States does not answer these questions they will be answered by foreign countries that sell in the United States. Lacking any policies of its own, foreign industrial policies will, defacto, determine the structure and composition of the U.S. economy.

Needed: Revitalized corporate structures

In the mid-1980s the Japanese semiconductor industry showed its remarkable ability to simultaneously absorb vast losses while investing for the future. At the present time, a major Japanese electronic firm is gearing itself for a similar performance in flat-panel displays. Preparing to weather five straight years of losses in order to achieve a strong market position, the Japanese firm considers the investment well worth the risk. No American company could do this and expect to survive. As long as this is true, the United States will continue to face the difficult choice between losing domestic producers in important global markets, or restricting foreign access to the U.S. market. To avoid this dilemma, it will be necessary to develop ways to help American firms equal the staying power of major European and Asian corporate groupings.

If we wish to revitalize corporate America, we must also address the ways in which corporate America is required to operate. The short-term U.S. focus stems from the fact that American business people work in structures and under circumstances that favor short-term results. This is, in large measure, a result of theories and attitudes that have gained wide acceptance among U.S. political, academic and business leaders regarding the nature of the corporation and its relationships with other economic participants.

So long as these views persist, American business will never be able to operate as effectively as its European and Asian counterparts. These views, and the circumstances to which they give rise, must be carefully analyzed and revised in order to shift our focus from the short term to the long term. This would include developing mechanisms aimed at: making American corporations less hostage to the immediate demands of shareholders; taking steps to prove, both to American labor and consumer groups, that we all have a vital interest in the health of American business; making long-term capital commitments more attractive to American investors; and focusing our attention more carefully on the relationship between capital and risk

Reducing risk

Capital and risk are inseparable investment elements, and risk is one of the most powerful and least understood aspects of America's short-term business orientation. Risk is high here for three reasons: in addition to the high cost of American capital, and the immediate performance demands of the U.S. financial community, the American market is routinely targeted by foreign companies that are able to launch forays from protected domestic sanctuaries. Such companies frequently violate U.S. law with impunity.

American companies have been driven out of consumer electronics and other fields by predatory dumping, collusion, and customs fraud carried out by foreign firms and domestic distributors—against which the U.S. government has never enforced its own trade laws. The United States must take active steps to assure that such violations never again allowed to go unpunished, and it can do this by simply enforcing the laws that are now on its books. Failing positive enforcement action, no board of directors would ever support an American company's efforts in a field where it may be victim of such tactics.

Needed: A contemporary international trade policy

When the United States adopts a production-oriented macro-economic policy, when it has begun to coordinate its micro-economic policies, when it has begun to revitalize corporate structures, it will automatically create an international trade framework. Then we can get on with the job of developing a specific trade strategy. At each step of this process, we must come to grips with the contemporary economic structures and international dynamics that are shaping both the 1990s and the 21st Century.

More than 40 years ago, the overwhelming relative power of the United States enabled it to create institutions, and establish rules based on its own definition of such concepts as "free" and "fair" and "open." The United States must recognize that today many other market-oriented societies operate on somewhat different economic principles. More and more, the United States appears to be out of step with the rest of the world. All too often, U.S. attempts to get other nations to act like us are perceived abroad as "crying," as an attempt to find scapegoats for our own shortcomings.

It is increasingly clear that U.S.-created institutions and principles are less and less adequate in the new economic order that has begun to emerge. We must reevaluate our views, and carefully analyze the social and economic structures of other nations in order to understand the origins and objectives of their industrial policies and the manner in which they can alter the dynamics of the international marketplace.

If we can do this, based on a strategy geared to the objectives of economic leadership, we can function more effectively in the world without abandoning our ideals. Being realistic is not the direct opposite of being idealistic. These two notions can coexist if we as a nation examine ourselves, our priorities and our values, and revise them to better cope with the changing world beyond our shores.

We must realize that our international trade efforts are more likely to succeed if we deal with the world as it is, not as we would like it to be, or as it was in 1948. We must begin by acknowledging that in certain areas we are unlikely to be able to either open markets or pursue free trade as we understand it; unlikely because matters of national sovereignty, national pride, industrial policies, industrial structures, and deeply seated cultural differences make these practices impossible.   Once we analyze the structures and dynamics of different international markets, we can establish broad trade categories and act accordingly.

Needed: A sense of purpose

We must take up the decades of challenge ahead with the sense of purpose and the sense of great things to come that have marked every other challenge to our country throughout its long and remarkable history. With optimism, with creativity, with debate and ingenuity, we can and will find ways to maintain American economic strength and solve problems both at home and abroad. We must believe in our ability to do these things. We are too young and vital a nation to lose our sights or lessen our expectations. We must believe that we can and will continue to lead, for the only alternative to leading is to be less than America has the ability to be.

Most in this nation believe our people still have the will to excel. We must show them *how*, and we must show them that there are many ways consistent with American ideals to *encourage* rather than *discourage* American business. If there have been abuses in the past, we must rectify them. If there has been a short-term orientation, we must lengthen the view. If business and government have often been adversaries, let us make them partners. If there have been major changes on the world economic stage, we must acknowledge them and adjust to them. If a new world order is emerging, we must take up the challenges it offers.

Beyond the call for new macro- and micro-economic policies, revitalized corporate structures and new trade policies, we can remain strong only if we develop strategies based on the reaffirmation of the stake we all have in one another: as employees, as managers, as consumers, as tax payers, as investors, as citizens of the United States, as parts of a whole. "E Pluribus Unum" is still on our coins and we must reestablish it in our hearts. If we do not stand united, if we let divisive self-interests divert us from the pursuit of national goals, we must like Abraham Lincoln ask, "if any nation so conceived and so dedicated can long endure?" Or, as Benjamin Franklin said when the representatives had finished singing the Declaration of Independence, "Now we must all hang together. For if we do not, assuredly we shall all hang separately." It is time for Americans to take up such thoughts again. It is time to redefine ourselves. It is time to ask anew—what kind of a people are we, and what kind of nation do we wish to have in the 21st Century?

Become Competitive? Here's How

William C. Norris

The issue of how to improve American industrial competitiveness in global markets has become a prominent theme in pubic policy debate. Competitiveness is so popular in the political arena that some 5,000 bills were introduced in Congress last year to address the problem. It has also been discussed in countless speeches, conferences, task forces, news articles, scholarly studies and popular books.

Despite all this activity, very little real progress has been made and few significant programs have been advanced to respond effectively to the crisis, especially in the critically important area of manufacturing.

Substantial research and development has been under way in our universities and Government laboratories for years to develop advanced automated equipment and computer-integrated design and manufacturing technology. As a result, the United States possesses the most advanced manufacturing technology in the world, and, through ongoing research, will likely maintain the position for many years.

Ironically, except for the handful of larger companies this advanced technology is not being widely used in manufacturing. Our advanced technology largely remains in laboratories, while our foreign competitors—especially Japanese companies—are capitalizing on it.

There are many reasons why we are so slow in utilizing advanced manufacturing systems. They include the low level of technical capability in most manufacturing companies; a dearth of engineers in advanced manufacturing; the substantial cost of equipment; computer software and training, and a high risk and low return on capital that is well below what is

William C. Norris, *chairman of the William C. Norris Institute, is founder and Chairman Emeritus of Control Data. He is a member of the Advisory Board of the Economic Strategy Institute. Copyright* © *1987 by the New York Times Company. Reprinted with permission.*

traditionally acceptable. Aside from the risk and low return considerations, most small and medium-sized companies simply don't have the money.

How can the United States respond to this formidable array of barriers? We need to establish a nationwide network of regional computer-aided design and computer-integrated manufacturing centers. These facilities would perform manufacturing on a service basis, allowing companies to pay for the manufacturing service without having to pay the full cost of the initial investment to build the center. Each company would have access to the center through a work station at its own premises that would be connected by telephone.

In addition to computer-aided design-engineering and manufacturing services, education and training could be provided. A small or medium-sized company could use the center's facilities initially and later decide to install selected robotic equipment on its own premises. Larger companies would be licensed to replicate the entire facility.

Initially, 10 regional centers would be optimum, built over seven to eight years. At a cost of $80 million for each center, the estimated $800 million total cost would be financed through a combination of Federal, state and private funds. A large percentage of the initial funding would have to be Federal money, given the necessity to move rapidly on a large scale and because of the high risk and uncertainty involved.

Once full operation was reached, the manufacturing centers would be taken over by the private sector and operated as a for-profit business. At that time, the number of centers could be expanded.

While such a program is critically important to a broad range of manufacturing companies, it has a unique value for small, cash-strapped companies, which lack an advanced manufacturing capability.

A similar situation occurred in the early days of the computer industry. Small companies needed access to the computing power of large computers. However, during the period, only large companies, major universities and Government agencies could afford the initial investments, which often exceeded $1 million.

The answer was to establish computer centers that provided access on a service basis for small companies. Today, as the cost of computers has decreased dramatically and their power has increased, every small company is able to afford a computer that costs a few thousand dollars and that can handle all its needs.

The same scenario could take place in advanced manufacturing. During the next 15 to 20 years, the cost of hardware and software will be significantly reduced, and small companies will be able to afford their own systems. Meanwhile, the gap in the availability of this essential capability could be bridged if states move rapidly to form consortiums that would establish regional advanced manufacturing centers. Such a program would require a much greater degree of cooperation among states than has so far existed. But since benefits would be spread over a region, rivalries between states could be avoided.

While Federal legislation is essential to get the required amount of Government financing, such a significant program, initiated and managed by the private sector, would surely be viewed favorably by Congress. This approach would provide the means to manufacture high quality, low cost products in a minimum amount of time.

When the goal was reached, we would finally have done something to arrest the dangerous decline of American manufacturing, and industry would once again have the tools to be competitive in global markets.

A 21st Century Infrastructure for America

Kevin L. Kearns and James Lucier

Once Americans had the vision to implement infrastructure policies and projects which formed the very foundation of America's rise to greatness. They knew that without government commitment to economic development and a framework within which that development could take place, neither businesses nor individuals would take the personal and financial risks necessary to make that development a reality.

Every school child, without being aware of the fancy name, studies the infrastructure policies that facilitated America's expansion into an industrial and technological giant. The Cumberland Road and the Erie Canal opened the way for westward economic expansion. Later came the railroads, the telegraph, mail services, the telephone, water treatment and irrigation systems, gas then electric lighting for cities, vast hydroelectric projects and national electrical power grids, commercial airlines, and the national highway system.

But are we planning for and securing our economic future in the same way now? Shockingly, we are not. In the next century, technological innovation, increases in productivity and national cooperation among government, business and labor will determine which nations are leaders and which nations are second-rate powers. However, today America is dithering as our current infrastructure collapses around us.

In addition, while other nations are creating high-tech infrastructure programs that will allow them to dominate economic competition in the next century, Americans seem unable to grasp the importance of the new,

Kevin L. Kearns, *a Fellow of the Economic Strategy Institute, was a career Foreign Service Officer from 1977 to 1990, serving most recently as the director of the State Department's Office of Defense Trade Policy. His previous postings include Bonn, Seoul and Tokyo, where as Deputy Chief of the Mutual Defense Assistance Office, he was deeply involved with the FSX fighter plane negotiations.* James Lucier *is a policy analyst at the Economic Strategy Institute. Excerpted from a forthcoming Economic Strategy Institute study.*

technology-driven infrastructure: fiber optic networks to office and home, digital libraries, intelligent highways and smart cars, mag-lev trains, supercomputer networks and many other advanced technology projects. Without this type of modern, cohesive, national infrastructure, America will not be able to compete economically with the Europeans and the Japanese.

This critical component of our economic future is being badly neglected by the Administration and the Congress. Unless we shortly begin a major national effort to repair our crumbling 20th century infrastructure and to create a new 21st century infrastructure for America, our country will soon join the has-beens of history.

At this point it may be best to define infrastructure and explain why it is so important. Broadly, infrastructure is society's basic equipment for producing wealth and knowledge. It comprises the physical assets, human capital, coordinating institutions, and information resources which underlie productive activity in the economy. Just as farm goods cannot move to market without roads, thus hindering economic well-being in an agricultural society, in an advanced information society, fiber optic networks, which facilitate the quick and efficient exchange of critical information, are indispensable to the creation of wealth. In general, infrastructure underlies and makes possible value-producing exchanges of goods, services, or information upon which a society's standard of living is based.

This raises the question of who is responsible for the creation of infrastructure. While there are many different agents involved in both the public and private sectors, for much of our nation's history it has been the role of the federal government to design and implement a forward-looking national infrastructure policy. Such projects as the railroads, canals, and the telegraph mentioned above were centerpieces of our nation's plans for economic development. Unfortunately, today the criticality of a central federal role is not well understood and very idea of an infrastructure policy is decried as something alien to the American tradition by the advocates of laissez-faire economic principles who control the government's economic policy making apparatus.

Our toughest economic competitors are all planning major infrastructure upgrades. In the case of Japan and the newly industrializing countries, these infrastructure upgrades will be funded by trade surpluses with us. The United States cannot afford to let its deterioration continue while our major competitors are about to accelerate the pace of their development.

These trade deficit-funded infrastructure projects are mainly conventional, but new technology is about to make new types of infrastructure possible. Other countries are making the necessary investments and preparing to exploit these technologies as quickly as possible. They have the financing and coordinating mechanisms to do so in place. In short, not only are we failing to keep up, but we are about to drop out of the next leg of the race altogether.

Let us look at some of the advanced technology infrastructure systems which promise to radically alter the world as we know it.

• Broadband integrated digital services networks will replace the telephone as the telephone once replaced the telegraph. Where standard telephone lines once carried voice and slow data transmissions, the new broadband optical fiber networks will easily carry HDTV and high-speed data transmissions between supercomputers. The market for high resolution systems and newer, cheaper supercomputers to plug into this network will be enormous, as will the demand for the special data and communications services which will become suddenly possible.

• Intelligent vehicle and highway systems will make traffic flows faster and safer while reducing pollution and congestion. They will increase the capacity of existing highways and obviate the environmental consequences of building new ones. Traffic flow will become a major application for supercomputers and artificial intelligence, and cars themselves will undergo a radical transformation. The modern automobile will have computerized navigation and guidance systems at its heart, literally becoming a mobile computer connected to other computers. Its body will incorporate advanced materials; its engine of advanced design will burn newer, cleaner fuels (if it burns fuel at all), and its sensors will be beyond current technology.

• The next generation of commercial aircraft will include hypersonic transports capable of crossing the heavily-traveled Pacific routes in a matter of hours, and commercial vertical takeoff aircraft will facilitate shorter intercity travel.

• Mag-lev trains will likely be the first major deployment of superconductor technology, leading the way to advances in power generation, power transmission, electric engines, and supercomputers.

- Space-based manufacturing will provide many special materials, pharmaceuticals, and other products hardly dreamt of today.

Opportunity and challenge: The new infrastructure industries

The new high technology infrastructure differs from previous, more basic systems largely in the amount of information technology it incorporates and in the fact that much of it, rather than simply being public works, will stimulate the manufacture of highly complex, high value-added goods. Also, each type of infrastructure generally cuts across several fields of technology, embodying not only advanced information systems, for instance, but advanced materials and manufacturing processes in addition. The increasing public investment that goes into developing such technologies in their pre-competitive stages can thus be considered a type of infrastructure as well.

The market for producing infrastructure-related equipment will be highly lucrative. Rapid growth will be possible as whole countries install new systems more or less at once. Deploying new infrastructure or selling the base-line equipment will be a major exercise in manufacturing and the commercialization of new technology.

The products themselves will also be desirable from a producer's standpoint. High technology infrastructure equipment will likely have a high income elasticity, meaning that people will continue to buy it as the market matures and economic growth continues. The market will continue to expand even once the growth phase is over.

Moreover, experience has shown that high technology products have rapid economies of scale once market penetration begins, and the making of one generation of a product contributes much experience to the making of the next and vastly more sophisticated generation. Manufacturing plants typically require much greater capital investment as the field develops, and latecomers to the field will find substantial practical barriers to entry.

In short, the new infrastructure-related industries offer producers the possibility of rather secure market position with steady revenues. Control of the initial commercialization generally leads to control of the technology itself, and with it the market for peripherals and services, as well as the lion's share of resulting economic growth worldwide.

Yet those countries which did not develop the technology themselves will eventually have to deploy it to remain even marginally competitive, even if it means having to purchase it from supplier countries at great cost.

Worldwide moves toward 21st century infrastructure

The moral for the United States is clear. Though we are still the technology leader in many of these fields, that fact is that actual commercialization and deployment is key to developing them. Our failure to move while the opportunity is ripe may mean permanent loss of our competitive position. However, the United States is already lagging behind in many fields.

* Japan and Europe are racing toward the development and implementation of a broadband digital communications network. Nippon Telephone and Telegraph alone will spend $210 billion to bring optical fiber to every home in Japan by 2015 and every major office center by 1995. Meanwhile, the United States has the technology, but regulatory fallout from the AT&T breakup keep large-scale commercialization from proceeding.

* Japan and Europe have put large amounts of money into intelligent highway and vehicle systems and are very close to deploying commercial systems. The United States realizes the importance of such systems but has no comprehensive plan to begin one.

* The leading next-generation commercial aircraft may well be the German Saenger and not a U.S. product. In addition, the United States has developed the V-22 Osprey tilt-rotor aircraft, but the Administration has decided to terminate the Osprey program. Meanwhile, the Japanese have shown considerable interest in an Osprey-type vertical takeoff aircraft. Japanese industry leaders have said that if the United States does not complete development of it, they will.

* Japan and Europe have programs in place to develop a mag-lev train and the corresponding superconductor spinoff technologies. In the U.S., there is no timetable for a similar development, though we do have a superconductor research consortium.

* Europe, Japan, and other producers are pursuing control of the commercial launch industry, which is critical to development of space. Meanwhile, the U.S. space program continues its resolutely anti-commercial bias.

- Europe and Japan have technology-development infrastructures to accelerate progress. The U.S. has no explicit technology policy.

In field after field, the results seem clear. Though the United States has pioneered research in many fields, we still risk missing major opportunities for commercial development—indeed, as noted, the United States could be locked out of these fields altogether. We will have no choice but to buy the highest value-added products from abroad. Our productivity and standard of living will eventually slip lower, both in relative and absolute terms. We will forego the opportunity to have high-wage tax-paying industries here, while other countries could parlay their wealth and technological superiority into an even more competitive position.

Toward a 21st century infrastructure policy

What needs to be done to remedy an already serious situation? Crucial to America's future economic development is an increased federal role on the model of earlier infrastructure policies, with a renewed commitment to basic investment. In particular, the federal government must provide the sort of active coordination and positive incentive structures which enabled this country to develop into the world's leading power with the advent of earlier technologies. In addition, all infrastructure proposals must be designed to ensure full participation by business. Commercial exploitation of infrastructure systems and related infrastructure technologies in order to raise productivity and competitiveness (and with them the nation's standard of living) is after all the goal of infrastructure policy.

To get government at all levels involved, a full scale campaign of education and then political action is necessary. First, a core group of interested individuals from industry, labor, government and academia must be brought together to formulate a program. It is suggested that the central element in that program be a multi-disciplinary 21st Century Infrastructure Project. The objective would be to run the project for a period of no longer than six months and at the end of that time to publish a report which would serve as the basis for the education/political campaign. The core group would raise the funding necessary to support the project through donations of money/specialists from industry, foundations, trade associations, etc.

In the meantime the core group would also begin to mount an effort to bring as much media attention to the issue as possible. The objective should be to make 21st century infrastructure a legitimate political and economic concept, and in fact a household word.

Ultimately, the objective is to create a unified legislative agenda and to rally the nation behind that agenda so that it is enacted into law intact. The campaign must be run so that 21st Century Infrastructure does not become a massive pork barrel project for the 1990s. Key elements of the infrastructure program would be:

>   federal parameters and guidelines on infrastructure so that business can make intelligent decisions;

>   a unified national infrastructure budget, submitted as part of the federal budget submission;

>   the appointment of a federal infrastructure czar with the authority to coordinate all executive branch infrastructure projects;

>   the creation of a mechanism, i.e. a National Infrastructure Bank, to finance certain types of infrastructure projects, especially those on the state and local levels;

>   a unified national R&D policy for both civilian and military agencies, which in turn would be part of an overall technology policy with an emphasis on commercialization;

>   the removal of regulatory obstacles to the creation of such infrastructure projects as fibre optic networks to the home and office;

>   the creation of national infrastructure consortia to ensure that we are competitive with the Europeans and Japanese in key areas;

>   financial incentives to induce business participation.

There are, of course, many other components, too numerous to list here. The key is that the nation as a whole has to formulate and then act upon its infrastructure goals for the 21st century. Without a cohesive national infrastructure policy, we will be at the mercy of those nations that have developed and deployed the new technologies. The net result for the United States will be greatly diminished power and influence in a more hostile world environment. Absent a major national effort to form the basis of a 21st century infrastructure now, we will soon be the first generation of Americans unable to control our own destiny.

An Ambivalent Congress

David A. Heenan

With the elections over, both Republicans and Democrats are proposing various measures to restore America's competitiveness. Their nostrums share a powerful common belief: that America's economic well-being rests on the ability of U.S. business, government, and labor to forge a national consensus . . . .[S]urveys in the 1970s and 1980s have revealed that between two-thirds and four-fifths of Americans believe that the tensions between business, government, and labor are at the heart of our "sickness." As a result of these concerns, virtually every proposal of today's 200-member bipartisan Congressional Caucus on Competitiveness contains some element of "cooperation" or "partnership."

But are America's political leaders truly committed to building an economic partnership? Are they prepared to share their power with business and labor? Further, are the opinions of federal lawmakers in agreement with those of legislators in state government? Have politicians' attitudes on consensus-building changed over the decade? And what are the implications for corporate America?

Views from Capitol Hill

To answer these questions, a survey was taken of over 300 members of Congress as well as their peers in several state legislatures. The survey spelled out three possible scenarios of a socioeconomic future for the United States. Respondents were asked to identify which one they (1) preferred, (2) expected to dominate in the United States over the next 10 years, and (3) felt would be most effective in solving America's problems over the same time period.

Scenario I describes the regulated free-enterprise system or mixed economy now in effect in the United States. It represents the status quo in

David A. Heenan *is president and chief executive officer of Theo H. Davies & Co., Ltd. in Honolulu. Excerpted with permission from* Business Horizons, *May/June 1989.*

which dealing between business, government, and labor typically are either adversarial or remain at arm's length.

Scenario II portrays "America, Inc." Consensual attitudes dominate regulations among business, government, and labor. Typically, their cooperation leads to an economic partnership such as that observed in Japan or West Germany.

Scenario III can be summed up as "managed capitalism" or "modified socialism." Government holds the economic reins, and central planning abounds. (Sweden and Yugoslavia possess many of the elements of this opposition.). . .

[T]he most important findings are the following:

• Almost three-fourths of the congressional members surveyed prefer the status quo (Scenario 1). A little more than one-fifth think an "America, Inc." is best, while only 0.8 percent favor a centrally planned economy.

• Slightly less than three out of every four politicians believe the present ideology will dominate during the next 10 years; roughly one-quarter of the respondents anticipate that an "America, Inc." will prevail; and about 1 percent expect to see the emergence of Scenario III.

• When asked which scenario would be most effective in solving America's competitiveness problems, two-thirds of those polled named Scenario I. Approximately 30 percent picked "America, Inc.," and a small minority (0.7 percent) chose "managed capitalism."

• Opinions vary considerably between federal and state legislators. Washingtonians generally are more bullish on our mixed economy and its ability to withstand the test of time. Conversely, policymakers at the state level are much more inclined to see the merits of the partnership approach (Scenario II).

• Neither age, business experience, geography, nor political party is a predictor of opinion. In technical jargon, there are no statistically significant differences at the 5 percent level. Although a study conducted a decade ago found younger lawmakers more disposed to collaborative economic systems, that is not the case today. Also, significant experience in the private sector did not influence respondents' ideological leaning—the same result as in the earlier survey. Similarly, there are no regional differences in attitudes despite the uneven economic performance of various parts of the country. The same results hold for party affiliation.

Congressional legislators have remained remarkably consistent in what they think is the proper course for the U.S. economy. These most recent opinions are virtually identical to those gathered in a study conducted from 1979 to 1981. However, state legislators today are significantly more supportive of Scenario II than were their colleagues at the beginning of the decade . . . .

America's political leaders have delivered a clear verdict: the nation should not cast out its adversarial system in favor of the more collaborative methods of Japan and West Germany or the more directed economies of Northern and Eastern Europe. Most prefer our present ideology, for all its shortcomings. Hence, these results parallel those obtained in a 1987 survey of *Harvard Business Review* readers. Politicians doubt that the United States would be willing to adopt the cultural values and institutional reforms needed to build an "America, Inc." They argue that the Japanese or German models, attractive as they are, cannot be assimilated by a nation with the values and traditions of the U.S.: Yankee ingenuity, rugged individualism, egalitarianism, and independent, competitive spirit.

Supporters of regulated free enterprise also cite its superior effectiveness in resolving competitiveness problems. Many express their concern over further government encroachments in the economy; others single out the proven track record of the mixed economy; still others are unconvinced that the U.S. could assume the traits of a more organic society; and some associate Scenarios II and III with the potential loss of political liberties. No doubt the after-effects of the presidential elections may have generated pressure to change our adversarial ways. An ideological overhaul, however, does not appear to be forthcoming. Any shifts that occur will be subtle ones.

Congressmen admit they have not effectively articulated the competitiveness issue to grass-roots America—or at least that the opposition has failed to do so. "The Republicans don't have a point of view (on competitiveness)," claims Senator Bill Bradley, a New Jersey Democrat. "It's consistently offering inconsistent and contradictory responses.". . . Several respondents fault the previous Administration for sending out mixed signals....

Nevertheless, Capitol Hill is equally mindful of the positive lessons of the Reagan legacy. Despite the staggering trade and budget deficits, lawmakers do not want to reassert Washington's stake in the economy, and they expect this hands-off policy to continue into the 1990s. "We're prepared to play this hand out," says Representative Robert Matsui, a California Democrat. "We simply won't turn the clock back."

Institutionalizing U.S. business-government partnerships is also difficult. Consider the ill-fated attempt in 1987 to link the independent, nonprofit Council on Competitiveness with the federally supported Congressional Caucus on Competitiveness. . . .

[T]he coalition floundered on a technicality. Congressional rules prohibit lawmakers from joining with groups that have the potential for self-interest, no matter how slight. . . .

As a result, Washington's first stab at a business-government partnership—a partnership to breed further partnerships—stumbled over America's antiquated rule book. (At the time of this writing, both groups remain at arm's length, although informal communications between them are good).

Washington's role

The central issue surrounding America's competitiveness is the role of government in the process. Most lawmakers surveyed agree with Representative Sam M. Gibbons of Florida: "Government's proper role is as a rulemaker or umpire—but not as a partner." Besides, its "safety-net mentality," as Gibbons calls it, runs counter to the entrepreneurial spirit of American industry. Although not all congressmen concur with this analysis, they largely agree that any economic partnership will be dominated by business.

Still, many lawmakers look for more, not less, cooperation between the public and private sectors. They approve of closer linkages between U.S. business, universities, and government research laboratories. A favorite example: the National Science Foundation's establishment of engineering-research centers at 21 universities, 45 industry-university cooperative centers, and 12 materials-research centers—at a total cost to the taxpayers of about $115 million annually. . . .

Even at full maturity, such business-government coalitions fall short of what is needed to enhance competitiveness. Some legislators believe, therefore, that government's best point of attack may be at the state, not federal, level. . . .

Congress is genuinely eager to tilt this nation gradually toward a new spirit of cooperation. However, deeds—not words that blindly beg for partnerships—will be the answer. For the next decade, economic collaboration will take place primarily between business and state and local government on the one hand, and labor and management on the other.

Many years ago, Walt Whitman rejected the notion that America was a fragmented, special-interest society:

> O I see that this
> America is only you and me,
>   Its power, weapons, testi-
> mony, are you and me,
>   Its Congress is you and me,
> the officers, capitols,
>   armies, ships, are you and
> me. . .

The principle of indivisibility is deeply ingrained in the American psyche. But we must put our talents in tandem in ways consistent with our culture. Only then will the competitiveness challenge be resolved and new dreams realized.

Staying on Top

Kevin P. Phillips

In the face of Japan's enormous inroads into U.S. markets and industries—50 percent of the new cars on California roads in 1984 are Toyotas, Datsuns, Hondas and Mazdas—it's extraordinary how many serious U.S. commentators are wasting time and effort debating whether or not Japan has something called an industrial policy and whether or not government involvement and planning have played a major role in Japan's economic ascent. The hairsplitting goes on for high stakes, of course. Each side of the debate here hopes to shape American policy by its interpretation of how Japan succeeds. On one hand, liberals, convinced that government planning and regulation are the key to our economic future, find it useful to argue that the Japanese government in general, and the famous Ministry of International Trade and Industry (MITI) in particular, guided the Japanese economy to its present eminence. Accordingly, liberals can be found urging the creation of a federal economic planning council, a national industrial development bank and the like. To this, conservatives say, wrong again: look at the trend of tax reduction in Japan; look at Tokyo's low cost of raising business capital (less than half our cost); look at the Japanese national commitment to savings, to productivity and to group consensus. Government planning isn't responsible for Japan's success, they claim; MITI made any number of mistakes, and fortunately for Japan, business often, as with Honda and Sony, ignored MITI's advice.

This ideological polarization seems absurd. Rarely has so large a truth lain in the middle of so big a debate. For starters, by all the evidence, liberals are correct when they say that government's role was important as it promoted industrial growth and success during the 1970s not only in Japan but also in Korea, Taiwan, Brazil and a number of other countries whose

Kevin P. Phillips *is president of the American Political Research Corporation and publisher of the* American Political Report *and the* Business & Public Affairs Fortnightly. *Excerpted from* Staying On Top: The Business Case for a National Industrial Strategy. *Copyright © 1984 by Kevin P. Phillips. Reprinted by permission of Random House Inc.*

economic advance during that decade became a byword.

Europe's experience with industrial policy is admittedly mixed. For East Asian nations, however, even William Krist, the Reagan administration's Assistant U.S. Trade Representative for Industrial Policy, acknowledges the industrial policy approach as having proved generally successful.

> Other countries, however, have adopted industrial policies akin to those of Japan and are succeeding in winning a larger share of world export markets. For example, after Japan quadrupled its share of world exports in the 1960s to 11 percent, Taiwan, Korea, Hong Kong and Singapore tripled their share of world exports in the 1970s. Other large industrializing countries, such as Brazil and Mexico, have been guiding their growth though current international indebtedness is complicating their trade growth.

Does it matter if some of that official role came in planning, some in labor or resources allocation, some in targeting subsidies and some in simply establishing (or maintaining) the sort of tax and capital-formation climate that enterprise needs to flourish? Effective tax policy coordination between business and government is no mean achievement in itself. For conservatives here to say that Japan owes little or nothing to official industrial policies—to dismiss the economic coordination and consensus-building achievements of one of the world's longest-enduring conservative regimes—strikes me as an exercise in analytical irrelevance.

At the same time, conservatives seem eminently correct when they argue that much of Japan's success flows not from the sometimes fallible bureaucracy of MITI but from the enterprising and frugal character of Japanese society and from the capitalist economics of Japan's enormously successful ruling Liberal Democratic party, which, despite its name, is very definitely right of center. In practical terms, the managers of Japan, Inc., have used the leverage of government planning and power to promote a generally conservative economic system and set of cultural values. Indeed, one could almost say that government guidance has been effective in part because of Japan's mildly authoritarian cultural milieu. Progressive academicians prefer to skirt such recognition, that the values of MITI are not those of the Harvard Faculty Club. Yet it's true, and it in turn supports a notable irony: that "industrial policy"—a neomercantilist business-government partnership—has enjoyed its most substantial successes under conservative or right-wing regimes like those found in Japan, Gaullist France, Korea, Brazil and Taiwan. That's probably because such governments have meant business, in both senses of the word. One can conclude that around the world effective, not theoretical, industrial policy fits part and parcel with what can be called de facto business nationalism.

The rebuttal to an industrial policy, as commonly perceived, is both political and economic. Given a moderately resilient national economy, the realities of U.S. governance—from our town-meeting, Jeffersonian political heritage to our fifty-state crazy quilt of business-development subsidies and practices—work against close replication of a MITI or establishment of new federal agencies designed to enthrone federal officials as the arbiters of which industries wax and which wane. Foreign-type industrial masterminding is not all that compelling, either. To be sure, some foreign practices involve powerful planning agencies, but these are a minority. And those with a record of enviable successes are even fewer. By contrast, a number of the less interventionist elements of industrial policy can be found in many Western nations—attitudes and institutional arrangements that give a nation's industries and exporters a global competitive advantage and therefore merit our analysis and in some cases our adoption of them.

It's easy to list a number of these approaches our competitors use and we do not: first, government coordination of industrial competitiveness and trade objectives; second, official commitment to upholding national economic interests by taking full advantage of existing international trade law—either in loopholes or opportunities to restrict the unfair practices of competitors; third, active government assurance of export credits, subsidies and loans to ensure that a nation's industries are fully competitive with foreign competitors similarly favored; fourth, a greater sense of cooperation—of a shared national economic stake—among business, government and organized labor.

Shaping a more activist U.S. policy to increase business-government collaboration strikes me as a matter more of common sense than ideology. Nor would this kind of industrial strategy—unlike the central planning ambitions of left-of-center industrial policy proponents—undermine parallel emphasis on revised fiscal and monetary policy. So if I had to come up with a phrase to describe the program, it would not be "industrial policy" but "business nationalism"—a strategy for industrial competitiveness.

Most of the national industrial policies offered by the left and center-left have failed to come to grips with (1) the pivotal role of capital formation or incentive economics found in successful industrial policies like that pursued by Japan, and (2) the interaction of an emerging world market and an intensifying economic nationalism. Liberals are too often uncomfortable with both realities. In their various industrial Baedekers, center-left spokesmen rarely note the conservative economic policy components of foreign success. Ignored as well is the ethnic, economic and political Balkanization—economic nationalism, in short—unsettling the world since the early 1970s. Nor is the left attuned to the practical political necessities of policy making. Nitty-gritty constituency considerations are skipped over blithely. Few proindustrial policy speeches, articles and position papers ever seem to address the interest-group politics of who's going to be for what—and why. Flawed scripts have been the result. Accordingly, too much left-of-center advocacy has ranged from crude protectionism and New Deal deja vu to technological romanticism.

Which brings us to the conservatives, whom I hope to prod into action. In recent years, while traditional smokestack, high-tech liberal and futurist proposals have been churned out, right-wing ideologists and politicians have been too busy defending a free global marketplace that more pragmatic senior business executives believe no longer exists. For the most part, the free-marketeers have failed to frame a serious set of counterproposals. But the fundamental argument against a business-as-usual free-market response to our current economic problems lies in the changing political basis of competition in the global market. It is simply a new game being played. all of the major Western nations have and will continue to have market-driven economies. An honest appraisal of human nature foretells as much, and rival socialist economics—flawed by their naive view of human motivation—are on the ebb. A market-driven economy is not, however, the same thing as a free-market economy. In the former, government-aided pursuit of markets can sometimes be exceedingly effective. And from Tokyo to Brasilia, a substantial state economic role—sometimes nationalization of industries, but more often now a mix of capitalism and international marketing—is making the old free-market political model less able to stand up to scrutiny. Corporate leaders and business spokesmen seem even more inclined to think out loud about the problem than academicians and professors on the left.

For roughly a century and a half, free-market views have been the dominant Anglo-American theology—though hardly an accurate model of economic reality—to our very great reward and profit. The ebb of our theology may signal a larger ebb. Up to now global free trade, for all its periodic abridgements, has rested on the world manufacturing and trade hegemony of Britain and the United States. But basic industry today is shifting into the Brazils, Taiwans and Koreas, while high-tech leadership is up for grabs among the United States, Japan and Europe. It is my assessment that a pluralistic and Balkanized world economy is more conducive to neomercantilism—to the effectiveness of some state intervention and to new forms of economic nationalism—than to the requirements of free trade. Thus our national problem.

Mr. Horton's Neighborhood

Bruce Stokes

In late November 1987, Joe Trippi, the deputy manager of the presidential campaign of the U.S. Congressman Richard A. Gephardt, was worried. Gephardt's campaign in Iowa, where the first 1988 Democratic presidential caucus was only two months away, was about to air a hard-hitting political TV ad comparing the relatively low U.S. price of a Korean-made Hyundai with the relatively high price of an American car sold in Korea. The problem was Korea's trade barriers. Trippi's goal was to use the ad to underscore in voter's minds his candidate's commitment to fair trade.

Trippi broadcast the ad, and rest is history. Gephardt's faltering campaign caught fire. The 60-second Hyundai spot captured the imagination of the press and the public. And Gephardt won the Iowa caucuses.

Later in the primary season the Hyundai ad came back to haunt Gephardt. His opponents used it to paint him as a protectionist and economic nationalist. But, clearly, the ad helped give him the visibility and public support he needed at a crucial time in his campaign.

Ironically, in the waning days of the presidential general election, Democratic candidate Michael A. Dukakis, the man who defeated Gephardt in the primaries in part by attacking his positions, began to echo many of Gephardt's broader themes. He talked about the need for the U.S. to recapture control of its economic destiny through greater attention to trade, foreign investment, foreign influence in America. And he stressed putting America first. It was classic economic nationalism. But in the eyes of Democratic political strategists, Dukakis' loss no more discredited the economic nationalist message than did Gephardt's defeat.

"Economic nationalism did not get its political test in 1988 because

Bruce Stokes *is the international economics correspondent of the* National Journal *Excerpted with the author's permission from "Mr. Horton's Neighborhood?" by* Bruce Stokes, The International Economy, *March/April 1989.*

Michael Dukakis was uncomfortable with espousing it," said Stanley B. Greenberg of the polling firm of Greenberg-Lake, the Analysis Group, which conducted public opinion surveys for the Dukakis campaign . . . .

Political experts disagree over the electoral potency of trade or foreign investment issues, but most think it cannot and will not be ignored. And the context in which economic nationalism issues are raised may determine whether the Japanese—or foreigners in general—become the Willy Horton of future campaigns.

The seeds of economic nationalist debate were sown in August 1985 in a special election to fill an open congressional seat in Texas' 1st District. The Republican candidate had dismissed trade as an irrelevant issue, and national Democratic leaders trumpeted the Democrat's victory as a repudiation of Reagan administration trade policy. In 1986, when Democrats gained a majority in the Senate, the trade deficit was cited as an important contributing factor. In 1987 the stage was set for Gephardt's run for the White House. As author of the controversial Gephardt amendment to the trade bill then stalled in Congress, which called for phased reductions in trade surpluses with the U.S. under the threat of import restraints, Gephardt was already identified with what came to be known as economic nationalism. But, said Shrum, "Dick's fate in 1988 was to be John the Baptist," preaching in the wilderness. . . .

Exit polls of people who voted in Iowa and the southern primary states suggest economic nationalism's role in his fate was less clear. In Iowa, voters told CBS News/*New York Times* pollsters that Gephardt's attacks on foreign trade competition were at best a tertiary reason for casting their votes for him. More important was his stance on farm policy and reducing the federal deficit. A similar southern regional poll showed that voters were more interested in Gephardt's position on Social Security and the budget deficit than on trade. Moreover, in both polls no more than one in eight voters cited trade as the issue that mattered most to them. Nevertheless, Gephardt said in an interview, "you should not confuse my ultimate failure with the failure of the [economic nationalism] issue."

And later developments suggest that . . . he may be right. As the campaign progressed, other Democratic candidates picked up some of Gephardt's themes. Sen. Albert Gore began delivering a small-guy vs. big-guy economic populist message. And the Rev. Jesse Jackson stressed the loss of U.S. jobs to overseas production facilities, not blaming foreigners but American corporations.

And, in the ultimate compliment, Lee Atwater, George Bush's campaign manager and now head of the Republican National Committee [said] in a recent interview that Gephardt "did a better job than any other candidate developing a populist theme. [He] gave me some pause."

In the general election, Dukakis delivered a populist message in his Labor Day campaign kickoff speech, and then dropped the issue. Only after his disastrous performance in the second debate and prolonged internal struggle within the campaign did he begin to articulate his own brand of economic nationalism—pursuing an "on your side" message while decrying foreign investment and the loss of jobs because of the trade deficit. . . . "It was during that period of time that the [public opinion] gap [between Dukakis and Bush in California] closed," said Tom Kiley, whose firm of Marttila & Kiley coordinated the Dukakis forces' polling effort. Largely because of Dukakis' new economic nationalist/economic populist appeal, his campaign turned a "catastrophic loss into a moderate loss," concluded Shrum. Atwater said: "I'm very glad that they did not develop the populist theme that they developed in the last two weeks. . . . "

Buoyed by these electoral signals, economic nationalism proponents think the issue can be framed to make it an important factor in future elections. The cornerstone of their case [is a] survey of 1,600 likely voters conducted by the Analysis Group over the three days prior to the November election. The poll found that 47% of those questioned thought protecting U.S. jobs from foreign competition by enacting tougher trade laws was of the utmost importance, rating it 7 on an ascending scale of 1 to 7. . . .

Devising a campaign strategy to tap these sentiments and their adherents will be a delicate task. Democratic political consultants have just begun to think out loud about how to do it. They say the approach in 1990 and 1992 is likely to take two tracks: an economic populist appeal and economic nationalist approach.

A candidate talking about economic nationalism—a level playing field for trade, the threat of foreign investment—will bring some voters to his or her camp, but it won't be enough to win . . . .   So the economic nationalism of future Democratic candidates is likely to be paired with an economic populism espousing traditional populist themes . . . attacking big corporations and Wall Street—"pick-ourselves-up-by-our-own-bootstraps" issues—education, investment, savings—so that America can be competitive again. . . .

Democratic strategists are less clear about [dealing] with the racism .

.. that an economic nationalism appeal seems to tap into . . . .

The broader strategic question facing political analysts looking ahead is whether economic nationalism will work as a campaign theme because of the substance of the issues or whether economic nationalism merely created a large playing field upon which candidates can test themselves and show their character, giving people reason to vote for them. If the former, then candidates must develop detailed positions on trade . . . and so forth. If the latter, the message can be vaguer, the language more symbolic.

Used in this way, noted Shrum, economic nationalism could be "the economic analogy of the Reagan appeal of national security and military strength in 1980," plucking the same heart strings. At the same time, this would give Democrats a way to use the issue without turning foreigners into Willy Horton. "I think you can be very though on this issue without engaging in stereotypes and being unfair," said Shrum.

Whether Democrats will ever run on an economic nationalist platform will depend on the state of the economy. If good times prevail, few political analysts think a Democrat can win the White House in 1992. And if the country plunges into a deep, prolonged recession, any Democrat can win and economic nationalism is irrelevant. So the issue looms largest if economic conditions are mixed. The issue will first be tested in the 1990 congressional races—in the Michigan Senate race and possibly in Montana's. And Rep. John Bryant, the Texas Democrat pushing registration of foreign investment, may be using the issue to position himself to run for the Senate in Texas.

The role of economic nationalism in the 1992 presidential race is less clear. Most political analysts assume Gephardt will run again and that a more streamlined version of his 1988 appeal will be a major campaign message. Another possible Democratic candidate, Sen. Bill Bradley of New Jersey, has a reputation as a cerebral free-trader. But, said Lake, "if Bill Bradley could find it in his discourse to have some real emotion on America's economic interest, he might be well positioned." "There is no Democrat who can afford to walk away form economic nationalism," contended Greenberg.

And when they do, they are likely to broadly frame the issue. The appeal will have to include, Kiley said, "a restatement of national purpose that is more than tough retaliation against the Japanese. It requires a real challenge to the American people to compete more aggressively, to consume less. [And] that appeal has to include a very strong call to nationalism."

About the Editors

Clyde V. Prestowitz, Jr., founder and President of the Economic Strategy Institute, was formerly senior associate at the Carnegie Endowment and a fellow at the Woodrow Wilson International Center for Scholars, where he wrote his influential book on the U.S.-Japan economic conflict, *TRADING PLACES*. He is a frequent contributor to major newspapers, magazines and journals. From 1981 until 1986, following a career in international business, Prestowitz was successively Deputy Assistant Secretary of Commerce, Acting Assistant Secretary and Counselor to the Secretary of Commerce. He received a B.A. degree with honors from Swarthmore College, an M.A. degree from the East-West Center of the University of Hawaii and an M.B.A. degree from the Wharton Graduate School of Business. He also studied at Keio University in Tokyo.

Ronald A. Morse was the private-sector liaison and a special assistant to the Librarian of Congress before becoming Executive Vice President of ESI. From 1981 to 1988 he served as the development officer at the Woodrow Wilson International Center for Scholars in Washington, D.C., where he founded and directed the Asia Program. He has also held positions at the U.S. Departments of Energy, State, and Defense. Fluent in Japanese, Morse is the editor of several books and numerous articles on U.S.-Japan relations and Asian affairs and the author of numerous pieces of testimony and articles in the United States and Japan. He holds an undergraduate degree from the University of California at Berkeley and a Ph.D. in history from Princeton University. He lived and studied in Japan for five years.

Alan Tonelson joined the Institute after completing a book for The Twentieth Century Fund on redefining U.S. foreign policy interests. Previously, he served as associate editor of *Foreign Policy*, *The Wilson Quarterly* and *The Inter Dependent*. He received his B.A. in history from Princeton University. Tonelson's articles and reviews have appeared in many leading national publications, including *The New York Times*, *The Washington Post*, *Foreign Policy*, *The Atlantic* and *The New Republic*, and he has lectured on U.S. foreign policy at the State Department's Foreign Service Institute, the University of Virginia, and the Paul H. Nitze School of Advanced International Studies at The Johns Hopkins University.